DYNAMIC NYMPHING

Tactics, Techniques, and Flies from Around the World

CZECH • POLISH • FRENCH • UK • US and more

GEORGE DANIEL

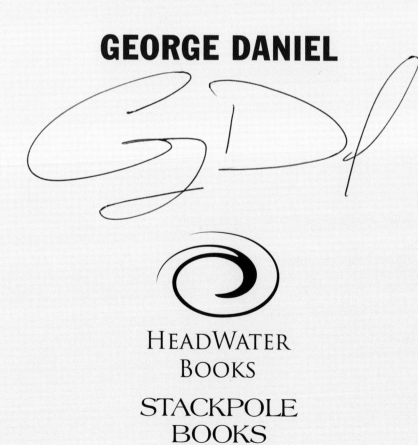

HEADWATER
BOOKS

STACKPOLE
BOOKS

Published by
STACKPOLE BOOKS
5067 Ritter Road
Mechanicsburg, PA 17055
www.stackpolebooks.com

Printed in the United States of America

First edition

Illustrations by Dave Hall

10 9 8 7 6 5 4

Library of Congress Cataloging-in-Publication Data

Daniel, George.
 Dynamic nymphing / George Daniel. — 1st ed.
   p. cm.
 Includes index.
 ISBN-13: 978-0-8117-0741-1 (hardcover)
 ISBN-10: 0-8117-0741-5 (hardcover)
 1. Nymph fishing. I. Title.
 SH456.15.D36 2012
 799.12'4—dc23
                                        2011027724

Contents

Introduction

If one thing sustains me, it is the rather obvious fact that trout do not know who I am. This is good. Because, whether I am fishing in my home waters of the Hampshire chalkstreams, the mad helter-skelter of water chaos on the Madison in Montana, or the pastoral slip and slide of a Pennsylvania creek, trout are comfortingly and reassuringly familiar.

Because trout don't know where you come from, the tactics that you bring to your own particular party are global. The styles adopted from far-flung rivers—be they the techniques used to coax fish in the mosquito hell that is the Kola Peninsula in Russia, the cunning methods that wheedle tiny nervous trout from the upper Lot in the Lozère area of France, or the ultra-specialized and refined fly-fishing tactics used to ply the mighty rivers of Poland and Slovenia—can be equally applied elsewhere. That is what makes this book so important. George Daniel has pulled together his experiences on an international fly-fishing theater and brought them to a stage near you.

Fishing techniques have changed considerably since I first started fishing. When I first flexed my young muscles to propel a fly with a wobbly cane rod, it was powered by silk, hope,

Techniques are universal, and the more you know, the better you are able to adapt to changing conditions on any stream. British angling legend Charles Jardine uses a curly Q along with a sunken Trico spinner while targeting rising trout with Tulpehocken Creek Outfitters (TCO) guide Josh Day on Pennsylvania's Spring Creek. GEORGE DANIEL

and a very different age of upstream dry fly, tweeds, and an ethos that owed more to the Victorians than to the glimmer of modernity lying just around the corner. It was a good time to be starting; everything was so fresh. I was fortunate that my first formal tutor was Frank Sawyer, the man that rocked the cozy foundations of traditional fly fishing by advocating the use of nymphs on chalkstreams. And these were deep nymphs, not those namby-pamby, soft-hackle, Flymphy things of Skues—we are talking heavy metal here, people! Sawyer's utilitarian and distinctly ordinary-looking nymphs made of pheasant tail and copper wire flew in the face of others' delicate creations of thread, gossamer, hackle, and dubbing. It was a bolt of fly-tying common sense, fished with devastating brilliance, and the simplicity and effectiveness of Sawyer's nymphs shook the polite UK-society fishing world.

However, Frank Sawyer was a riverkeeper. His business was water and the life therein, and he had the opportunity to unravel the mysteries of the river on a day-to-day basis—something many of us, because of time restrictions or geographic location, cannot do. But we can open our minds to the possibilities by reading books like this and continually striving to learn when we do fish. We live in an open university of fly fishing. All we have to do—and what the author of this book has done—is attend the streamside "lectures," dip in deeply, and learn from the process.

Being a student of the sport is a good and often surprising thing, especially if you dig deep into its origins or the genesis of a method. When you do, you begin to see that there are a lot of misconceptions in fly fishing. It is odd how erroneous impressions are sometimes formed about an angling method or methods because of either prejudice or just plain ignorance. For instance, take the common belief that Czech and Polish nymphing are two different styles. Let me clear up one thing here and now: It is all fixed-line fishing. There is not a massive difference between the two styles. Honestly. The edges are entirely blurred, and the trout and grayling could not give a flying fig. The main difference is that Czech nymphing styles tend to have the heaviest fly on the point position, whereas Polish styles tend to have the heaviest fly primarily in the middle position and the lighter on the point.

Or, take the common misconception that Czech nymphing is complicated. I have fished with Jiri Klima, who has received wide acclaim for devising the Czech style. Fishing with that man (whom I referred to in one publication as the "river god") certainly opened my eyes. Instead of cunningly complicated terminal tackle and rigs, he used simple rigs with one or two flies, occasionally three, and on leader lengths no longer than the fly rod, be that 10 feet, 9 feet, or shorter. Look at some designs used in other areas of the sport, and you might assume that a degree in higher applied mathematics was required just to put the leader together. Phooey! Surely the fly rod should be long? No. Surely you should always use multiple-fly rigs? No. Surely you have to have water of a certain height and velocity? No. It doesn't need to be complicated. Where did the nucleus of Klima's idea to simplify things come from? Izaak Walton's *Compleat Angler*. Modernity rooted in history—I love it.

Though we frequently hear claims that something is revolutionary or the latest innovation, history often rears its head and makes a fool of us all. For instance, during a bit of fly-tying detective work for an article about the illustrious Pheasant Tail Nymph à la Frank Sawyer, I found . . . horror of horrors! . . . that the French had beaten Sawyer to the heavyweight fly ballast "punch" some years previously.

Take the curly Q, which you will read about in this book. This deft style of fishing fine tippets for wary fish in clear-water situations, where the tiniest flick or discordant note would spook the quarry, is often credited to the French, but it was actually crafted by the English on the River Thames. Bleak fishers came up with the idea when match fishing (competition fishing) with baited hooks for the midget fish. The bleak is a tiny silvery fish that resembles the alewife, smelt, or black-nose dace. Because of the fish's small size, even the most delicate bobber would have deterred the quarry from taking the bait, so anglers designed a spiral of thicker nylon to serve as a visual indicator. When greased, it would rest on the surface and extend when the fish took, so as not to offer resistance and deter the quarry. The French coarse match fishers seized on the idea and adapted the concept for equally nervous "gun-shy" trout in hard-fished waters.

Fly fishing is about adaptation—in any role, capacity, or genre. Jiri Klima adapted his Czech nymphing styles to suit the water column, height, and speed. If he fished a tiny brush stream with a ribbon of ankle- and thigh-deep runs, for example, then he merely shortened his leader and equipment to suit. Simple brilliance. But that came from within the fisher, just like Sawyer. Give either of these fishers a bent bit of twig and piece of string, à la Huck Finn, and they still would have caught fish. A bit like George Daniel, really.

But equipment does influence tactics as well. We in Britain have had a penchant for longer rods ever since pre-Halfordian times. I guess the hangover from Izaak Walton and Charles Cotton must have been more influential than I realized! The reason is that many of our UK-based styles have centered on a short-cast, maximum-control style of fishing. Yes, casting in our fly-fishing world is as pivotal to what we do as it is anywhere else; the difference is that we have tended to put presentation at the heart of our efforts. As the great River Test riverkeeper William Lunn, known for his trout fly called the Particular, said, "The proper fly, properly presented, will bring forth the proper result." This was true last century, it is true today, and it will remain true as long as fly fishers fish. We have taken that axiom to heart.

There was a period in the United States when the short rod ruled. I remember the almost heroic efforts of Lee Wulff and his exploits with 6-foot rods, for almost any species. Some tried to get the idea of fishing with short rods to take hold in the United Kingdom, but short rods largely failed in all but the smallest Devon or Welsh stream arenas. The reason was simple, and it all comes back to that word "control." You simply cannot use many of the tactics formed either in the UK or on the Continent effectively with a short fly rod. Just try to dance a team of three North Country wet flies (soft-hackles to you

As you fish up- or downstream, you must change your approach, tactics, and rigs to effectively fish in different types of water. You must be dynamic! JAY NICHOLS

Americans) artfully and tantalizingly through a riffly run on a rod shorter than 9 feet. It can be done, but it takes away from the art of the style.

Among other materials that have had a truly huge and universal impact on the sport are brass and tungsten beads. The first time I came across these devastating trout baubles was in the mid-1980s with Roman Moser, the master of Austrian-Bavarian streams. He introduced me to these beads, and they transformed my subsurface fishing. But it was his application of all the materials that made him such a good fisherman. And that is the point here: what is most important is not the equipment or materials; it is the angler.

My plea is that you become a student of the sport. Reach out and grab every bit of information and knowledge that you can. And do not let age be a barrier. I have learned so much from the young, as I know George has, with his close associa-

tions with the US Youth Fly Fishing Team. For my part, what I learned during trips made with my son Alex to places like the Czech Republic, France, and the United States, as well as from his trips to Portugal with the English Youth Fly Fishing Team, has influenced my views of fly fishing and my own angling practices, and subsequently my articles and lectures. And George's experiences on similar trips have also influenced his fishing and are precisely what led him to write this book.

Books like this one are huge steppingstones in our path to a better understanding of the sport. We would do well to embrace them and then, arguably more important, use the knowledge we've gained in our natural playgrounds.

Thank goodness for fishers like George Daniel!

Charles Jardine
England

Dynamic Nymphing

S everal years ago, my wife, Amidea, and I were fishing a local limestone stream, filming a segment for a nymphing program. Out of the corner of my eye, I saw a car with an out-of-state plate pull off the road, and a couple soon got out and watched me catch several fish. After thirty minutes, we decided to try another spot to film, and the couple stopped us on the way to our car. They asked how the fishing was in the area and what patterns we would recommend. It was an early spring day with low temperatures and little bug activity, so I recommended several nymphs. His response shocked me: "I used to nymph, but it became way too easy, and now I only fish dry flies."

Though nymphing can at times be an easier method for taking fish, it is not as easy as this guy claimed. Some rivers are easier to nymph than others, especially those that are almost uniform in water type and current. For example, central Pennsylvania's Spring Creek is relatively uniform in depth and speed throughout most of its reach. On the other hand, pocketwater

Streams are dynamic systems. The speed and depth of a river are constantly changing, even when it looks uniform. When fishing whitewater, look for any signal of in-stream structure slowing down the current. Here the author looks to cast a nymph so that it lands in the slow pocketwater on the Ausable River, New York. AMIDEA DANIEL

Many anglers pass over water that looks too fast to them, but it can be perfect trout habitat. Look for soft spots, such as the slower water behind boulders, and use tight-line tactics to get your flies on the bottom. The best method to get down to the bottom in this type of water is to fish a single nymph with weight (shot or a weighted fly) focused in a small area. JAY NICHOLS

with various current speeds and depths requires an amazing amount of concentration and effort because no two pockets are identical in speed, size, and depth.

When you fish with dry flies, you can watch how the fly floats and make any necessary adjustments. When you are nymphing, you can't always see your nymphs or underwater currents, so you often have to make an educated guess based on what you believe is happening below the surface. As you gain experience and use the right tools, reading the currents and making these adjustments becomes easier. Noticing these subtle differences is what separates good anglers from average ones.

Streams are dynamic systems. The speed and depth of a river are constantly changing, even when it looks uniform. One variation that's important for an angler to be aware of is the difference in speed between the surface and the bottom of a river. I first noticed this difference while snorkeling with my wife on a local warmwater stream. A trail led to a heavy riffle with some whitewater, where my plan was to enter the riffle and start to swing downstream to a deep pool. Instead of going straight to the pool, however, I decided to see if I could find fish in the heavy riffle first. Standing in the strong current, I was barely able to maintain my balance. What happened next was an eyeopener. I held my breath and dropped three feet to the stream bottom, where I found little resistance from the current. In fact, the bottom velocity was about one-fifth of what it was at the surface.

Why is this important? Many anglers pass over water that looks too fast to them, but they are not considering that the water may be moving much slower closer to the bottom of the

river, which is where the trout are holding. For example, when my wife and I went to fish the Madison River in Montana several years ago, during the peak time of mid-June, all the slower sections of prime dry-fly water were packed with anglers. However, no one was fishing the riffle sections. My wife and I had one of our best days ever nymphing this water in solitude. Granted, wading is a lot easier in slower water, but if you are up for it, learning to fish fast water can be like having your own private stretch.

Currents also change velocity and direction when they collide against structure, which is one reason why trout hold near structure. In his video *Underwater World of Trout*, Wendell "Ozzie" Ozefovich shows how some currents actually move upstream by submerging a 4-foot pole with ribbons attached on the bottom half. Surprisingly, although most of the ribbons move downstream, others move upstream. Ozefovich refers to this phenomenon as "reverse currents" and identifies this as one of the adversaries fly fishers regularly face. He also observes that the reverse currents are usually slower, giving trout an easier target when capturing food, which causes the fish to favor them.

To make matters worse, not only do we have reverse currents to deal with, but we also have what Ozefovich describes as "changing cross currents." While filming, he noticed that trout sometimes did a 360-degree spin within seconds, reacting to a temporary whirlpool effect. Again, this is in current that appeared to be moving downstream only. Is it any wonder that nymph anglers are probably missing at least half of the takes? Staying in touch with your flies in the maelstrom of currents can be extremely challenging.

THE COMPETITIVE EDGE

From 2006 until 2010, I competed in five world fly-fishing championships, in Portugal, Finland, New Zealand, Scotland, and Poland, along with countless sanctioned Fly Fishing Team USA trials and national championships in the United States and Canada. I have also fished in other competitions, including the Fly Fishing Masters and ESPN Great Outdoor Games. During that time, I was head coach of the US Youth Fly Fishing Team in two world championships, in Portugal and the Czech Republic. Each year, traveling to a different country always resulted in a new and exciting fly-fishing lesson, which mostly came from local guides the team hired to act as our interpreters and teach us how to fish the water effectively in preparation for the competition. Normally, we spent about five to seven days with our guide learning how to fish the foreign water. During these five wonderful years, I was enrolled in the greatest fly-fishing school, with world champions as teachers.

Competition fly fishing not only was beneficial to me personally, but I think it has had a significant impact on angling in the United States. Some things that are fairly common among anglers because of fishing competitions are bead-head flies, sighters, longer rods, and Czech-style nymphs. And then there are the casting techniques and equipment, such as double hauling and shooting tapers, that came from casting competitions. And these are just the tackle- and technique-related developments. I could write another book about how competitions have made me more efficient on the water and trained me to focus.

Granted, fly-fishing competitions are controversial, at least in the United States, where they are not as common as in Europe. But these competitions, at least the ones I have participated in, are not like NASCAR races or Bassmaster tournaments. They are run more like the Olympics, with no cash prize. Most anglers in the competitive fly-fishing circuit spend

Right: The 2006 US Fly Fishing Team in Portugal, the author's first experience fishing the World Fly Fishing Championships. From spring creeks and small freestone streams to large tailwaters—the author needed a complete nymphing system to deal with the wide range of conditions. GEORGE DANIEL

Below: The US Youth Team in Portugal during the 2008 World Youth Fly Fishing Championships. Today's younger generation is privy to more information at an earlier age than were previous generations. It's amazing to see how skillful our young anglers are today. GEORGE DANIEL

Right: Jorge Pisco of Portugal, gold medalist in the 2007 European Championships, shows members of the US Youth Team some of his favorite patterns for fishing his home waters. Many of Jorge's nymph patterns incorporate cul de canard (CDC). GEORGE DANIEL

large amounts of their own money and time competing simply because they enjoy spending two weeks with four or five other anglers to represent their country and continue to perfect their angling skills. After the fishing sessions conclude and the awards have been given, a large celebratory dinner is held, where all the teams sit down for the last time that year and exchange contact information and even the tactics they used throughout the competition. The anglers then take these new concepts back with them to their respective countries, where they often share them with their friends at home.

Even if you consider fly fishing to be a leisurely recreational pastime and don't like the idea of turning it into a competition of any sort, you most likely have already benefited from the competitions in one way or another. And no matter how you feel about the issue, you probably still would like to improve your technique in order to catch more fish. This book is my attempt to share with you what I have learned about nymph fishing through five years of competition, as well as a lifetime of fishing a broad range of trout streams, everything from Colorado tailwaters to Pennsylvania mountain streams.

DYNAMIC NYMPHING

Despite all I've learned during the last five seasons, however, I know I still have a lot more to learn. My desire to improve and sense that there's always something new to discover keeps me heading out to the streams. It is the losses—the fish I fail to catch—that invigorate and motivate me to learn as much as I can about fly fishing, fly tying, and the environments in which fish live.

Some anglers like to fish just one way, and far be it from me to pass judgment on that. But they are not catching as many fish as they could if they mixed things up a bit. Let me give you an example. Many people accuse strike indicator anglers

of being one-trick ponies, but I have seen tight-lining anglers also refuse to adapt and only use that one method. A number of anglers from my region in central Pennsylvania still refuse to use suspension devices (strike indicators) on fishing trips out West. Most waters in our area are small enough and easily wadeable so that most anglers can get sufficiently close to nymph without having to use a suspension device. However, when they find themselves on the Bighorn River while it's running 5,000 cfs, they discover that it's difficult to get close enough to nymph a section of water without an indicator. Also, I've found that many of our local anglers nymph mostly the faster runs, where tight-line nymphing can be very effective, and leave the slower pools alone, as they would likely require a suspension rig.

I, too, used to rely on just one favorite technique—the Harvey and Humphreys form of high sticking—because it was what I knew and had confidence in. But after traveling around to different parts of the United States and other countries, I began to realize that I could transform a good day into a great one by using a wider range of techniques. These included the use of suspension devices for both short- and long-distance presentations, as well as many of the now popular European tactics, including Czech and French nymphing. You may not plan on traveling to Europe, or even to other waters in your state, but having a few different options and knowing alternative techniques can help you catch more fish.

Because continued success hinges on your ability to change techniques to meet the conditions, you need to think on a dynamic level. Each section of water—riffle, run, pocketwater, or pool—dictates a different approach, as do various water conditions. Riffle sections consist of faster-moving water where you can get closer to present the fly. In such cases, a tight-line tactic such as Czech nymphing is a good one to use. As you move downstream, the gradient lessens and the water may become shallower as it slows down and widens. Trout in these slower sections frequently will not permit you to get close enough to tight-line nymph. Here a better choice is a strike indicator (which I call a "suspender") coupled with a longer cast.

The most effective nymph fly fishers I know are prepared to use a wide range of tactics depending on stream conditions. For example, during the 2008 World Fly Fishing Championships in New Zealand, many of the Czechs and even the French team members who won gold and silver team medals abandoned

Whether they are not aware of other techniques or are too stubborn to change, most anglers I see don't change their nymphing approaches based on the conditions. Many of the ideas shared in this book can be tweaked to handle a variety of stream situations—from low, spooky Portuguese waters all the way to the high, rushing waters of the Rocky Mountains. Here Amidea Daniel releases a beautiful brown trout on a Colorado spring creek. GEORGE DANIEL

Above: Your casting approach also needs to be dynamic—you need to be able to cast from all angles. AMIDEA DANIEL

Right: The Prince Nymph is one of my favorite confidence patterns, whether I'm fishing in the East or West. In fact, it's almost always on my rig when fishing large freestone Rocky Mountain rivers and streams. GEORGE DANIEL

their tight-line techniques in favor of the dry-and-dropper technique popularized here in the States. British stillwater competition anglers I know and have competed against may have up to ten tactics and rigs ready to use. They have them ranked in order as to when they will use each one. They give each tactic a certain amount of time before moving on to the next, until they find one that works. It may not be necessary for you to have ten tactics ready to use, but why not have a backup plan?

When you are fishing, you must be able to move fluidly through multiple approaches and not be dogmatic in your thinking. There really is no one best way. I cannot emphasize enough the importance of changing your rig and tactics as conditions change. Joe Humphreys states it best in *On the Trout Stream with Joe Humphreys*: "This kind of fishing [nymphing] can drive people crazy. They don't see the necessity, or if they do they don't want to take all that time and trouble to be constantly

Richard Formato fishes the headwaters of the South Fork of the Holston River. A long cast and light leader is a must when facing similar conditions. GEORGE DANIEL

fiddling with their weights. But why fish with something that doesn't work? If your nymphs are drifting along three feet off the bottom or if they're shooting through that pocket too fast, what good is it?" When I fish, I frequently change weights, try different drifts, switch between tight-line and suspension tactics, and tie on a variety of fly patterns, depending on the water type, behavior of the fish, my level of concentration, and other factors. The key is to be flexible and dynamic. Have fun, experiment, and blend the various techniques together in your own way.

The techniques that I will share with you in the following pages come from around the world, from both competitive anglers and friends who are superb anglers but could not care less about fly-fishing competitions. The book is a melting pot of Czech, Polish, French, and American nymphing techniques from some of the world's top anglers. In order for these techniques to improve your fishing, however, it is up to you to put in the time onstream practicing with these tools and thinking about how to effectively adapt them to the conditions on the water, which are constantly changing. I would be most pleased to know that this book helped you develop confidence in your skill and inspired you to experiment and adapt rather than simply copy the way I do it. I encourage you to develop your own fishing style and find a system that works for you.

A Nymphing System

I make it a point to fish at least one or two new sections of river a month. Not only do I like to see new water, but more important, I also want to avoid becoming complacent on familiar waters. The only way I can continue to improve my skills is to fish in unfamiliar waters, where I don't know where every fish is holding or what the hot pattern is. I keep a broad range of tackle with me at all times, but I am continually working to refine and simplify my universal system to reduce the amount of tackle I carry to deal with all the diverse conditions.

This chapter gives details on the equipment I use. When you put together your own system, you should modify it to suit your own needs. Those needs are influenced, among other things, by psychology (do you like to carry enough stuff to out fit an army or only the bare essentials?), physiology (do you need a wading staff or something to help you see better?), where you are fishing (do you fish small mountain streams or brawling freestones?), how you fish (do you walk a lot while fishing or use a drift boat?), and what species you are pursuing (brook trout, which will take flies readily, or tailwater browns, which require a greater selection of flies?).

Every angler will develop a personal nymphing system, which instills confidence in his or her own approach. Listening to others' advice is a good start, but only you can develop a system in which you have total trust. Above, Howard Croston sets the hook on a nice fish. *TOTAL FLYFISHER* MAGAZINE

GREAT EQUIPMENT WON'T MAKE YOU A GREAT ANGLER

In August 2007, Pennsylvania hosted the World Youth Fly Fishing Championships. The heat and low stream flows made it extremely difficult to catch trout. One afternoon, I had the chance to watch a member of the Czech squad. He wore patched neoprene waders and a fly vest that looked as though it had been made in the early 1980s, and it was completely unadorned with gizmos and gadgets. I would guess that he carried no more than 100 flies in several small tin candy containers with foam glued to both sides—about a tenth of what I carry.

The young Czech's beat was shallow and flat, the worst of the lot, so stealth was important—and he knew it. He spent the three-hour session on his knees and stomach, stalking the fish. The only time he got up was to take a fish to a controller to be measured and scored. He was the picture of pure focus and patience. Because the water was relatively featureless and he had no distinct areas to fish, he had to cover every foot of it. It appeared that he broke his short 80-yard beat into a small grid consisting of 3-by-3-foot targets. He would cast and drift his single weighted nymph into the 3-by-3 target no more than three times before targeting the next grid. In three hours, he picked up six measurable fish, winning his session and later going on to win the individual silver medal.

I firmly believe that you should buy the best equipment you can, but don't expect high-end equipment to do all the work. If you want to be a great angler, focus on how to use the equipment you have. Though I believe that experimenting with new tactics and equipment leads to development, effective anglers

Every angler should have a working box—a small range of patterns you believe will be useful for the day's fishing. I normally pull four to six of each of the patterns I plan to fish that day out of my bulk storage boxes and put them in my working box. This one-box system simplifies my selection process and forces me to focus more on approach. JAY NICHOLS

know how much time to spend experimenting versus perfecting. I still have yet to totally figure this out, but I am working on it.

Growing up, I had little gear. My secondhand 7½-foot Fenwick fiberglass rod doubled as my bait rod for the early season. Even though I was catching fish, I was under the delusion that I could become a better angler if only I had better equipment. Soon after high school, I began guiding part-time to pay for college tuition and also for new fly-fishing gear, and it wasn't long before I began competing in fly-fishing competitions. Ten years later, I had amassed a collection of gear that could supply a small fly shop. Eventually I ended up with some forty fly rods in a range of lengths and line weights, along with every imaginable gadget. But all this gear complicated things too much.

SIMPLIFY FOR EFFICIENCY

No matter what system you end up developing, I will say this: all the successful anglers I know eventually keep those things that consistently help them catch more fish and eliminate those things that do not. This might sound like common sense, but knowing what you need and what you do not is the mark of an experienced angler. After I had amassed enough gear to fill a fly shop, instead of focusing on how to use my equipment, I was more concerned with what equipment I was going to use. Recently, I sold all but five of my fly rods and reels, as I became overwhelmed with the number of rods I had to choose from. I also decided to streamline my fly boxes and went from carrying twenty boxes to six. First, I couldn't carry twenty fly boxes at one time, and it caused me to think for hours the night before about which ones I should carry. I would spend hours rearranging flies—moving patterns back and forth for the water I was fishing the next day. It became such a chore that I decided to give most of my patterns (the ones I never used) to friends and family and kept just my confidence flies in six boxes. The result was an organized system that I could carry everywhere and required little rearranging, which meant more time focusing on the fishing.

I try to minimize the gear I carry while trout fishing, and part of that is using general equipment—rigs that can cover a wide range of conditions rather than being specifically designed for one river. This is mostly because I fish lots of different types of water. As a result, I developed a general nymphing system to handle most conditions. For example, for flies, I prefer variations of Hare's Ears and Pheasant Tails because they suggest lots of different types of food in trout waters. Few nymph patterns in my box are geared toward a specific insect or hatch, as I feel that would limit the pattern's effectiveness, though there are exceptions.

GET TO KNOW YOUR GEAR WELL

While competing in the World Championships, I saw that many of the competitors that I respected simplified their equipment and often only fished with one or two river rods. Why? By spending lots of time getting to know their rods, they can consistently time and adjust the power on their hook sets, apply maximum amount of pressure without breaking fish off, and cast more efficiently and accurately. For me, I feel more relaxed on a stream with familiar equipment, and this allows me to focus more on technique.

FOCUS ON TECHNIQUE

Though I am very thankful for modern advancements in rod technology and other fly-fishing equipment, it is still how you use this equipment that counts. All fly anglers, at some point in their lives, are guilty of coming up with great excuses as to why they were not successful catching fish. I was no exception. While in college, I would frequently stop by Joe Humphreys's house to visit and talk fly fishing. One day when I was fishing, I struggled to catch only one trout. Later, I visited Joe and was talking to him about this "new" pattern that didn't work for me that day. "George," he said, "the fly did not fail you. You failed the fly." He then told me that instead of making excuses for failures, it's more constructive to try to find solutions. His reply was a bit of a blow to my ego, but he was right.

Along these lines, great anglers rarely have "secret" flies. The French, who are well known for their incredible angling abilities, tie the simplest fly patterns. After several world competitions, a number of French competitors were gracious enough to show to me their favorite patterns, because they knew success had more to do with good technique than with a killer fly pattern. Fishing simple patterns that take little time to tie is common among some of the best competitive fly anglers.

Joe Humphreys (above) is a master of efficiency, and modifying the angling of the tuck, rather than changing weight, is normally his first adjustment when dealing with varied speed currents. This approach saves you countless minutes you would have spent changing weights and lets you spend the time fishing instead. GEORGE DANIEL

SUSPENDERS AND SIGHTERS

An "indicator" refers to anything that indicates a change, which in fly fishing means a change in drift. This can result from the current velocity changing, the fly hitting an object, or a trout taking the fly. Because "indicators" can range from a large piece of buoyant yarn to a piece of colored monofilament integrated into the leader, I divide indicators into two groups: suspenders and sighters.

Suspenders, or suspension devices, are what most people think of when they hear the term "indicator"—pieces of yarn, foam, cork, or buoyant dry flies whose job is to hold up your flies through the drift as well as indicate takes. To control the depth at which your rig drifts, you adjust the distance between suspender and flies.

Sighters are integrated into your leader, and their job is to indicate change, not hold up your flies. You are responsible for controlling depth and drift. A sighter can be anything that provides a visual reference to a take and does not suspend your fly, such as the tip of your fly line, a knot on your leader, or something more apparent, like one or more pieces of brightly colored monofilament integrated into your leader.

Nymphing rigs can be divided between two types: those that incorporate a suspension device and those that do not. This book is basically divided between tactics, rigs, and approaches with suspenders and those without. A rig that relies on a suspender, such as a strike indicator, a buoyant dry fly, or even a greased and coiled piece of colored leader, allows the suspension device to control the depth of the fly throughout the drift. Sighters come into play in tight-line nymphing. You are in control of how deep your fly drifts and ideally maintain a tight line to it throughout the drift, relying on feel or a sighter to detect the take.

A sighter is a brightly colored piece of material (in this case, colored nylon) that is built into your leader to add better visibility for strike detection. JAY NICHOLS

Use as long a rod as you think you can get away with. I rarely use a fly rod that's less than 9 feet, even on small streams. A long rod allows you to reach over currents that would cause drag and hold less line on the water. JAY NICHOLS

RODS

I use as long a rod as I can get away with—even on small streams. I most often fish with a 9½- to 10-foot rod rated for 4- to 5-weight line. A long rod allows me to be farther away from the fish while still being able to reach over "nagging" currents (currents between the angler and the targeted seam that cause drag), providing optimal line control. Shorter rods cannot hold as much line and leader off the water. This means more mending and less line and leader control.

Long rods have improved greatly over the last several years. Older 10-foot models could be clumsy and tip-heavy, and they often were available only in heavier line weights. These heavy rods made it hard to tight-line with an extended hand for a long period. Today, however, more and more anglers are coming to realize that a 10-foot rod allows for better line and leader control, and manufacturers are responding with light 10-foot rods in line weights as low as 2, which are easy to fish all day. Some argue that you can't fight a fish efficiently with a long rod, and I will concede that this is true when dealing with large fish, but it is not really an issue when trout fishing.

I also like fast-action rods, which allow you to set the hook quicker than slower-action rods. At short distances, this delayed reaction isn't too detrimental, but at distances exceeding 50 feet, the slower rods take too long to react to the hook set, often missing the fish or not getting a secure enough set. Some rods labeled "Czech nymphing" are designed with a very slow action to protect light tippets, but I've found that fast-action rods can easily handle 6X and 7X tippets if you apply the correct amount of pressure. I concede that softer tips are better with really light 7X and 8X tippets, but I rarely fish these sizes and find that I can adjust when I do.

Fast-action rods also maintain more tension on the line when playing a fish. Soft-action rods can be wobbly in the tip, which means you lose tension to the fly. With barbless hooks, it's important to maintain tension while playing a fish. With stiff, fast-action rods, you do tend to lose more small trout, the 7- to 10-inchers, because there is no bend in the rod, but I found this important only during my competition days, when 8-inch trout scored points and I often fished with a medium-fast-action rod to bounce less fish. At this stage in my angling life, however, I'm not too concerned if an 8-inch trout accidentally falls off my line.

Find the rod length and action that fit best in your system. Pictured are three of my teammates as we were preparing for the 2007 World Championships in Finland. Ask each guy about his favorite rod and you'll get three different answers. They have their own preferences and so should you. GEORGE DANIEL

REELS AND LINES

When tight-line nymphing, the right reel is essential not for playing fish, but to counterbalance the long, tip-heavy rods. A balanced outfit reduces fatigue and provides greater enjoyment on the stream. To see if the rod is balanced with the reel on it, I focus on the area where my thumb is resting on the handle, mentally mark the spot, and then try to balance the rod on my index finger at that same point on the handle. If the rod tips quickly to one side, like a seesaw, then it's either tip-heavy or reel-heavy. The rod doesn't have to sit perfectly straight on my finger, but I want some measure of balance to reduce fatigue on my hand.

I like to carry two rods rigged and ready to fish: one with a tight-line system and the other with a suspension system. If I don't carry two rods with me while fishing, I carry two reels, each set up with a different leader (discussed below). I use the same fly line for tight-line and suspension nymphing. Currently I like a weight-forward, floating line with a regular taper that's at least 40 feet long, like RIO Gold or Scientific Anglers Trout tapers. Some lines marketed for nymphing have heavy front tapers, but the weight of the line out of the rod tip pulls down on the leader and creates sag between the rod tip and nymph that will pull the flies or rig away from the stream bottom. A standard double-taper is also a fine choice for long-line mending. I prefer a 4-weight over a 6-weight, as medium line tapers in this weight provide adequate power for presentation and will not create too much of a belly in a tight-line connection to the nymph.

When possible, I prefer to have two rods rigged and ready to fish: one with a tight-line system and the other with a suspension system. Usually I wrap the unused rod around my wader belt, keeping it out of the way until I'm ready to make a switch. I especially like to have two rods when fishing rivers that have both broken and very slow-moving water. JAY NICHOLS

LEADERS

I carry three main leaders: my standard tight-line nymphing leader with a sighter, a short but aggressive knotless leader for long suspension drifts, and a French-style leader. To make it easier to change rigs, I carry two reels: one set up with a tight-line leader and the other with a long suspension drift leader. In low water, I change the tight-line leader to the French-style for longer presentations. These three leaders (along with some basic modifications described below) allow me to fish up close and from far away, with both tight-line and suspension tactics. Leaders are like guns and cars—everyone has a preference. My formulas are only suggestions; experiment to find the leader that works best for you.

For the butt sections of my tight-line leaders, I like to use two types of material: fluorescent blue Stren and ultragreen Maxima, which is stiffer but less visible. Dave Rothrock introduced me to fluorescent blue Stren back in the late 1990s. It is easy to see, which allows you to quickly locate your leader and follow the butt section down to your sighter. It is imperative that you spot your sighter immediately, because some drifts are so short in tight-lining that they last only a few seconds.

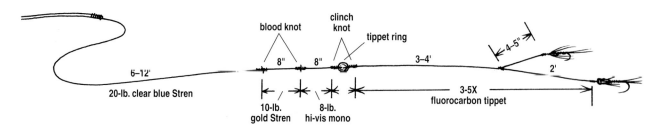

Here is a standard tight-line leader. I try to keep the taper as simple as possible, with just three sections: a butt that's half the total length, a sighter, and a level fluorocarbon tippet connected to the sighter with a tippet ring. To the level fluorocarbon tippet, I attach a 3-foot section of fluorocarbon tippet using a surgeon's or Orvis knot, leaving a 4- to 5-inch tag if I want to attach a dropper. I prefer to place the heaviest fly on the point to keep the entire rig tight.

A long leader allows me to present nymphs from farther away without having to place any line and leader on the water. This is especially important when fishing over spooky fish on streams like the famed Letort. A typical French-style leader is longer than 20 feet to allow gentle presentations in spooky water. Because smaller, lighter-weight patterns are used, such an aggressive leader is all the taper that's needed to deliver the presentation. JAY NICHOLS

When I anticipate having to use suspenders and I don't want to switch to a dedicated leader for them, I like a tight-line leader with Maxima in the butt because it is stiffer. The butt sections are long (about 50 percent of the overall leader) and not tapered. This really simplifies the leader design and construction process. The long butts help turn over the lightweight nymph rigs with a 14- to 16-foot leader, the length I'm most comfortable fishing, and the knotless leader also moves smoothly through the guides, which is critical when fishing long leaders, when a part of the leader often remains within the guides. The French-style leader is also constructed with a very long butt section that acts as an extension of the fly line.

Conversely, suspension leaders should be shorter and have more aggressive tapers. Unlike short casts with heavy weight, where the rig turns over the leader, for long casts you need to let the tapered fly line do most of the work turning over the rig. For this situation, I modify a 7½-foot 3X knotless Umpqua Power Taper leader, incorporating a tippet ring, level tippet, and suspender. Knotless leaders sink less than knotted ones, which makes it easier to mend them and pick up your line after the drift or during the hook set. They also do not collect as much debris as knotted leaders, which can be a problem in late summer when many spring creeks have a lot of algae on the surface. The important thing is to experiment, and once you've decided on a system, be consistent so that you can effectively use it.

Because I often switch between tight-line and suspension nymphing, even in the same run, I often attach a Thingama-

A modified Dave Rothrock leader is great for those with visual difficulties or any nymph fisher who wants to see the entire leader better. The combination of blue and gold Stren creates a highly visible leader for any lighting condition. JAY NICHOLS

bobber strike indicator or dry fly to my tight-line leader and high-stick it, as long as I'm within 30 feet of my target; any longer than that, and I use a specialized leader (discussed below). When using a dry fly as a suspender, I attach a short section of tippet, at least 2 feet, from the tippet ring to the dry fly, and then attach my nymphs to the dry. The 2-foot tippet section creates separation from the colored sighter.

Long-Range Nymphing Base Leader

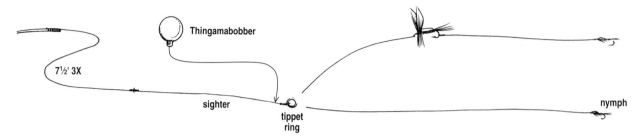

For casts exceeding 30 feet, I modify a 7½-foot 3X knotless Umpqua Power Taper leader, an aggressive taper with a thick butt, by cutting off 8 inches of the tippet and attaching a 2.25 mm tippet ring. If I do not plan on tight lining, I will not add a sighter; instead, I connect the tippet ring directly to the knotless leader butt.

   If I want to use a Thingamabobber, I attach it above the tippet ring, attach a piece of fluorocarbon tippet that is from one to three times the depth of the water to the tippet ring with a clinch knot, and then tie a nymph or nymphs to the other end.

   If I want to use a dry fly as a suspender instead of the Thingamabobber, I attach 2 to 3 feet of tippet to the tippet ring before tying it on.

Loren Williams' French Leader

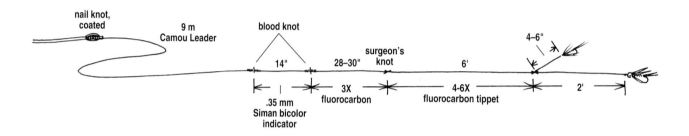

Loren Williams' French leader uses a manufactured 9 meter Camou Leader as the base. Cutting approximately 8 feet off the tip of the leader allows you to tie in a sighter section with a diameter as large as .35 mm and still maintain a continuous taper.

Curly Q Leader

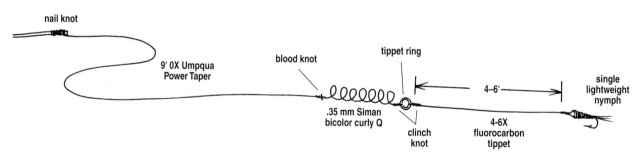

This shallow-water leader rig is perfect for long casts beyond 25 feet. I prefer a leader less than 16 feet but still long enough to allow a delicate presentation. To make this rig, you attach a 9-foot 0X Umpqua Power Taper leader to the line with a nail knot. Cut back about 1½ feet of tippet; this will allow the diameter of the curly Q to match up with the leader tip section so that the blood knot will attach the two sections. Attach the curly Q (made with a minimum of six wraps; see instructions on pages 21 and 22) to the leader with a blood knot, and then attach a tippet ring to the other end of the curly Q with a clinch knot. Attach a straight piece of 4X–6X fluorocarbon tippet to the tippet ring (clinch knot), and then tie on a lightly weighted fly.

SIGHTERS

The sighter is a critical component of the tight-line system, as it provides a visual indication of when to lead your nymphs or set the hook. Sighters are anything you integrate into your leader to help you detect strikes. For years, anglers watched the knot connections or the line-leader connection, but sighters are much more visible. Various kinds of sighters include colored sleeves, braid, fluorocarbon, and monofilament nylon. Monofilament is my favorite material because it's available in a wide range of colors and sizes, it's affordable, it floats (great for switching over to dry flies), and you can easily tie it into the leader system with standard knots. Another advantage of a nylon monofilament sighter is that you can use it as a shock absorber when fishing fine tippets and faster-action rods. Boiling the leader for five minutes will soften it and provide a little extra give when playing fish, which is especially useful when fishing with 6X diameter or smaller tippets. Placing the sighter after the butt section of your leader situates it much closer to your flies, where it is more sensitive.

A sighter that is all one color has two points of contrast for your eyes to focus on: where the sighter connects to the tippet and to the leader. Using two or three colors increases these points of contrast and provides more reference points for you. You can also add visibility by drawing small black bands on the sighter with a permanent marker or tying overhand knots throughout its length. Such minor details can really help you see it better. Because we all see color differently, experiment to find what works best for you. Today there's an abundance of colored material on the market that can be used as sighters, most of it developed by the terminal tackle industry and some from the fly-fishing industry. Check out the terminal fishing line department at a Cabela's or Bass Pro Shop and you will be amazed at how many color options are available to choose from.

Left: Josh Stephens showing us why everyone needs to visit New Zealand. Josh built a brightly colored sighter into his leader to allow for better strike detection, even while sight-fishing spooky brown trout on the famed clear-water streams of New Zealand. AMIDEA DANIEL

Below: Jan Siman bicolor strike indicator material is the brightest and most visible sighter material currently on the market. The material combines fluorescent chartreuse and fluorescent orange to provide the ultimate visibility in any light condition and against various backgrounds. It is my first choice when trout are not wary of brightly colored leader material, such as during runoff periods. JAY NICHOLS

Left: Compared with a monochromatic sighter, a two-tone sighter provides additional points of contrast and offers better visibility through various light conditions. For fishing when the water is lower, I like to build my own sighter made of gold Stren and hi-vis mono. You can also make your own sighter from materials of two or three different colors. Experiment and find what color scheme works best for you. Not everyone sees color in the same manner. GEORGE DANIEL

Basic Sighter

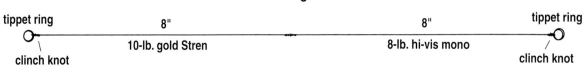

The sighter I favor these days (above) is made from 8 inches of 10-pound-test gold Stren and 8 inches of 8-pound-test hi-vis mono. I like to taper the sections because this helps turn over dry flies a little better if I switch to them during a hatch. The 16-inch length not only serves as a generous target for my eyes, but also telegraphs the drift of my flies when it is lying on the water's surface, as the tip of the sighter often points in the direction of the flies. Additionally, it can act as a depth gauge. A tricolor sighter like the one below provides various points of contrast, and the different colors show up well in different lighting conditions.

Tricolor Sighter

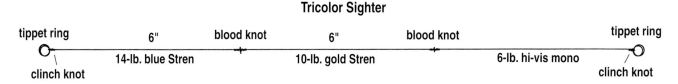

Some fly shops also are carrying Czech nymphing indicators, which are a form of sighters, and more and more fly shops are likely to begin carrying similar nymphing accessories.

The diameter of the material you use for the sighter is an important consideration, as the larger the diameter, the more surface drag it creates. A thin sighter bites into the surface current more quickly and creates a tighter angle to the nymph. For example, the highly visible gold Stren in 8-pound-test is small enough in diameter that it quickly sinks through the surface layers when fishing deeper water; 14-pound-test, on the other hand, is almost a third larger in diameter, which creates greater surface drag. A sighter and section of tippet that are similar in diameter will sink at a uniform speed, resulting in little to no slack from the sighter to the nymph. Even the smallest amount of slack in your system is detrimental to strike detection. This is why I normally use no larger than 6- to 8-pound-test for the second section of my colored sighter when nymphing with my normal 4X or 5X tippet section. It's important that the last section of the sighter is stronger than the tippet so that you don't break it off. That's why I like 8-pound-test: I can still fish 3X and smaller diameters without worrying about breaking off the sighter. Always fish a tippet section that has less breaking strength than the sighter.

OTHER LEADER FORMULAS

Steve Parrott's Czech Leader

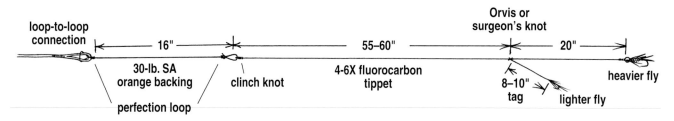

Parrott is shop manager of Blue Quill Angler in Evergreen, Colorado. Parrott's sighter is 30-pound-test backing (Scientific Anglers) with loops in both ends (for a competition legal setup, he used a needle nail knot to tie this backing section to the end of the fly line). "I like for my leaders (measured from the tip of the fly line to the bottom of the leader where I am going to attach my anchor fly) to be around three quarters the length of the rod I am fishing," Parrott says. "This leader above will measure out around 8'4" which is perfect for a 10' rod. If I am using a shorter or longer rod, I will adjust the section of the level tippet coming off of the sighter. I place my anchor fly in the point position with a lighter fly up top. I will switch this order if I want to fish shallower water."

Devin Olsen's Leader

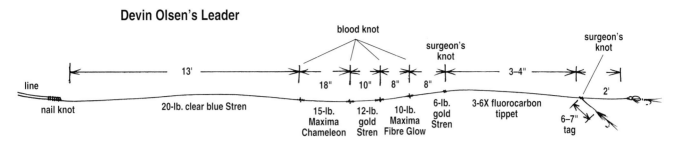

Devin Olsen is fast becoming one of the more reconizable names in competitive fly fishing. He's been a member of Fly Fishing Team USA for five years and has competed in three World Championships.

Lance Egan's Standard Nymph Leader

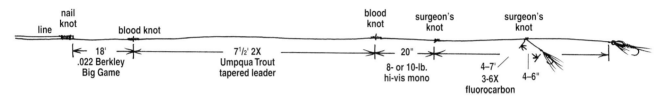

Egan attaches an 18-inch-butt section of .022-inch diameter Berkley Big Game to the fly line with a needle nail knot and then blood knots a 7½ foot 2X Umpqua Trout tapered leader to the butt section. His prefered sighter is 20 inches of 8- to 10-pound-test hi-vis monofilament. His tippet ranges from 3X to 6X depending on fly size and river conditions. If using two flies, he spaces them out 20 to 24 inches, and tippet length from the sighter to the point fly (dependent on water conditions) is generally between 4 and 7 feet.

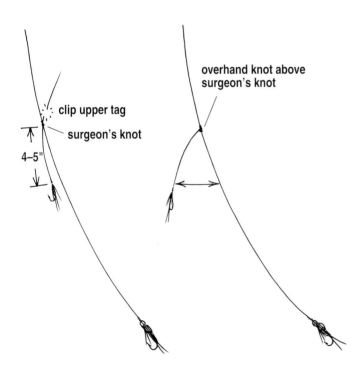

For my tippet-to-tippet connections, I use surgeon's and Orvis knots, and I frequently attach a dropper nymph to the excess leader material (tag). Use the tag that points toward your point fly, and clip the other one. To prevent tangles, tie a simple overhand knot in the bottom tag above the original knot. This keeps the fly away from the leader. I like to use a tag 4 to 5 inches long. This length provides enough movement for your flies, allows for multiple fly changes, and doesn't tangle as much as longer tags.

I use a tippet caddy to carry guide spools of fluorocarbon ranging from 3X to 6X to deal with any stream condition. The caddy keeps the various sizes easily accessible. Compared with nylon, fluorocarbon sinks faster, has better knot strength when wet, and is more resistant to abrasion. Ideally, the tippet length should always be longer than the greatest water depth you fish. For example, a tippet section spaced 2 feet from sighter to point fly and fished in a 4-foot-deep run will pull the sighter below the surface, costing you the ability to detect strikes. At the same time, you don't want your sighter too close to the fly. In low, clear water, I prefer to keep my tippet length 4 to 5 feet. The waters I fish in central Pennsylvania rarely exceed 5 feet in depth, so this 4- to 5-foot tippet length will work in both shallow and deeper water, although sometimes I may need to extend the length of the tippet when fishing deeper water. JAY NICHOLS

TIPPET RINGS

A tippet ring is a miniature steel ring used to connect a leader's butt section to the tippet. Tippet rings allow you to attach thin-diameter 4X–6X tippet to the relatively large-diameter sighter, which tapers down to 8-pound-test in my favorite rigs. If you were to try to connect these two with a knot, it not only would look horrible, but also would be likely to fail because of the difficulty of connecting two sections of extremely different diameters together. I like to use a straight piece of level tippet attached to the tippet ring because it sinks a lot faster and more uniformly than a tapered leader.

Tippet rings also save you a lot of time and leader materials, since you don't have to use up any of the leader material when retying your rig. You can switch among various nymphing setups without having to meddle with the integrity of the leader. They are lightweight, so they will not hinge your cast if you decide to switch over to a dry-fly setup. I use the same butt section for both dry-fly fishing and nymphing.

MULTIPLE RIG ORGANIZERS

I like to store my rigs on an Orvis Dropper Rig Fly Box insert, and I label each one with a black permanent marker so that I know exactly what type of rig it is and how heavy it is. However you organize them, you can save a lot of time by having multiple setups prerigged and ready to go. This, along with the tippet ring, allows you to quickly and easily change your rig to match the conditions.

I have heavy, medium, and lightweight rigs ready to go at any moment. My heavy rig is pretty specialized, and I generally use it only during spring runoff or when fishing fast, deep water (deeper than 4 feet). This rig often includes at least one anchor pattern that is tied with a $^5\!/_{32}$- or $^1\!/_{16}$-inch tungsten bead along with lead wire. My medium-weight rig includes a $^1\!/_8$-inch tungsten bead-head fly with additional leader wire, along with another, smaller tungsten bead-head pattern. I use this rig in early spring and any time after a strong rain to deal with medium-speed currents averaging 2 to 3 feet in depth. My lightweight rig often contains at least one $^7\!/_{64}$-inch tungsten bead-head pattern along with a lightly weighted or unweighted nymph. Based on the concept of elevating and leading (see page 74), this is all the weight I need to deal with in over 60 percent of the stream conditions I encounter in both the East and West.

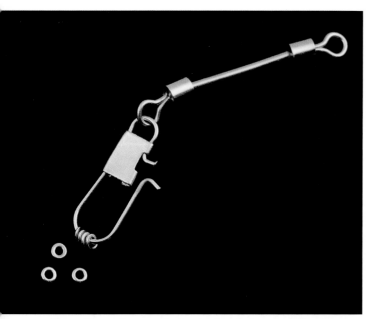

Above: Tippet rings vary in size, but I prefer to use a 2.25-millimeter ring for all my trout and steelhead rigs. Rings are available in a few different sizes. I like to use one size, the 2.25-millimeter, for all my trout and steelhead fishing, including streamer and dry-fly fishing. JAY NICHOLS

Right: A pretied rig saves time on the stream. I like to carry at least one of each of the following: heavy and medium-weight tight-line rigs, a dry-and-dropper (a rig with a dry fly used as an indicator and a nymph underneath as a dropper), and a rig with a single dry. This system allows you to quickly adjust to stream conditions when moving up- and downstream. GEORGE DANIEL

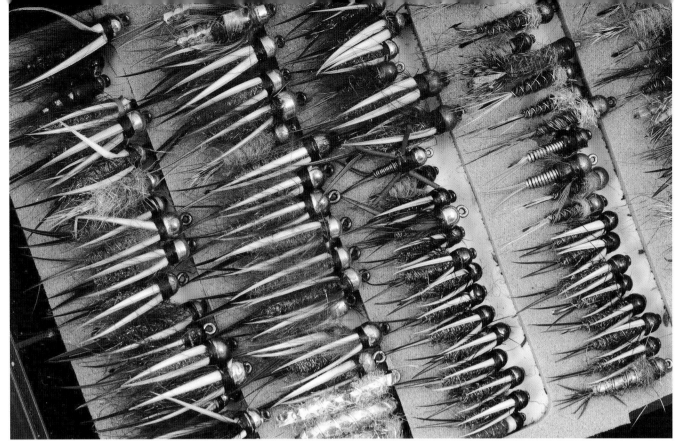

Carry a wide range of sizes and styles of your "go-to" bugs. A successful nympher always adjusts the weight based on the speed and depth of the water. Most often, it's nothing more than a microadjustment of a gram or two. In such cases, I have found it far easier and faster to switch between weighted flies than to add and remove split shot. JAY NICHOLS

SUSPENDERS

I use four kinds of suspension devices on a regular basis: dry flies, Thingamabobbers, pinch ons, and curly Qs. First, I carry an assortment of small to large dry flies to combine with a range of weighted nymphs as dry-and-dropper rigs. I seldom add split shot when fishing a dry-and-dropper rig, as I prefer this rig to suspend a weighted nymph slightly higher in the water column. Besides, most dry flies can hold only so much weight.

I use a dry fly any time I feel there's a chance that a trout will eat the indicator. During heavy hatch periods, I sometimes use a dry-and-dropper rig to provide a multistage approach to the trout. A high-floating dry fly represents the winged adult, an unweighted soft-hackle is the emerger, and a heavy bead-head point fly is the nymph. Thus I can cover three possible feeding levels all with one rig and one cast. Before using this kind of rig, check local regulations to make sure more than one fly is permitted.

Thingamabobbers are simply plastic spheres filled with air. Diameter for diameter, I have yet to find another indicator that can suspend the same amount of weight and also requires zero maintenance. Thingamabobbers come in $\frac{1}{2}$-, $\frac{3}{4}$-, and 1-inch sizes. I carry all three sizes to deal with just about any weighted nymphing rig I want to fish. The $\frac{1}{2}$-inch size will handle most suspension nymphing rigs I throw here in the East and easily suspends all my #8 and smaller heavily weighted tungsten flies.

Pinch-on indicators were first introduced to me by my friend Chuck Farneth, a former ESPN Great Outdoor Games champion from Arkansas. This small indicator floats forever

The CDC Indicator pattern is more buoyant than the CDC and Elk and often takes just as many fish on the surface when I'm fishing a dry-and-dropper rig. I use this pattern when drifting larger, heavier nymphs in broken water, and the CDC and Elk more for softer water. JAY NICHOLS

and is one of the most sensitive for fishing very lightly weighted rigs. It's a favorite of Chuck's when fishing many of the famed Arkansas tailwaters with very small nymphs.

And finally, there's the curly Q. Charles Jardine wrote about this indicator in an article titled "Bites on a Curly Wurly"

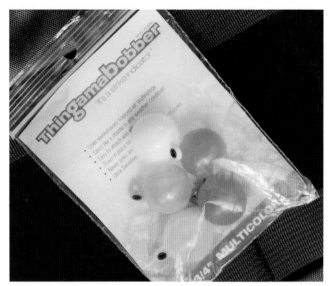

The Thingamabobber suspender has become a favorite because of its ability to float heavy rigs with no maintenance, along with its O-ring connector that makes it easy to take on and off. It comes in a variety of sizes and colors to use in just about any light condition. JAY NICHOLS

in the UK magazine *Fly Fishing and Fly Tying*. Curly Qs are created by wrapping colored sections of mono around pieces of wooden dowel or other cylinders, such as empty pen tubes, screws, or any other similarly shaped object.

My instructions here for making curly Qs are based on that article. I use this coiled, colored nylon suspension device for low, clear water where distance is a must and a soft presentation is critical to avoid initially spooking fish. Curly Qs have coils that sit up off the water's surface, making them easier to see from a distance. Greased sighters, which are straight and lie flat on the water, can be seen from up to 20 feet away but are difficult to observe at greater distances. I carry several prepared, coiled curly Q rigs that are still wound on their wooden dowels in a small plastic bag.

I prefer to use larger-diameter colored nylon, such as 14-pound gold Stren or .35-millimeter Jan Siman bicolor strike indicator material, for my curly Qs. The thicker-diameter material is easier to see and has more surface area, and once greased, it will float better than smaller-diameter material. Since nylon has more memory than fluorocarbon, it holds its springlike shape longer.

An Anglers Image pinch-on indicator is one of my favorite suspenders for lightweight rigs. I normally fish two size 16 or smaller tungsten bead-head nymphs (3/32-inch bead or smaller) with a pinch-on suspender. JAY NICHOLS

CREATING THE CURLY Q

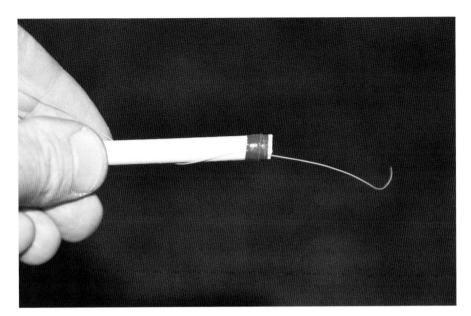

A 4-inch section of ¼-inch-diameter wooden dowel creates a large enough curly that will ride sufficiently high on the water to be seen at great distances. Cut a 20-inch section of 8- to 15-pound-test colored nylon monofilament. These sizes are large enough in diameter to float lightweight nymphs once treated with Mucilin floatant.

Lay the tag end of the colored mono over the dowel, with at least 4 inches hanging over the edge. This tag provides a straight piece of tippet to allow for an easy knot connection to the main leader. Secure it in place by wrapping a ⅛-inch-wide piece of duct tape around the end of the tag and one end of the wooden dowel.

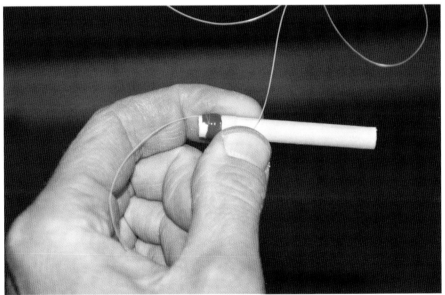

Now wrap the loose end of the colored mono around and around the dowel, keeping the wraps tight against one another. Use a minimum of eight wraps but no more than twelve. More than a dozen wraps would create too long of a curly Q, causing it to become a little too wind-resistant and have too much stretch, thus reducing its sensitivity.

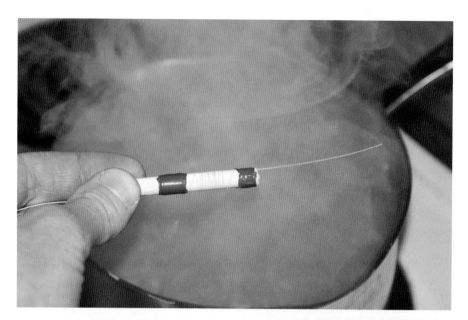

Place the dowel and monofilament in boiling water and then store in the freezer overnight.

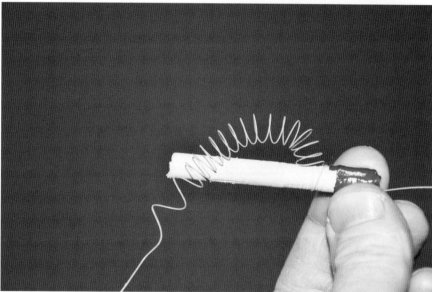

To use, simply unravel both duct tape sections and pull the curly off the wooden dowel.

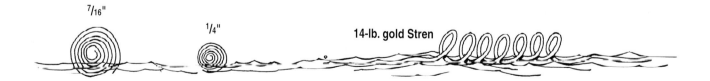

Larger diameter curly Qs sit higher in the water and allow anglers to notice strikes from a distance. Some of my favorite colors are gold Stren, fluorescent blue Stren, Maxima Fibre Glow, and green Berkley Big Game.

OTHER EQUIPMENT AND ACCESSORIES

Stomach Pump

Occasionally, mostly when I am having trouble finding the right fly to consistently catch fish, I use a stomach pump to figure out what the fish are feeding on. If I am fortunate enough to catch a larger adult fish during one of these slow periods, I use the stomach pump to quickly gather a sample of what that fish has eaten most recently. This tells me not only what patterns I should be fishing, but also, just as important, at what levels I need to be fishing the fly. Picking up rocks to look at potential food sources is a great place to start, but the pump provides you with the latest intelligence on what food items are being consumed. Keep in mind, however, that the stomach contents of one fish will not always be the consensus among all fish.

Some anglers argue that a stomach pump removes the food content the trout has worked hard to obtain, but I use one only in streams that contain high aquatic insect concentrations. In tailwaters, limestoners, and spring creeks, I believe that a pump rarely negates a trout's daily feeding.

Hook File

Nymphing requires that you fish your patterns near the stream bottom, among boulders and other structures that will inevitably dull your hook points. Luckily for us, today's quality chemically sharpened hooks retain their sharpness longer than their predecessors. However, pocketwater can wreak havoc on hook points, and even the high-end hooks quickly become dull after a few good bumps on the bottom, rendering them almost useless. A few quick strokes with a hook file, or hone, can quickly bring them back to life.

When sharpening hooks, I like to file the point on the bottom and both sides. I start with one side, then do the bottom, and finish with the opposite side. Often all that's needed is one or two brushing motions on each side. Hold the hook file steady with your nondominant hand, and place one side of the hook point on top of the file, creating a little tension between them. Then begin to stroke the fly against the file, starting with the tip and stroking from the point toward the bend. Sharpen just the portion of the hook point before the barb.

Some anglers use a stomach pump to determine what trout are currently eating. Use the pump sparingly, and only on larger adult trout. Do not use a stomach pump on a fish smaller than 12 inches. Also, never use the pump if the water is warm. JAY NICHOLS

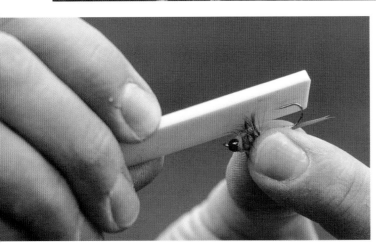

If you want to be a successful angler, it's important to take the time to do the little things like keeping your points sharp. Spending just thirty seconds sharpening the hook point will drastically increase your landing percentages. It often surprises me to see how many missed fish it takes before an angler either reties a new fly or sharpens the dull hook. My TMC hook file is one of my most used accessories.
JAY NICHOLS

Leader Wallet

I carry a leader wallet, which is a compact storage unit for all leaders, leader material, and sighter material I may need. It serves as a backup plan in case disaster strikes, such as if I wrap an entire leader around a tree branch that's too high to reach. I carry the following items in my leader wallet at all times:

- 7½-foot 3X knotless leaders for long-line suspension nymphing
- pretied nymphing leaders with Maxima Chameleon and fluorescent blue butt sections
- 20-pound-test fluorescent blue Stren and 25-pound-test Maxima Chameleon cut in 15-foot lengths
- sighter material cut in 20-inch lengths in gold Stren and hi-vis mono
- extra tippet rings

Polarized Sunglasses

A great pair of polarized sunglasses may be the most underrated nymphing tool. While working in a fly shop, I found that the most difficult high-end product to sell was quality optics. However, those who eventually purchased a good pair of sunglasses inevitably said they would never go back to inexpensive ones.

Having good optics enables the angler to look into the trout's world, providing a detailed map of the depths, drop-offs, and structure. I rely on my lenses to see the bottom water levels to determine how fast I should lead my nymphs and to spot fish when sight-fishing. Sunglasses also protect your eyes from miscast flies and weight. My favorite lens tint is brown, which allows me to see well in all light conditions.

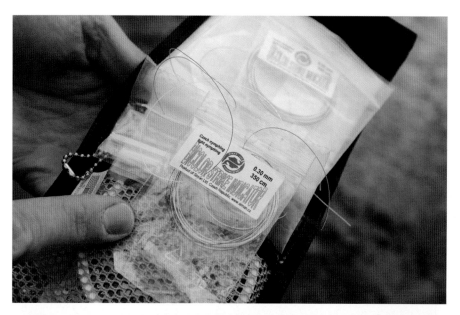

Along with prerigged leaders for both tight-line and suspension nymphing, I carry a variety of colored sighter sections in my leader wallet. Pictured is the Jan Siman bicolor strike indicator material I carry in sizes from .35 to .20 millimeters. When I'm fishing, I prefer not to carry spools of colored mono or butt-section material for building leaders. Instead, I build all my leaders at home and carry at least two of each style wherever I go. JAY NICHOLS

A degreasing agent such as Loon Snake River Mud is useful when nymphing with small amounts of weight, as it helps the tippet break the water's surface tension. JAY NICHOLS

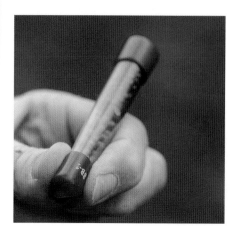

While I try to stick with weighted flies—mostly tungsten bead-head patterns—there are times I feel split shot can replace or complement weighted flies. I use split shot when fishing unweighted emerger patterns to allow the fly to ride slightly off the stream bottom. I carry several packs of Anglers Image Anchor split shot in sizes 1, 4, and 6 for most trout-fishing conditions. For most nymphing conditions, I place the shot 4 to 8 inches away from the fly, and the smaller shot is a little less noticeable. To hold the split shot, I like the push-style dispensers that quickly drop a weight into your hand rather than carrying various sized pots of shot. JAY NICHOLS

Chest Pack

For carrying my gear, I prefer a chest pack with a small backpack mounted on the rear. I tend to wade aggressively and often find myself up to my chest in water. Most vests come down to the waist, however, and anytime you exceed that depth, your vest gets wet, along with all the contents within. A chest pack rides higher, permitting you to wade in waist-deep water without getting any storage area wet. Also, with fishing vests, most anglers put the majority of their tackle in the front pockets, which places most of the weight on the neck. A chest pack with front and back compartments, on the other hand, allows you to equally distribute the weight between front and back, which places the weight on your shoulders, not your neck. This is especially important if you begin to carry tungsten flies around.

Though I still carry a number of larger fly boxes in the rear compartments of my chest pack, my working fly box is a C&F Chest Patch, a small, vented fly box that attaches on the outside of a pack or vest. In it, I put a good sampling of all my favorite nymphs. These nymphs are not always organized according to pattern design, as I constantly change the weight of my patterns. The only organization is that each row holds patterns with similar weights, mostly with the same size bead. Like all C&F fly boxes, this flip patch has Micro Slit Foam, which works much better to keep the flies from falling out than most other designs. Because it is vented, I also put my used flies in here to dry. JAY NICHOLS

Left: I used this William Joseph chest pack for about four seasons (approximately 1,000 outings), until it finally fell apart, as I knew exactly where every part of my nymphing system was. JAY NICHOLS

Fly Dryer, Desiccant, and Floatant

I carry three products to keep my flies riding high: Amadou fly dryer, Frog's Fanny Fly Treatment or Loon Easy Dry desiccant, and Tiemco Dry Magic silicone gel floatant. After fishing a dry fly, I first use a piece of Amadou to squeeze out some of the moisture. Then I use the desiccant to remove even more moisture from the dry fly, especially with CDC flies. I carry the container with applicator brush so I can really stroke the powder into the fly. Brushing a little desiccant into a nymph is also a great tactic to use when an insect emergence is in full swing, as it will produce bubbles around the fly while under the surface. Finally, I use gel floatant to grease all flies, leaders, and indicators before fishing them. Tiemco Dry Magic is one of the few gels that work on CDC flies. Most other silicone gels actually sink CDC flies, as they mat down the tiny fibers that keep the feathers afloat.

Waterproof Camera

For several years, I kept a fishing journal in a notebook, but I recently have begun using a computer instead. In my journal, I don't talk much about the number of fish I caught or my philosophical views of the day's events. Instead, I focus more on the conditions, hatches, and other variables related to my success or sometimes lack thereof.

To supplement my writing, I add photos I took of various water types where I had success with a fish. After downloading each photo, I write below it a brief description of the tactics that did or didn't work. I'm a visual learner, and this has proved to be one of my most effective tools for recalling past experiences and building on them for more successful outings in the future. The Panasonic waterproof camera I carry also has a video option that lets me record the setting in live mode, along with a microphone I can use to record a quick narrative for the day's events. Sometimes a picture or short video is worth a thousand words.

Heavy anchor patterns come out only during the heaviest water conditions.

Casting Weight

3

Even though Kareem Abdul Jabbar had played lots of ball, the great UCLA basketball coach John Wooden started Jabbar's first day of practice by showing him how to properly put on his socks in order to prevent blisters. Coach Wooden never assumed his players knew all the fundamentals, and he tried to break down his instruction into the simplest parts for his players to understand and execute. It's tough to argue with ten national championships. What does this have to do with fly fishing? Though some of you reading this book have been casting flies for a long time, it still may benefit you to go over some important fundamentals related to casting nymphs.

Before delving into the different ways of fishing nymphs, I would like to offer a few general pointers on casting nymph rigs. I go into further detail on more specialized casts in the relevant chapters, but because casting nymphs and all the split shot and suspenders is so different from making the conventional dry-fly cast, I will cover some general ground here first.

FOUR PRINCIPLES OF THE BASIC CAST

Casting is simply the means by which you deliver a fly or flies to the fish. Though you do not need to be a tournament distance caster to be a great nymph angler, you must be able to deliver the flies and the line accurately, manage your loops and apply the appropriate power to accommodate multiple flies, and when necessary, cast delicately to avoid disturbing the fish. Fair casters hit their targets only a fraction of the time, and therefore they take only a fraction of the trout; this has as much to do with learning to identify the proper target as it does getting the flies there. Luckily for us trout anglers, trout often hold in a general area while feeding, providing us with stationary targets, unlike many saltwater species that are constantly on the move. Therefore, we don't always have to rush our casts. You can—and should—take your time getting into the best possible position before casting.

The four principles of the basic cast are *tension*, *acceleration*, *stop*, and *pause*. They are easy to remember, but you must

Casting is simply the means by which you deliver a fly or flies to the fish. Though you do not need to be a tournament distance caster to be a great nymph angler, you must be able to deliver the flies and the line accurately, manage your loops and apply the appropriate power to accommodate multiple flies, and when necessary, cast delicately to avoid disturbing the fish. JAY NICHOLS practice on the water and in the yard to develop your muscle memory, which means your muscles become familiar with repeated movements over time, making these movements easier to execute without conscious effort. It may take you only a day to grasp the four principles, or it may take several days, which still is a small investment for a lifetime activity. Hire a qualified casting instructor or fly-fishing guide if you struggle with the basic cast. You won't be able to make the advanced casts until you master the basics.

Tension

With a bow and arrow, drawing the bowstring back to create a bend in the bow creates tension. In some ways, the fly rod behaves like a bow. As you move the rod tip back and forth, the line weight forces the rod to bend, creating tension. This tension produces the needed energy to roll the line back and forth. The line must be tight with the rod tip to create the necessary tension to pull on the rod tip, bend the rod, and make the cast.

When beginning the casting stroke, do not allow slack between the rod tip and fly line. The rod tip should load as soon as you begin moving it. If you have slack in the line, much of the rod tip movement is spent taking out slack, not creating tension and loading the rod. The line should be lying in a straight line on the water up to the rod tip before you make the cast. If you need to remove slack, retrieve the line until it is hanging directly off the rod tip.

Acceleration

A good casting stroke is a smooth acceleration of the rod tip. Just as a good driver is able to speed up the car without the passenger's head rocking back and forth, you should provide a smooth ride for your flies on their way to the target. The accelerated movement is not a pushing movement. Our bodies are designed to pull. As an example, think about throwing a football. Do you push the ball or do you pull the ball through the air and release at the end? As when throwing a football, the acceleration movement in casting is more of a pulling motion, wherein you lead the fly line with the rod tip and release it at the very end.

The main idea is to put the greatest amount of tension you can on the rod in order for it to load. The more tension on the rod, the greater the load, which leads to a better cast. If you instead attempt to push the cast, the rod tip quickly loads and unloads, which lessens the amount of potential energy the rod is able to create. Instead, a longer pulling motion is able to put the rod under pressure for a longer time, creating a greater load. Turning again to the bow-and-arrow comparison, a quick pushing motion would be the equivalent of being able to pull the bow back only halfway before releasing. Sure, you can still shoot an arrow, but distance, speed, and accuracy are greatly diminished. On the other hand, a longer pulling motion of the rod is like fully pulling the bow back before releasing.

With short-line nymphing, the pull is a forward or backward drift of the forearm and arm. It begins with the hand drifting and

Square your shoulders to the target before proceeding with the cast. In this photo, I am racing to the next holding spot on the Whanganui River during the 2008 World Championships, but I still square up to the target before making the presentation. BRENT GLOVER

quickly speeds up to a stop at the end of the cast. Because heavier weights are associated with short-line nymphing, it's essential to wait until you feel a tug on the backcast before beginning the forward cast. With such a heavy-weighted rig, your finger or thumb on top (depending on rod grip) will actually feel the tension of the weight as you first drift before accelerating to a stop. Also, the shorter cast requires less energy during the smooth pulling acceleration. All you need to do is put the flies in motion, and the weight of the rig will carry them to the target. With long-line nymphing, you are relying on the taper to deliver the flies, so the feel is similar to casting a dry line.

Stop

After the accelerated movement of the rod tip has created tension, you need to release the built-up energy to unroll your line back and forth. A good, sharp stop is the best way to release that energy, and only a sharp stop will fully unload the rod. Imagine you're facing a brick wall that's 2 feet away. Now imagine your rod hand accelerating toward the wall but stopping suddenly before hitting the wall. This is what the appropriate abrupt stop when casting resembles. In some short-range casts, you can get away with a lob and soft stop, but for other nymphing casts, such as a tuck cast, a good stop is critical.

The path of the rod tip during the casting stroke determines where the line goes, so make sure your wrist travels in a straight line to your target if you want the line to lie straight out.

A common mistake is to turn the wrist inward during the casting stroke. This will throw an undesirable curve into the line. In this case, the flies are being cast off to the side of the rod tip instead of directly over. During this cast, the hand curved inward toward the body, and the curved shape of the line reflects the path the rod tip traveled.

Pause

As soon as the rod tip stops, a loop forms off the tip. Most overhead casting requires a pause at this point to allow the line and rig to unroll fully, either forward or backward, so that the line straightens out and enough tension is released before you proceed with the next casting stroke. This pause is extremely important when casting weights. When short-line nymphing, the weight of the rig is heavier than the line out of the rod tip, and you cast it more like a spinning rig, where the weighted lure pulls the line to the target. The rig will unroll over the rod tip only when you feel the weight pull on the backcast. The tug of the rod tip signals that enough tension has been created to proceed with the forward cast. If you make your forward cast before feeling that tug, the rig can hit you or your rod.

With extremely heavy nymphing rigs, it's usually best to cast large loops. Narrow loops allow the flies to travel too close to the rod tip, and at times, the rig may fall enough to smack the rod tip. Your hand directs the rod tip, which determines the shape of the loop as it unrolls. A wide arc motion with the rod hand means that the rod tip should also move in a wide arc, creating a wide loop. Note how high the loop forms over the rod tip. A wide loop like this provides adequate space for the heavy nymphing rig to unroll during the forward cast without coming in contact with the rod tip or bottom tag of the line.

If the rod hand follows a straight path during the casting stroke, the rod tip will also move in a relatively straight path, which should create a relatively tight loop. A tighter loop may be appropriate for presenting lightly weighted rigs. If you are having problems achieving a tighter loop, watch your hand during the cast. Depending on your grip, the pad of your thumb or index finger, whichever is on top of the rod, should look like it's moving in a straight line during the acceleration.

TIMING

Timing is another important factor in casting proficiency. Casting a lightweight nymph is similar to casting a dry fly. The line hanging out of the rod tip is heavier than the nymph and therefore is responsible for delivering the cast. In such cases, you should begin the casting stroke as soon as the line begins to unroll, just before it straightens out. One of the quickest ways to tell how to time your cast is to make a hard backcast and see if the weighted nymph tugs on the rod tip. If you feel no tug, then it's a good bet that you should use a timing strategy similar to dry-fly casting, and vice versa. Leader length also influences timing. When fishing lightly weighted nymphs, the longer the leader, the longer the pause should be.

How much wind resistance is built into the leader will also affect the timing. Sometimes the suspension device creates so much wind resistance that it acts like a parachute in the air and slows down the speed of the loop. In such instances, you must pause to allow the line and leader to unroll. This is a common scenario when using a large, bulky yarn indicator and a lightly weighted rig, but it also occurs with dry flies and Thingama-

bobbers, especially when an angler switches from a heavy-water nymphing rig to a shallow-water nymphing rig but fails to replace the bigger suspension device with a smaller one. Now the lighter-weight nymphing rig does not have enough energy to carry the wind-resistant device through the air. If this occurs, you need to switch to a smaller, less wind-resistant suspender.

The best way to develop your sense of timing is to spend time on the water casting various nymphing rigs. If you find yourself trying to force your casts, take a deep breath on the backcast and exhale on the forward cast. Relax and try not to think too much about the casts; just let the rod do the work for you. Only when you stop thinking and worrying about how to make your casts work will they feel natural to you, and you will have found the perfect timing. One of my favorite quotes is from the movie *The Legend of Bagger Vance*, during a discussion about the mental approach to the game of golf: the key is to "stop thinking without falling asleep." I think this applies to casting the fly rod as well.

CASTING A HEAVY RIG

When the rig—shot and fly—weighs more than the length of fly line and leader out of the rod tip, it's the weight of the rig, not the line, that brings the flies to the fish. In this situation, it's critical that you feel the weight of the rig tug on the backcast before making the forward casting stroke.

To start, make sure the line is tight off the rod tip to ensure that tension occurs immediately as you move the tip through the casting stroke. If slack occurs, strip in the line needed to create a tight connection.

The backcast is a smooth acceleration to a stop. The pulling motion places tension on the rod blank, loading it and forcing it to bend. If you do this correctly, you will feel the tension of the rod load on your index finger throughout the entire cast. The elbow slightly elevates during this stage to assist in line pickup. The wrist does not break at all on the backcast.

Continue to accelerate until the rod hand is no longer in your peripheral vision, and then come to a sudden stop. When the wrist, forearm, and arm work together as one unit during the backcast, the rod tip remains at an upward angle during the pause. This upward position is essential to give the weighted rig time to tighten and pull on the rod tip before making the forward cast. If the rod tip is at too low of an angle, the weighted rig may touch bottom and often will snag.

Once the rod tip stops, keep the tip at that position before you feel the pull. This pause is critical to any cast, but even more so with a heavily weighted rig. Here it's especially important to wait long enough for the rod to properly load.

The pause while casting a heavy rig takes longer than when casting a lightly weighted rig, where the pause is similar to that when casting a dry fly. Sometimes I take a deep breath on the backcast and begin my forward cast while exhaling. You cannot force this step; you must be patient and wait for the rod to load.

Your cue to begin the forward stroke is a tug on the rod tip.

Begin the forward cast by smoothly accelerating the rod tip forward with a pulling motion. If you are accelerating smoothly, you will feel the tension of the weighted rig on your index finger if you are using the three-point grip (see page 41). The thumb and index finger remain in a vertical position, which directs the rod tip to remain in a vertical position as well.

During the casting stroke, your hand should continue to slowly drift outward, not downward, as if to hand a telephone to someone while saying, "It's for you." Again, the thumb and index finger remain close to a vertical position during this smooth, accelerated drift of the rod tip.

Just before you stop the rod tip, your wrist breaks slightly as you apply the power phase of the forward casting stroke.

During this power phase, the rod will speed up quickly but smoothly, as your back three fingers pull from under the handle and your thumb and index finger push outward. Your wrist breaks slightly, with the index finger and thumb angled upward and not downward. This slight break of the wrist helps the rod tip turn over the nymphing rig.

The flies should be unrolling outward and upward, not downward. As the rig unrolls past the rod tip, let your hand and the rod tip drop toward the water.

While tuck-casting or tight-line nymphing at a short distance, up to 25 feet, do not drop the rod tip, as that would create slack in the line and leader, detrimental in any tight-line system.

If you are fishing from a distance and have excess line on the water, you can drop the rod tip. In this situation, a low rod tip allows for the maximum arc to set the hook.

CASTING A LIGHTWEIGHT RIG

Nymphing is not always about "chucking and ducking" heavy weights. Often, a lightly weighted nymph is all it takes to achieve a natural drift. With a lightweight rig, the timing of the cast differs from the timing you use when casting heavy weights. Most often, a lightly weighted nymphing rig weighs less than the amount of line and leader out of the tip guide, which means that the weight of the line and leader is responsible for delivering the goods. The timing is almost identical to casting a dry line. The only difference is that the timing may be slowed down if a wind-resistant suspension device is attached to the leader. Imagine that you drop two stones off a bridge at the same time. One rock has a small parachute attached, but the other does not. The rock attached to the parachute will take longer to reach the water because of wind resistance. The same principle holds true when casting weights with and without a suspension device: the suspension device acts as a parachute and slows the delivery of the fly.

The mechanics of casting lightweight rigs are almost identical to those of casting heavy weights, except for the tug on the backcast. A lightly weighted rig will not have enough pull to create the tugging sensation. Instead, to create the tension needed to begin the forward casting stroke, pause long enough to let the fly line almost completely unroll. Because the line is responsible for delivering the goods with lightweight rigs, the line is also responsible for loading the rod.

Continue to wait until all the line is just about to straighten out on the backcast. A slight pull (not a tug) will occur on the rod if you wait too long. This pull signals that all the energy you built into the cast just dissipated, which is not what you want when casting lightweight nymphs. The diameter and hence wind resistance of any suspension device will determine how long a pause is needed. A large-diameter suspender will act like a parachute and slow the unrolling of the line.

Begin to drift the rod tip forward as soon as you begin to see the line straighten. Tension—the line becoming taut with the rod tip—occurs as soon as the rod tip begins to drift forward. The longer the rod is under tension, the greater amount of energy it stores. If you begin drifting before the line straightens out, slack will occur for a period during the stroke until the rod regains tension. The rod tip should remain under tension during the entire stroke length.

Making the forward casting stroke is like casting a dry fly. Your hand continues to drift outward while gaining speed during the movement. The loop should begin forming directly overhead toward the target.

THE OVAL CAST

The standard overhead cast can be a fast and powerful movement that may jerk the rod tip because the rig is not always under tension. If the rod tip jerks, a heavy rig can move off to one side, because the backcast is no longer 180 degrees from the target. The oval cast uses a semicircular swinging motion, and there is no loading and unloading movement for the backcast as in the standard overhead cast. The weighted rig maintains tension on the rod tip throughout the entire backcast. As a result, instead of jerking the rod tip, the rig simply straightens out after you stop your rod hand, allowing the rig to unload. In some ways, casting a heavy nymphing rig is like attempting to cast a chain—you have to build momentum by winding it in an oval pattern, not shaking it back and forth.

The flies ride under the rod tip during the backward swing motion, and then the forward casting stroke forces them high over the rod tip. This is especially useful when casting extreme weights, where you want your flies to move over the rod tip and not through it. The heavily weighted rig will begin dropping as it unrolls to the target. The heavier the rig, the quicker it will drop toward the rod tip, running the risk of hitting and breaking it.

OVAL CAST

Begin by making sure that there is no slack between the rod tip and line. This is a short movement, done only with your rod hand, so the rod tip needs to generate line speed as it begins the casting motion. Note that the rod tip is pointed slightly to the right-hand side of the angler.

Begin to break your wrist so that the rod tip is pointed away from your body, and start slowly sliding the line off the water. This is a slow but steady accelerated movement. The aim is to keep the rig under the rod tip during this movement.

Your rod hand continues this slow acceleration away from your body. Ideally, your rod hand during this entire accelerated movement travels in a semicircle or 180-degree arc. Think about the rod tip traveling in the shape of a horseshoe during the stroke.

Continue moving the rod tip in the 180-degree arc. This should be a smooth stroke with the rod tip remaining under tension during the entire backcast.

To complete the 180-degree arc, your rod hand drifts forward toward the front of your face. Note that the rig drifts under and off to one side of the rod.

Your hand continues to drift until directly in front of your face, completing the full 180-degree arc. Once you have completed the arc, stop the casting motion and pause until the line completely straightens out behind you. This will allow you to deliver an accurate cast on the forward stroke.

Once the line straightens out directly behind you, you can begin the forward cast. Because of the constant rod tension, the rod tip will not jerk on the backcast to tell you when to begin the forward cast. In fact, this cast is partially designed to eliminate the tug and provide a more accurate cast. The rod tip still travels in a straight line during the final presentation stroke for accuracy.

Continue to accelerate forward toward the target. Note how high the loop forms off the rod tip. Keeping the rig under the rod tip during the backcast and casting over the rod tip during the forward cast forces the rig to ride high over the rod tip—considerably higher than with a standard back-and-forth casting stroke.

Accelerate forward and come to a sudden stop to unload the rod tip. In this case, the rod tip stops higher to accomplish a tuck. Note that the fly line tip is angled directly down toward the stream. This steep angle of the fly line allows the nymph to enter the water at a steeper angle, enabling it to drop to the bottom more quickly.

Keep the rod tip in the same spot where you stopped on the forward cast, as the nymph continues to tuck downward and enters the water directly under the line.

THE ROD GRIP

For most of my fly-fishing casts, I use the three-point grip, keeping my index finger on top. I find that having this finger on top reduces fatigue over the course of the day. Having the index finger on top is a good grip for beginners to start with, as it positions the hand in a manner that makes it difficult to break the wrist. When casting with my index finger on top, I hold the grip a little higher up on the handle to allow the tip of the index finger to touch the rod blank, as this increases sensitivity and allows me to feel more fish takes.

I hold the grip with my thumb on top only for additional power for longer distances. With the thumb on top, you can achieve a greater range of motion, including breaking the wrist, and thus many great casters and fishers keep the thumb on top, as they are able to control their hand movements.

Before making a cast, turn your wrist inward to cause the reel to tuck directly under the wrist. This motion creates a wrist lock, reducing the chances of breaking the wrist during the casting stroke. Using a wrist lock grip forces your forearm to perform much of the work during the casting stroke, thereby reducing fatigue in your hand, which can especially be a prob-

lem with longer rods. The forearm has larger muscles than the wrist and hand, and it can withstand more stress. Without the wrist lock, a normal grip would force the hand to support the majority of the weight of the often tip-heavy rod. The wrist lock grip instead places a majority of the weight onto the forearm, reducing the workload of the hand. Locking the wrist in this manner will also help you deliver your casts with less effort.

When teaching the basic casting stroke that I use, I like to use another telephone analogy for the hand position. I picked this up from Floyd Franke, former head casting instructor at the Wulff School of Fly Fishing. Imagine that you are facing a table with a telephone on top, and the phone is ringing. You extend your hand to grab the phone, creating an almost 90-degree angle at the elbow. Then you pull it toward your ear to say hello. While casting, keep your elbow close to your body, simply sliding it up and down, backward and forward. Have you ever tried to throw a ball with your elbow away from your body? You just don't have the same amount of power with the elbow away as you do when it is close to your body.

ROD GRIP

The three-point grip begins with your rod hand in the same position you would use to hold a small firearm, with both the thumb and index finger slightly off to each side of the rod handle.

When preparing to make the cast, turn your wrist inward to cause the reel to tuck directly under the wrist. This motion creates a wrist lock, reducing the chances of breaking the wrist during the casting stroke.

Before you begin the forward cast, first make sure that the line is either trapped by your line hand or secured under your rod hand. There should be little to no slack in the line hanging off the rod tip, as slack will decrease the amount of rod load. Ideally, you should see the line coming straight off the rod tip. Keep your elbow positioned close to your body but still flexible.

Now pretend you are grabbing a ringing phone and pulling it toward your ear to say hello. Think about smoothly pulling rather than pushing your flies through the air. The bending of the rod that occurs while pulling the flies through the air is what loads the rod with stored energy. A pulling motion will keep tension on the rod tip longer than would a quick jerk. The longer the tension remains on the rod, the more potential energy is created.

The last phase of the backcast is the stop. Basically, the stop unloads the rod and allows the fly line to unroll behind you, creating tension for the forward casting stroke. Stop the cast as soon as the rod hand is no longer visible in your peripheral vision or when you see the line-and-leader connection being lifted completely off the water's surface. Going back to the telephone analogy, this is where you would hold the rod as if you were answering the phone and saying hello. Now you need to wait for the line to unroll or the weights to pull on the backcast. Keep the rod tip angled upward to allow the weighted rig to unroll without touching the ground.

The rod tip remains fixed until you see the line and leader almost straighten out or feel the weights tug on the backcast. If you are using a three-point grip, your index finger should be angled upward toward the sky and not parallel with the current. Keeping the rod tip at this higher angle will allow the law of gravity to set in with the weighted rig but not allow it to drop to the water yet.

You are now ready to begin the forward casting motion. Returning to the telephone analogy, this is where you would hand off the phone to the person next to you, saying, "It's for you." At this stage, your elbow is slightly raised but remains close to your body, your index finger is on top of the rod handle, and your wrist is locked into place by the reel.

The forward motion is smooth and accelerated, with your hand beginning near your head and extending outward, not downward. Your hand continues to drift outward until your elbow is at a 45-degree angle. During this motion, your elbow also drops slightly, similar to a chopping motion. Your hand should not completely straighten out, as doing so would force the rod tip to travel in a wide arc. This also would force the hand to travel in a downward motion, often collapsing the cast in the water instead of allowing it to straighten out. Aim out and not down.

After the stop, the line and leader unroll toward the target, and this is the stage where you can drop the rod tip to present the flies. This downward movement needs to occur only after the stop occurs and not during the casting motion. Dropping the rod tip during the acceleration stage will collapse the cast and it won't completely unroll.

The rod tip continues to drop. On long casts, the rod tip should end up close to the water's surface, as more leverage is needed to set the hook in case of a strike. On shorter casts (up to 20 feet), the rod tip should be higher off the water.

If desired, you can change your rod hand position to the regular three-point grip during the presentation stage.

CASTING STYLE

It's not my goal to teach you what casting style is best for nymph fishing. Eventually, through practicing proper execution of the four casting principles, you will develop your own style. Casting style cannot be taught; it's something you develop over time, and eventually you will feel at ease, as if the rod is doing all the work and you are just providing it with directions.

A lot depends on your physical makeup. For example, I have long, lanky arms and do not consider myself very strong. As a result, I don't possess the power needed to make short casting strokes like my mentor Joe Humphreys stresses while casting. Joe is renowned for his famous short casting stroke and strongly encourages this style. However, I need to use more arm movement to create the energy needed to execute the cast and have always struggled with the short casting stroke. I simply experimented with various casting styles until one day, many hours of practice later, I found the style that suited me best, and you should experiment until you find the one you feel most comfortable with.

Your casting style greatly depends on the water types you fish. Small-stream fly fishers tend to cast off to the side while big-water anglers tend to use an overhead style. Remember the principles and develop a style that suits you and the water you fish.

Tight-Line Tactics

4

Tight-line nymphing refers to a broad category of tactics that do not rely on suspension devices. The goal of this set of techniques is to keep a taut connection between the nymphs and the leader or line so that the leader or line will hesitate the moment the nymphs stop during the drift. This style of nymphing requires complete focus and concentration, as you become the tour guide for your flies. Unlike when using a suspension device, you must control the speed and depth at which your flies drift. With suspension nymphing, once the nymphs bite in the bottom current, the indicator slows down and instantly relays the current speed. In tight-line nymphing, you often have to guess the current speed. To compound the problem, every piece of water varies in speed. Frequently the goal is to obtain a dead drift while eliminating slack in the system; however, some situations call for a more active presentation.

Tight-line nymphing is currently enjoying a revival in the United States, with the popularity of the Czech and Polish styles of nymphing. It is a very old method of nymphing and the one I learned while growing up on the limestone streams of

Here Anthony Naranja is French-nymphing the River Hoczewka in Poland. A long leader is essential when fishing low, clear water, as it allows for less line to lie on the water. GEORGE DANIEL

Above: Tight-line tactics provide direct contact with the nymph, and I use them as my first approach anytime I'm able to get close on smaller streams. This small limestone stream was off-color as a result of a recent storm and allowed me to get close enough to use a tight-line system. JAY NICHOLS

Left: You don't need Czech flies to Czech nymph. Copper Johns are just one of many common patterns that are effective with tight-lining tactics. JAY NICHOLS

central Pennsylvania. Though many new anglers are indoctrinated into fly fishing with a large strike indicator and a pair of nymphs, I did not discover the benefits of suspending nymphs under a float until later in my fishing career. In fact, most anglers in central Pennsylvania learned to nymph-fish the way two of the area's greatest anglers—George Harvey and his protégé, Joe Humphreys—did. In the Czech and Polish styles of nymphing, the rods are often longer, the heavy flies and level tippets reach the stream bottom without the use of a tuck cast, and highly visible sighters are built into the leader, but the concepts of leading the drift and watching and feeling for a take are the same as with the methods Harvey and Humphreys used. And the Czechs and Poles do not have a monopoly on the tight-line technique overseas.

This style is not only mentally trying, because of the concentration required, but also physically demanding. You must be able to get close enough to present the patterns in a natural manner without opposing currents creating drag. As a result, a straight-up or slightly up-and-across approach is common to ensure that the line and leader end up in current flowing at the same speed. In large bodies of water, this means having to wade farther out to cast directly upstream, if possible. Another aspect is that you often have to keep your rod hand extended to hold the line and leader off the water. This is often a physical limitation for those who have shoulder or hand problems. The right equipment can make this physically and mentally demanding technique easier.

George Harvey/Joe Humphreys Method

- Drift length: short to medium (approx. 1–30')
- Line will often lie on water and gradually get picked up during drift
- Leader length: approx. 8–12'
- Tippet diameter: 3X–5X
- Weight: non-weighted or lightly weighted flies in compination with split shot
- Strike indicator: knotted leader sections or line/leader connection
- Active and passive presentation
- Water type: broken water surface
- Casting: similiar to high sticking but incorporates the tuck cast

High-Sticking Method

- Drift length: short to medium (approx. 1–30')
- Line will often lie on water and gradually get picked up during drift
- Leader length: approx. 8–12'
- Tippet diameter: 3X–5X
- Weight: non-weighted or lightly weighted flies in compination with split shot
- Strike indicator: knotted leader sections or line/leader connection
- Active and passive presentation
- Water type: broken water surface
- Casting: standard cast for weighted flies

Tight-Line Nymphing

The practice of nymphing without a suspension device. The direction, depth, and speed of the drift is determined by the angler.

Czech Nymphing

- Drift length: short (approx. 1–20')
- Line will rarely lie on water due to short drift
- Leader length: approx. as long as rod
- Tippet diameter: 3X–5X
- Weight: light to heavy bead-head nymph without split shot
- Strike indicator: sighter (colored piece of mono) built into leader
- Active and passive presentation
- Water type: broken water surface
- Casting: short overhead lob with weighted flies

French Nymphing

- Drift length: short (approx. 1–10')
- Line will not touch water due to short drift and long leader
- Leader length: long, often exceeding 25'
- Tippet diameter: 4X–7X
- Weight: light to medium bead-head nymph without split shot
- Strike indicator: sighter (colored piece of mono) built into leader or curly Q
- Active and passive presentation
- Water type: low, clear water
- Casting: longer casts with long leaders

Managing slack in the system so that the nymphs will quickly reach the bottom is critical in tight-line nymphing. Have you ever pulled a lightly weighted fly out of your box, only to have it slip through your fingers and into the water? Even with a lightly weighted nymph, you will notice how quickly the fly drops to the bottom of the stream without additional weight, because there's no resistance pulling the fly downstream. Resistance often occurs in the form of the fly line, leader, suspension device, and especially the angler leading the flies through the drift. And yet you retie another fly on the leader and add a load of split shot to get a bottom drift. The truth is, your nymph doesn't need too much weight to reach the bottom if you allow enough slack in the system that the nymphs can drop quickly to the bottom. You need to quickly recover this slack to maintain line control, however, which is necessary to detect takes.

The styles described in this chapter are all forms of keeping this tight connection, whether you are close to the water or up to 40 feet away. Furthermore, drifts can be passive, in which you fish the fly dead-drift, or active, where you attempt to move the fly faster than the current, most often to imitate an emerging insect.

Former world champion fly fisher Vladi Trzebunia's Polish nymphs (top to bottom): Vistula, Crane, Kriva, and Shrimp. The Poles are known for their woven flies, which is one of the few differences between Polish and Czech nymphing. These tightly woven bodies create a two-toned effect and drop quickly to the bottom. JAY NICHOLS

The typical short-line nymphing leader is approximately a rod's length long. Shorter leaders are easier to control while rapidly presenting a multiple-fly rig. Anglers often use a level leader consisting of straight 3X–6X. Flies attached to a level leader will all sink at the same speed and prevent unwanted drag. However, a system that works for one angler may not work for another. For example, the top Czech competitors differ in opinion regarding leader length and construction. GEORGE DANIEL

Tight-line nymphing can require a lot more physical effort than suspension nymphing, often requiring that you wade through fast or deep water. This photo shows Anthony Naranja swinging a nymph at a tailout on the Simo River in Finland. Allowing the flies to drift below you and swing at the end of the drift is an effective tool only when the fish are actively moving up and down the water column to feed, especially during a hatch. JULIE NARANJA

The short-line technique was originally geared toward grayling, or what the English often refer to as "lady of the water." These are shoaling fish, and when in large schools, they tend not to spook as quickly as trout. Because of this, anglers can make short casts to them, often from only a rod tip's length away. The line seldom touches the water, with the nymphs drifting below the rod tip. GEORGE DANIEL

THE HARVEY/HUMPHREYS AND HIGH-STICK METHODS

High-stick nymphing and the Harvey/Humphreys method have many similarities, so I group them together. George Harvey was instructor of the first accredited fly-fishing course at Penn State University, teaching thousands of students how to fly-fish, and he developed, among many other things, the tuck cast and the slack-line leader. Joe Humphreys was mentored by Harvey and was also a Penn State angling professor who taught thousands of students how to fly fish. Because both gentlemen developed this nymphing style, I call it the Harvey/Humphreys method.

Joe called their technique high-rod nymphing, and it is very similar to high-sticking except for the casting. George and Joe relied on the tuck cast, developed to allow the flies to quickly penetrate the surface and reach the bottom quickly. The concept behind the tuck cast was one of the greatest contributions to nymph fishing in the last 100 years. Eventually, Joe fine-tuned the tactics George had taught him into one of the deadliest short-line strategies ever.

After you make the cast and the flies reach the appropriate depth, you elevate the rod tip and gather slack with the line hand for control. You then begin leading the nymphs through the drift, watching the fly-line tip or sections of knotted leader for any hesitation.

For longer drifts, perhaps in shallow riffles where you can't get close to fish, it is necessary to have some line on the water. When "shooting for distance," as Joe calls it, after you have made the cast and the nymphs reach the correct depth, you elevate the rod tip and gather slack with the line hand using a slow strip or a hand-and-twist retrieve. Because the clear leader is lying on the water and is virtually invisible, you focus on the fly-line tip, looking for any hesitation to signal a strike. This is why a brighter-colored fly line is often used to aid in strike detection. At greater distances, Joe often watches for the belly of the fly line to straighten or for the line-and-leader connection to pause to determine when to set the hook.

Above: On small trout streams that have spooky fish, an upstream approach positions you behind the fish's cone of vision, which allows you to get closer. GEORGE DANIEL

Right: Fly-fishing pioneers George Harvey and Joe Humphreys were among the first anglers to document the tuck cast. GEORGE DANIEL

The higher the rod tip stops, the deeper the tuck. Instead of worrying about adjusting the amount of weight when moving from spot to spot, first try changing the angle of your cast. This was one of the secrets that helped me win several competitions. Instead of changing weights or flies, I simply changed rod-tip angles, which saved me time and kept my flies in the water longer than if I had changed flies or weights.

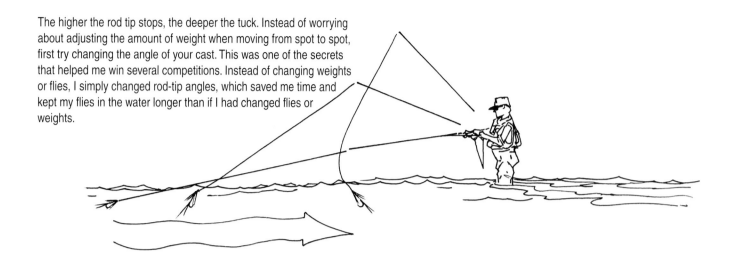

Unlike Czech and Polish nymphing, the Harvey and Humphreys method requires casting the flies rather than a simple lob, so the leader is different. George and Joe both used George Harvey's slack leader (half stiff butt sections to turn over the leader and half soft mono for drag-free presentations). Though George originally designed this leader for dry-fly fishing, both men used it for nymph fishing, providing a streamlined design that could be used for all techniques.

The Tuck Cast

George Harvey developed the tuck cast in the early 1900s, while fishing Pennsylvania waters. He discovered that slack would occur if the weighted rig tucked under the rod and provided a split second with no resistance as the nymphs dropped to the bottom. The amount of slack was minimal, but it was all that was needed to allow the nymphs to reach the bottom. Also, the pendulum effect this cast created forced the weighted rig to enter at the same angle at which the water was pulling. This angle of least resistance, in combination with the slack, offered the angler one of the quickest methods to get the nymph to the bottom without the use of additional weight.

Joe Humphreys explained to me how he learned the technique: "My first experience of seeing the tuck cast came when George and I were fishing together in low and clear stream conditions. I was high-sticking with minimal success. I was fishing some pocketwater and was getting too close to the fish, when I noticed that George was doing something slightly different than just high-sticking close to the pocket: he was standing farther back and presenting the flies from a distance, and distance was the key in that low, clear water. I noticed that he was catching far more fish than I was. In fact, he took me to the cleaners!

Joe Humphreys uses a tuck cast to quickly get his nymph to the bottom at the top of this riffle. Because of the short distance between the angler and the top of the riffle, the fly needs to drop to the bottom quickly in order to provide a long enough natural drift. It's best to use the tuck cast only with tight-line systems, because you can get tangles pretty easily when trying it with a suspender. GEORGE DANIEL

"He was stopping the rod tip higher and was tucking the nymphs into the pockets. The nymphs quickly gained the bottom, and he was in control of the nymphs from the top of the pocket all the way back to him. He was getting his flies down from a distance, while I was getting too close to the fish. At first I thought it was the pattern he was using, so I challenged him about the pattern, and so he gave me his fly, which still made no difference for me. Eventually, George talked me through the tuck cast and coached me on how to properly execute it, and I began to take fish. The tuck cast completely changed the nymphing game for me."

Many years ago, Joe Humphreys told me that the dynamic aspect of the tuck cast is that you can vary the angle of the rod tip based on the speed and depth of the water you're fishing. Joe experimented with the cast after George Harvey showed it to him and discovered that the rod tip must stop at a higher angle for the flies to reach the bottom while fishing the heaviest runs, and at a lower angle on shallower runs. As a result, instead of having to constantly change weights, often all you have to do is change the angle at which the rod tip stops. "The key of the tuck cast is that it is able to drop your flies quickly to the bottom of any water type," Humphreys explained. "With that said, the tuck cast must be refined to meet the conditions of the waters you fish. In particular, the angle at which the rod tip should stop is relative to the speed and depth of the water you fish. In deep water, the rod tip stops higher and allows the nymphs to drop in at a steeper angle, quickly gaining the bottom. However, the tuck cast can sometimes become a hindrance if you stop the rod tip too high while fishing shallow water. This will most likely get you hung on the bottom."

The fly sinks quickly for two reasons. First, if the nymph comes in at the same direction as the water, there's no resistance as the fly breaks the surface, so it quickly sinks. Think about diving off a deck into water. If you dive in at a steep angle, directly downward, you reach the bottom quickly. However, if your angle of penetration is shallow, you drop no more than several inches below the surface. Also, the nymph enters downstream of the line, which allows enough slack for the rig to quickly reach the bottom before tension develops between the leader and fly.

The tuck gives the flies the slack they need to sink quickly to the bottom, but this is a double-edged sword. Slack is necessary for the flies to drop quickly to the bottom, but you have to manage that slack in order to gain control at the right moment so you can detect any resistance. This is where line control comes into play with the rod tip and line hand. After the rod stops, the nymphs tuck under the rod tip, and slack allows the flies to quickly reach the bottom. At first you do not move the rod tip downstream, so that it does not lead the nymphs, but instead slightly elevate it to control the slack as the nymphs begin to drop. Begin leading the nymphs with the rod tip only after they are under the tip. Now move the rod tip parallel to the water, leading the nymphs through the drift. (For more details on leading your nymphs when tight-lining, see page 74.)

TUCK CAST

One of the keys to a good tuck cast is to drift the rod tip forward, accelerating smoothly, and really squeeze the rod handle at the very end of the casting stroke. Pull with your back three fingers while at the same time pushing with your thumb and the finger on top. This hard squeeze quickly kicks the nymphs under the fly-line belly. Keep the rod at this level; allowing it to drop would throw too much slack into the presentation.

Stop the rod tip high and keep it high as the nymphs tuck under the tip.

In this photo, you can see the slack in the line, with the flies downstream from the fly line.

With the rod tip fixed at the same spot where it stopped, the slack enables the nymphs to drop quickly through the water column without tension. Keeping the rod tip at a high angle will allow you to pick up the slack quicker than if it were at a low angle.

The belly of the line now begins floating downstream toward the nymphs, which are still at a slack stage. The rod tip remains at the same angle while the line begins floating downstream. At this point, you should keep your eye on the line-and-leader connector.

Now the line and leader begin to drift downstream of the nymphing rig. The loop tightens, and tension occurs between the line and nymphing rig. The bend in the belly is pulling the nymphing rig downstream. You can either elevate the rod tip or move it downstream to manage the slack as the nymphs drift downstream toward you.

This photo shows the fly entering the water at a lower angle. Note that the fly line is downstream of the nymph. In this case, the lack of slack between the nymphing rig and fly line will provide little time for the rig to drop before tension occurs. A cast at such a shallow angle will allow the flies to reach the bottom in medium depths, but not in deep water. Thus it's important to adjust the angle of the rod tip to the depth and speed of the water.

The Downer-and-Upper Variation

Joe Humphreys's important contribution to the tuck cast is the downer-and-upper variation. The downer-and-upper is most useful when you are fishing very short drifts that last no more than several seconds and need the flies to be on the bottom almost immediately. I also use this variation in situations where I am casting close to a target.

DOWNER-AND-UPPER CAST

When making a downer-and-upper cast, just as with the regular tuck cast, your rod hand should drift forward and come to a stop. Keep your elbow close to your body and your hand close to your face. This position allows your hand to drift outward as the forward casting stroke begins, providing yet another opportunity to adjust the speed and angle as your nymphs enter the water. After the rod stops, allow the weighted rig to unload toward the target.

Keep your rod hand in a fixed position until the weighted rig almost begins to completely straighten out on the forward cast. Your rod hand should be approximately at eye level.

As soon as the nymphs begin to tuck downward, begin to push the rod tip vertically toward the sky. With the three-point grip, the index finger stabs the sky. This upward movement is the only stage where the rod hand actually accelerates. This last-minute thrust gives the flies additional energy as they descend to the surface.

Your rod hand should continue to accelerate upward until you can move the hand no farther. This short burst helps the nymphs drop to the stream bottom more quickly. This is a great tool when fishing short pockets, where the length of the drift may be only several feet in length. For example, it may be ideal for fishing in between two boulders spaced 2 feet apart, which allows for only a 2-foot drift.

To maintain line and leader control, continue to hold the rod tip at the same level as the nymphs begin to move downstream toward you. Because of the short drift, the rod tip leads the nymphs through the quick drift. In this photo, you can see how close this downer-and-upper dropped the rig from me. This is another reason why I use this variation in broken water, where I can get close to the target.

Long Casts

The tuck cast is for presentations closer than about 30 feet. When you execute a true tuck cast, the flies land downstream of the line. As a result, slack occurs between the rod tip and fly, and after the nymphs reach the bottom, you need to readily manage the slack before leading the nymphs. When making a cast longer than 30 feet, it is more difficult to control slack with a tuck cast, so for greater distances, I instead use a standard tight-line long cast. A longer cast gives the nymphs more time to reach the bottom before entering the kill zone. This tactic is most useful when you have drifts longer than 20 feet to provide adequate time for the nymphs to drop. The advantage of this tactic is that you are automatically in touch with your nymphs as they begin to drop to the bottom. This is especially useful when trout are intercepting your nymphs as they drop, especially during hatch periods when the fish are feeding at all levels.

LONG CAST

Begin by casting your rig directly upstream and in line with the targeted current seam. When executing this cast, stop the rod tip high at the end of the forward casting stroke to allow the nymphs to unroll outward to the target. My body is facing toward the targeted seam, and the rod tip travels parallel to this seam.

After the rod tip stops, the loop begins to form and pulls the flies out toward the target. Immediately after the stop on the forward casting stroke, begin to drop the rod tip toward the water surface. The rod tip needs to remain low to the water because of the amount of line that is being cast upstream. With a long cast such as this, your line hand is responsible for maintaining line control until the line-and-leader connection gets close to the tip guide.

Continue to hold the rod tip low to the water until all the line and leader unrolls past the rod tip and begins to lie on the water.

Note how the line hand and rod hand are together in what resembles a praying position. The line hand begins to strip in line before the rod tip moves as a means of slack management. Also note that the rod hand is extended outward as far as I can reach. Holding the rod hand farther away from the body allows you to make longer strips with the line hand, allowing for quicker line and leader control.

The weight continues to pull the rig toward the target, with the rod tip pointed toward the water before the flies actually land. In some ways, the presentation is similar to fishing a streamer. Also note that the line hand is in position to begin stripping in the excess line, and the rod hand is fully extended. The idea is to have the rod tip and line hand in position before the flies enter the water. The line hand is close to the stripping guide so that it can make longer strips, which allows for quicker line management.

The water's surface immediately begins to create tension on the fly line, causing it to move quickly downstream. In this photo, you can see a little slack off the rod tip due to the line quickly moving downstream. The first step is to keep the rod tip lowered; then quickly make one long strip with the line hand.

The line hanging off the rod tip is tight after the strip, providing better contact with your nymphs. When fishing from a distance, you should make the strip before elevating the rod tip.

After making the first long strip, begin elevating the rod tip to manage slack as the line continues to drift downstream. Pinch the line under your rod hand while moving your line hand up toward the stripper guide in preparation for the next strip.

Note how quickly the water's surface is pulling the fly line downstream. Slack is beginning to occur again between the rod tip and fly line. The rod tip can manage slack only so fast. When you see slack starting to occur, get your line hand ready to begin another long strip.

Starting with your line hand near the stripping guide, pull all the way toward your pants pocket. In this photo, the line is tight again as the rod tip continues to elevate and lead the nymphs through the drift. My eyes are focused on two areas: the belly of the fly line and where the line and leader lie on the water. Seeing either of the two portions of the line stop or hesitate suggests that the drift of the nymph has been disrupted.

After the line hand strips in the excessive slack, the rod tip continues to lift upward to assist in line management while simultaneously leading the flies downstream. This movement manages slack between the nymph and leader. To achieve a natural drift, the rod tip should move parallel to the current, keeping the entire rig in current of the same speed.

Once the rod tip is fully extended upward, continue to lead the nymphs downstream with the tip, keeping it in front of the rig. Slack will occur if the rig moves downstream of the rod tip, so make sure to lead the nymphs through the drift. Do not tight-line with a lazy hand.

CZECH AND POLISH NYMPHING METHODS

The origins are not totally clear, but the Czechs popularized and refined the technique most Americans now know as Czech nymphing after being introduced to this style during an international competition in Poland in the 1980s. From that point on, the Czechs refined the tackle, leaders, and flies for this short-line technique into a masterful fish-catching tool, winning international competitions and bringing this style to the forefront of the fly-fishing world. I often refer to these techniques as short-line or tight-line nymphing, not Czech or Polish nymphing, in order to avoid controversy—even though I am Polish.

The concepts of keeping the rod tip high and leading the flies to maintain direct contact with them are similar to the Harvey/Humphreys tactics, but there are several important differences. The Harvey/Humphreys method employs the tuck cast with a tapered Harvey slack-line leader, but Czech and Polish nymphing uses the lob cast with a level tippet attached to a tippet ring. Whereas the former method sometimes uses split shot for weight, the latter uses only weighted flies. In the Harvey/Humphreys method, the angler watches the fly-line tip or leader knot instead of using a sighter, and the nonrod hand gathers line, whereas in Czech and Polish nymphing, the angler uses a sighter and does not typically use the nonrod hand.

The slim design of traditional Czech and Polish nymphs set this style apart from other tight-line tactics. These streamlined flies (lightly or heavily weighted) quickly reach the bottom without split shot, so there is a tight connection between the nymphs and sighter, making for a highly sensitive nymphing rig. When you add split shot above your flies, you create a hinge and are not able to detect strikes as easily. Tungsten

beads allow tiers to create heavily weighted flies with less bulk. A common misconception, however, is that you need to fish authentic Czech- or Polish-style flies when using the Czech or Polish methods. The truth is that this short-range nymphing style can be done with any number of weighted flies, including Copper Johns and Beadhead Pheasant Tails.

The flies are attached to a level tippet so that the entire rig sinks at the same rate, which is not possible with leaders that are tapered. Depending on water conditions, level tippets can range from 3X to 6X, with 4X and 5X being the most popular. The thinner-diameter tippet cuts through the currents faster than a tapered leader, allowing the flies to drop quickly. To enhance strike detection, the angler builds a sighter into the leader. Typically, short leaders, those less than 9 feet, have the sighter built into the butt section, whereas leaders longer than 15 feet have the section somewhere near the middle portion.

Anglers do no false-casting with this form of nymphing as they would with the other tight-line tactics. In the short-line technique, you lob the heavily weighted, streamlined flies upstream, and after they settle to the bottom, you lead them downstream by the rod tip, holding it high to keep as much line and leader off the water as possible. The goal is to stay in touch with the flies throughout the drift, feeling the line and watching the sighter for a take. The drift is swift and short, followed by a sharp set at the end, which serves the dual purposes of hooking any fish that may have gone undetected as well as getting the line moving for the cast upstream. This combination of overhead lob, short drift, and quick set is pure efficiency, with the angler getting as many as 10 to 15 drifts per minute and remaining in direct contact with the flies the entire time.

Rods used with this method are often very long, more than 9½ feet, to help the angler reach over currents that cause drag. Since this technique is generally used up close (though there are exceptions), the angler traps the line with the rod hand, as the left hand does not need to gather slack. The Czech and Polish nymphing methods, however, can be adapted to both short- and long-line tactics, as well as to passive and active approaches.

The hard hook set at the end of every drift straightens out the line and leader, providing the tension needed to proceed with the forward lob. And the shorter drifts and hook sets often allow the angler to find a few additional trout on the end of the line. During my teenage years, I heard a local nymphing legend say that good nymphers are able to register only 40 percent of the takes. Though I have no hard evidence that these statistics are true, I do believe that a large portion of takes go unnoticed, and the use of the rapid short drift and set often increases the angler's success. Before trying this kind of hook set, however, check the local regulations to make sure it is legal. Some states, such as New York, prohibit this lifting motion on many steelhead and salmon rivers because of the possibility of snagging the fish.

Prepare to start the lifting motion as soon as the flies begin to drift past you. At the end of the drift, slowly accelerate the rod tip, lifting your forearm upward while moving it slightly downstream. Keeping a low rod hand but a high rod-tip angle

Jarkko Suominen shows off a grayling while Czech nymphing on one of his favorite rivers in Finland. Jarkko is a former Finnish national champion who led his team to a bronze medal during the 2005 World Fly Fishing Championships in Sweden.

Above: This photo shows Pete Erickson fishing a long line while sight-nymphing to spooky brown trout on the Ceira River in Portugal. A long leader and light tippet are necessary when facing such conditions. ANTHONY NARANJA

Right: Because of the tension between the rod tip and fly when using the Czech and Polish methods, you will often feel the fish take. Here's a tip that will increase your ability to feel the takes. The backside of your fingers is more sensitive than the inner side, so it's important to run the line over the backside during your retrieve. This photo shows how you can draw the line over the inside section of the middle finger to act as a guide and then slide it over the backside of the next finger. As the line hand strips in the line downward, following the same angle toward the rod butt section, this configuration acts as a trap, keeping the line moving smoothly over the backside of the finger. Placing the index finger on the rod blank will provide additional sensitivity. JAY NICHOLS

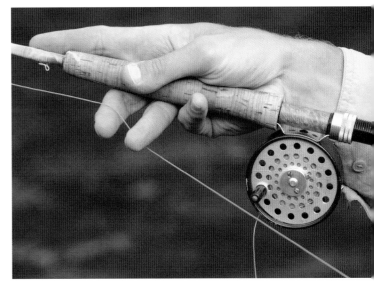

during the retrieve leaves room for your forearm to lift upward. This is just a short, powerful lift with the forearm. The goal is to move the flies quickly through the water column, where they will break the water's surface and hang tight under the rod tip. The rod tip remains angled upward to maintain tension with the rig. Once the flies break the water's surface, keep the rod tip high, with the flies hanging below the rod tip and under tension, while you reposition your body to face the target. Your elbow should be close to your body and ready to make the forward casting stroke.

Though not practical for low, clear, or placid water, the Czech and Polish methods of short-line nymphing work very well any other place you can get close to trout, such as in heavily riffled water on a freestone river or high or dirty water on any type of stream. Because of the precision with which you can control the depth at which your flies drift, you can use this technique in very shallow water, such as riffles, which hold a lot of fish but many anglers pass by.

FISHING WITH
YOUR NONDOMINANT HAND

The ability to cast with your nondominant hand is not a necessity, but it does provide several advantages when fishing across your body. Besides the advantages detailed below, at some point in your angling career you may injure your dominant hand and be forced to fish with your other hand, and you will be glad you've already become proficient at it. This was a useful tip that Dan Shields, another great central Pennsylvania angler and mentor, shared with me during my teens.

In the accompanying photo sequence, for example, I'm fishing upstream on the right-hand side of the river (looking upstream). In this situation, the stream is flowing on my left, and I need to cast over my left shoulder to present the flies. Because I want to place my flies in line with the current, my rod tip needs to travel parallel to the current seam. I'm right-handed, so if I were to fish with my dominant hand, placing the rod tip over my left shoulder while keeping my casting close to my body and positioning my shoulders upstream at a 45-degree angle, it would be more difficult to cast in line with the current. My body would be facing in one direction while the path of the rod tip would be facing in another. As a result, line and leader placement would not be accurate. That is, the line and leader would end up lying in two separate microcurrents. Though this would not be detrimental to the drift, it would create additional drag and slightly reduce the time my nymphs drifted in the kill zone. This position also would be uncomfortable while casting and leading the drift. This is where being able to use the nondominant hand becomes a useful aid. Switching to the opposite hand in such a situation permits the angler to square up to the target with the casting hand. It takes time for this hand to develop muscle memory, but it's worth the investment in time.

My body is squared up to the target, and by using my left hand, I can cast directly over my shoulder rather than across my body. This is a more comfortable casting position, and it allows the rod tip to travel parallel to the current instead of across it. Because my rod tip was able to travel in line with the current, the whole length of fly line that's lying on the water is in the same current. Also, using my left hand lets me lead the flies farther downstream.

In a situation like this, the use of the opposite hand allows you to add several feet to the drift, which will likely increase your catch rate. Also, your hand can travel farther upstream during the presentation as well as when leading the nymphs downstream. Try this experiment: Position your body as if you were going to cast across your shoulders to an upstream target. Pretend you are holding your rod in both hands, and simultaneously cast to the target and lead the rod tip through the drift. You will notice how much farther the hand on the same side as the current extends forward during the presentation and how much longer this hand can lead the nymphs during the drift.

Charles Jardine using his nondominant hand. Charles is a master of efficiency. GEORGE DANIEL

SHORT-LINE TACTICS

To cast using the short-line tactics of Czech and Polish nymphing, keep your rod tip high and wait until you feel the weight tug on the backcast before proceeding with the forward casting stroke. Your shoulders should be square to the target as you cast directly upstream. Because the drift is short, casting upstream rather than across-stream increases the length of the drift. The line hand is held off to the side and will not be used because of the short drift. Only the rod tip manages slack with this short-line tactic. (Note that I am casting left-handed in this sequence.)

With short-line tactics, since the drift is so short, your rig needs to be heavier to quickly reach the bottom. Rather than cast the rig, you just lob it, because all you need to do is put the weight into motion, and it will carry itself to the target. Begin the forward lob as soon as you feel the weight pull on the backcast. Also, because of the heavy rig, you should create a wider loop on the forward cast, slightly breaking your wrist to sweep the rod tip in a wider arc. This keeps the rig away from the rod tip and reduces the chances of collision, which could result in a broken tip.

At the end of the lob, the rod tip is often positioned close to the water's surface, and the rig begins to sink toward the bottom. Pause at this point to allow the nymphs to drop toward the stream bottom.

Once the nymphs reach to the bottom and the current starts to pull the rig downstream, begin to slowly elevate the rod tip. At this stage, keep the rod tip pointed at the nymphs and do not start to lead them downstream.

Continue to elevate the rod tip until you see your sighter or leader tighten up, indicating the rig is on the bottom. Once you see the line tighten, begin to lead the nymphs downstream with the rod tip. If the line jerks upstream, rather than simply tightening, this is an indication of a take.

When leading the flies downstream through the drift, you want them to move naturally with the current. The rod tip should lead the rig parallel to the current and not pull against it. Your hand should be fully extended as in the photo.

Instead of leading with just the rod hand, start to rotate your shoulders downstream. Here the rod hand is holding the rod, but the rotating shoulder begins to move the tip downstream. Using the larger muscles of your upper body to lead the nymphs results in less fatigue in the hand.

Continue to lead the nymphs at about the same speed as the bottom current. Avoid dragging them unnaturally. In shallow water, where the current speed is approximately the same on both the bottom and the surface, you can move the rod tip at about the same speed as the surface currents. In deep water, however, where bottom currents are slower than on the surface, move the rod tip slightly slower than the surface currents.

Continue to lead the nymphs downstream.

When the rod tip reaches a point directly across the stream from your body position, start to accelerate the rod hand downstream to begin the backcast. A five-second drift is common with these short-line tactics.

A common misconception is that the hand needs to be fully extended at all times while executing short-line strategies. This is not true. For example, when fishing up close, within 10 feet, the angler just needs to keep the rod tip at a steep angle, with the rod hand low. The hand rests around waist level, but the rod tip is angled upward toward the sky. This angle keeps most of the line and leader off the water. This is one reason why I like to get as close to the target as possible before casting. A longer rod also means the angler does not have to extend his hand as far.

How to Place and Use a Sighter

To determine how far you should place the sighter from your point fly, you need to first consider the average depth of the water you are fishing. The distance from the sighter to the point fly should be approximately one and a half times the depth of the water you intend to fish. This will ensure that your sighter remains above water level. When nymphing in central Pennsylvania, where the average depth of water I fish is between 2 and 3 feet, I place my sighter about 4½ to 5 feet from my point fly. If you're fishing water deeper than 5 feet, you may need to lengthen the distance from sighter to nymphing rig.

To determine how deep your nymphs are riding, you read the angle of the sighter. When you look at your sighter, you need to consider both the length of your leader and the depth of the water to be able to read the angle. For example, imagine you are fishing a 4-foot-deep run, your sighter and flies are 4 feet apart, and you want the rig to bounce on the bottom. To achieve this, you first need to elevate the rod tip vertically until the tip of the sighter is near the water's surface and pointing straight down into the water. Once you have determined that the sighter has reached the correct angle, you can begin leading the flies with the rod tip. I try to consistently keep an average tippet length of 4 to 5 feet so that I'm able to quickly identify when the sighter is at the correct angle. Constantly changing the distance between the rig and the sighter makes it more difficult to recognize when the sighter has reached the correct angle. For example, the angle will decrease the farther it is from the target. Keep it consistent. Also, using a longer sighter makes it easier to read the angle.

Once you make your cast, you must first let the nymphs sink to the bottom before beginning to lead them. Keeping in mind the distance from your sighter to your anchor (either split shot or the heaviest fly on the rig) and the depth of the water you are fishing, watch the sighter begin to angle downward toward the water's surface as the weighted rig pulls it to the stream bottom. Do not begin leading your flies until the sighter is positioned at the angle that you feel indicates that your nymphs are at the feeding level of the trout.

Some anglers have argued that a brightly colored sighter too close to your nymphs has the potential to scare fish, especially in low water. I am convinced that trout are able to see fluorescent sighter material and that it may at times actually spook fish. As a result, I use hi-vis mono in low-water conditions. This material is colored but not as gaudy as other manufactured materials. AMIDEA DANIEL

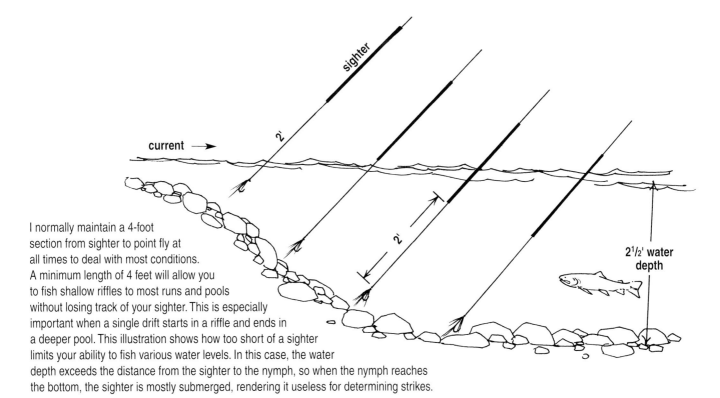

I normally maintain a 4-foot section from sighter to point fly at all times to deal with most conditions. A minimum length of 4 feet will allow you to fish shallow riffles to most runs and pools without losing track of your sighter. This is especially important when a single drift starts in a riffle and ends in a deeper pool. This illustration shows how too short of a sighter limits your ability to fish various water levels. In this case, the water depth exceeds the distance from the sighter to the nymph, so when the nymph reaches the bottom, the sighter is mostly submerged, rendering it useless for determining strikes.

Left: Here I am leading the sighter through a shallow run about 20 inches deep. The fluorescent yellow material is the sighter, and the orange material attached directly above is the leader. To keep the sighter closer to the water for photographic purposes, I used a short tippet, about 3 feet long—this photo illustrates well how a 3-foot tippet should be angled in 20 inches of water.

Right: In this shot, I am still using the 3-foot tippet, but here the nymphs are rolling on the bottom in water approximately 30 inches deep. The deeper the water, the steeper the angle you need between the sighter and the water's surface. In even deeper water, about 40 inches deep, the sighter will be angled directly downward and partially submerged in the water if your flies are truly rolling on the bottom. The sighter needs to be above the water for you to register takes, and the closer it is to your nymphs, the faster you will be able to detect takes. You know that split second can matter if you have ever watched a trout spit out a fly.

For example, let's say I am fishing a run 3 feet deep and my sighter is approximately 4½ feet from my anchor fly (I am not using split shot in this scenario). After I cast my rig and it enters the water, I allow my sighter to lie on the water's surface and watch it get pulled into the water as the nymphs settle to the bottom. I wait until my sighter is fixed at approximately a 45-degree angle to the stream bottom before actually leading my flies. This angle tells me that the rig is on the stream bottom and ready to be led through the drift.

Another key to knowing when your flies are on the bottom is to watch for the tension to increase in your sighter. This is why I prefer to use a sighter at least 12 inches long. After you have made the cast and the nymphs drop to the bottom, you will notice the sighter tightening up toward the stream once the nymphs are anchored on the bottom. This is just a tightening up of any slack in the sighter and not the short, jerking upstream motion usually associated with a take.

It's important to wait for the sighter to be at the correct angle before leading your flies. Anglers too often begin leading the flies way before the nymphs actually reach the bottom. My most common mistake, which I still make to this day, is not waiting long enough for my flies to drop to the bottom of a deep run before leading them. You won't catch many fish if your flies are not at their level. This is a thinking game, and you always have to be on the alert when using short-line tactics, as you control the depth and speed of your drift, unlike in suspension nymphing, where you use a set distance at all times.

Once you begin leading your nymphs, maintain the same height from beginning to end of the drift. If you drop the tip, you get slack. Watch the speed of your sighter, especially if it hesitates or stops during the drift, to determine how much control you have. If you notice your sighter slowly being pulled under the surface, there likely is slack in your system. This occurs if your flies wind up downstream of your sighter because you did not lead them through the drift fast enough. Strive to get your sighter to tick directly above the water's surface as the nymphs bounce off the bottom. If you have a tight connection, your sighter should suddenly hesitate or quickly move upstream anytime you correctly lead your nymphs.

Always watch where the nymphs exit the water relative to the sighter when you set the hook or pick up to make another cast. For example, say you're leading your nymphs through a riffle and see that your sighter is angled upstream, which should indicate that your flies are directly upstream of your sighter. When you pick up your cast, however, the nymphs

When fishing deeper water, you need to keep your rod tip elevated for a longer period than in shallow water before beginning to lead the flies. Wait and allow the rig to reach the feeding zone first. JAY NICHOLS

Pay close attention to where the nymph exits the water in relation to the sighter. In the top illustration, the fly exits the water upstream of the indicator. This signals that the indicator is positioned downstream and that tension is occurring in the rig, which is the ideal situation. The bottom illustration depicts the nymph exiting the water downstream of the indicator, which suggests that slack is occurring. This means that the angler probably is not leading the flies fast enough or placed them in a faster current.

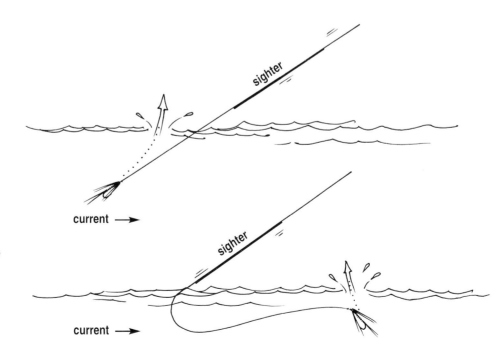

come out of the water downstream of your sighter. This indicates that you either are not leading your flies fast enough or need to add weight, or a combination of the two. Ideally, while you are leading the flies, the nymphs should be angled upstream of the sighter or directly below it, as tension occurs in both cases. If the flies are downstream, however, slack is occurring, which makes it difficult or impossible to detect a strike. These little tips will help you fine-tune your nymphing skills and make adjustments while you fish, like a sports coach making half-time adjustments.

Short drifts, those lasting only a few seconds, often require nothing more than elevating and leading the rod tip. Don't keep your nymphs in the water longer than you have connection with them. When you need longer drifts, retrieve slack with your line hand. Sometimes I purposely place my flies well

above the target to provide additional time for the patterns to sink. In such cases, I keep the rod tip fixed at the same spot where it stopped on the forward cast and use only the line hand to retrieve the slack line. After I have managed the slack and allowed the flies to reach the bottom, I then use the rod tip to lead the nymphs through the drift.

The speed at which you should retrieve flies with your line hand depends on the speed of the current. With slow currents, you can use a figure-eight retrieve to keep up with the nymphs. Faster currents, however, demand longer pulls with the line hand to manage the slack. I prefer to use a long, smooth pull for both situations, because I believe that pulling with the line hand, fast or slow, is a more controlled movement. There are no stops or hesitations when the line hand pulls; it's just one smooth gliding motion.

The tippet length here from sighter to point fly is consistently 5 feet in length. With the water depth at 2 feet, the sighter should ride 2 feet out of the water and angle slightly upstream to indicate that the nymph is close to the river bottom. If you use a longer tippet, the sighter will ride higher out of the water, and vice versa. Always think about the length of your tippet along with the depth of the water to determine the proper angle and height for your sighter.

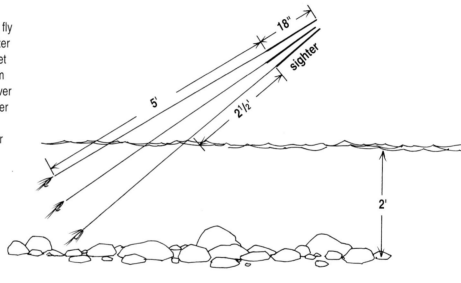

With the water depth at 4 feet, the sighter should ride less than 1 foot out of the water and be angled at 45 degrees upstream.

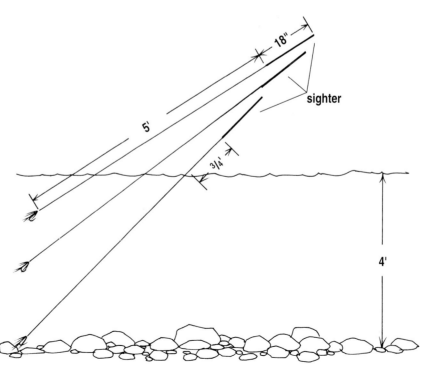

Surface currents are often faster than the currents on the stream bottom. This means that during the elevation to manage slack, the speed at which you move your rod tip should start out fast, as the nymphs begin dropping through the fast current and slow down once they near the bottom. As your nymphs drop, they first pass through the faster currents, which quickly push the rig downstream, and your initial rod tip movement must be quick enough to keep up with this pace. The nymphs then slow down as they reach the slower currents near the bottom; now your rod tip should also move at a slower speed. This tip is useful when fishing extremely fast currents, where many anglers are not fully in control of the drift. Loss of control occurs as soon as the nymphs are in front of the rod tip during the drift, and it's important that you regain control after the nymphs shoot through a fast run. Using a fast initial movement of the rod tip in fast water will enable you to regain control of the drift and help you catch more fish.

One of the biggest mistakes anglers make while tight-line nymphing is beginning to lead the flies too early during the drift, before they have reached the right depth. The angle of the sighter in combination with the length of the tippet provides information on the approximate location of the nymphs. In this case, you use the sighter as a depth gauge to allow you to estimate the location and depth of the nymphs. Maintaining a consistent length between sighter and flies during most fishing excursions will allow you to become more proficient at estimating these two variables. I try to keep the distance between my sighter and nymphs at 4 to 5 feet.

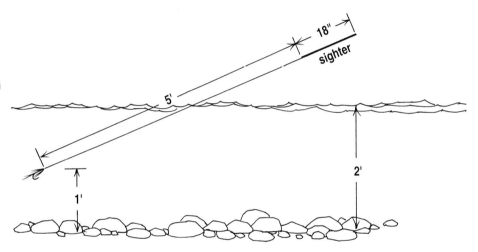

Trout feed throughout the entire water column and not just on the bottom. If trout are feeding 1 foot above the stream bottom during a hatch, you need to think about water depth, length of tippet, and the level at which the trout are feeding. This illustration shows the approximate height and angle of the sighter in order to fish the flies 1 foot above the stream bottom in 2-foot-deep water with a 5-foot-long tippet between sighter and point fly.

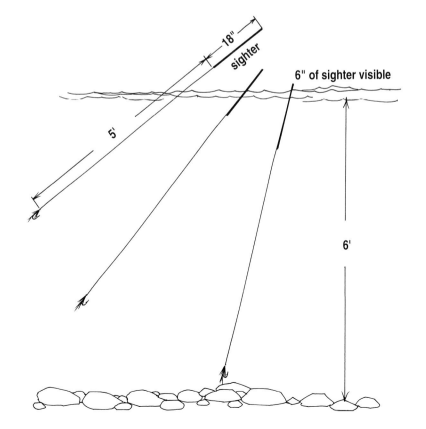

With the water depth at 6 feet, the sighter should be vertical, angled at 90 degrees to the water, and partially immersed, with only a few inches sticking above the surface. A 5-foot tippet plus a 1½-foot sighter equals 6½ feet in total length from top of sighter to point fly. With the water depth at 6 feet, only 6 inches of sighter should ride above the surface level if you want your flies drifting near the stream bottom.

Elevating and Leading

It's important to learn the proper techniques for elevating and leading your nymphs. The elevation phase provides the rig sufficient slack to drop quickly to the desired depth, and then lead-ing the flies creates the necessary tension to begin moving them downstream. If you master the techniques of elevating and leading, you won't need very much weight at all to drift your flies along the bottom, even in the fastest currents.

ELEVATING AND LEADING

Here the angler is positioned directly upstream toward the target. The presentation has been delivered to the shallows to allow time for the nymphs to drop before entering the kill zone. The rod hand is fully extended to provide the angler with leverage to first elevate the rod tip and then lead the nymphs, and the rod tip is still angled upward to keep as much line and leader as possible off the water.

At this point, the rod tip moves only vertically to manage slack as the nymphs move downstream. That is, you keep your rod tip pointed at the rig but begin lifting your forearm and rod tip toward the sky. To illustrate, imagine there's a tree standing directly behind where you presented your flies. You are standing directly upstream, and the rod tip is pointing close to the tree trunk in the early presentation stage. If you elevate the rod tip properly, it will continue to point at the tree but will trace the shape of the tree toward the top.

During the elevation phase, the rod tip does not move downstream, only upward. This allows you to manage the slack as the nymphs drop to the bottom. Moving the rod tip downstream will create tension and not permit the flies to drop any further. Continue to elevate the rod tip upward until the sighter is at the correct angle.

Only after the sighter has reached the appropriate angle should you begin to move the rod tip downstream to lead the flies. The elevation phase allowed the nymphs to drop quickly to the desired depth, and now leading the flies creates tension to begin moving them downstream.

The rod tip should remain at this height and not drop while leading the flies, as lowering the rod tip during the lead would throw slack into the rig. Maintaining the rod tip at the same height after elevating creates the tension you need to feel a take.

Continue to lead the nymphs until the rod tip is directly across your body. Look at the sighter for any reason to set the hook, such as a change of direction or a slight hesitation. Now make a quick downstream hook set to begin the backcast.

ELEVATING AND LEADING CLOSE UP

After making the cast, angle the rod tip upward to keep excess line and leader off the water. Your rod hand should be extended outward and positioned low. Keep the rod tip pointed at the target.

Using the three-point grip, your index finger begins to angle upward toward the sky while the rod tip remains pointed at the target. Move the rod upward to manage slack but not downstream at this stage.

Breaking your wrist, increase the angle of the rod tip as the nymph continues to drop. The timing of this technique depends on the speed and depth of the water. It will take longer for the nymph to drop in deeper water and less time in shallow water.

Continue to elevate the rod tip until the flies have reached the correct depth. The angle of the sighter will become steeper as the nymphs continue to drop to the bottom. This steep angle allows the nymphs to drop quickly but still maintains connection with them in case a trout decides to eat one on the drop. Your wrist does most of the work during the elevation stage.

When the sighter tightens up, your rig is on the bottom and ready to be led through the drift. Wait until the rig anchors itself on the bottom, as this will assist in keeping tension between rod tip and nymph.

Once the nymphs have reached the correct depth, keep the rod tip at a steep angle while your rod hand begins to lead the nymphs downstream. The rod tip does not drop, but moves downstream of or right above the nymphs to maintain tension and line control. In this photo, the nymphs are directly under the rod tip. Note the tight line from rod tip to nymph. The length of the tippet and the water's depth determine the correct angle of the sighter in relation to the water. Generally, the sighter should be at a shallow angle in shallow water and a steep angle in deep water.

Begin leading the flies through the drift once the rig anchors itself. Leading does not mean dragging your flies faster than the current. Instead, it means keeping the rod tip in front of the drifting nymphs to maintain tension as the current pulls the nymphs downstream.

Continue to lead the nymphs until the rod tip is directly across your body. Now make a quick downstream hook set to begin the backcast. With such a short length of line, a short upward lift with the forearm is all you need to set the hook.

Once you've made the downstream hook set, maintain a high rod-tip angle until you feel the tug, which signals that it's time to make the forward cast.

ROLLED WRIST FLIP CAST

I learned the rolled wrist flip cast while fishing with Vladi Trzebunia during our practice for the 2010 World Championships in Poland. This technique helps place your entire fly line in the same speed current when you have to cast upstream and across your body. With the traditional method of casting across your shoulder upstream, you shoulders are first squared to the target. Then they begin moving downstream as you follow the nymphs through the drift. You reposition them to face upstream again before making the next cast. The elbow and rod hand positions, with the elbow in and rod tip over the opposite shoulder, make it difficult to place the nymphing rig all in the same speed current. With the rolled wrist flip, however, you use less body movement before and during the drift and can easily place the flies in the same speed current when you have to cast across your body. Your flies also land farther upstream than with a conventional cast, which extends the life of the drift and gives the nymphs additional time to reach the bottom. I was surprised to see how little weight Vladi and other Polish friends were using on the San River during high water, thanks to this technique.

Begin with the rod tip and your body positioned perpendicular to the target. In this photo, my target is directly upstream following the current, but my shoulders and rod tip are pointing toward the opposite bank. The flies are being held by the water, creating a 90-degree angle from rod tip to fly line, and they are positioned at a 180-degree angle to the target. That is, the flies are holding in the same current as the targeted area but directly downstream of the target. The plane of the reel face is facing upward.

At this point, your wrist begins to flop in a 180-degree arc toward the targeted seam. Imagine that you're holding a cup of birdseed and you want to flick the seed on the ground. In order to get a good flick of the wrist, the opening of the cup needs to be facing in the opposite direction from where you want to flick the seeds. In this case, the rod tip is perpendicular to the target, but the fly line is positioned directly opposite the target.

Now, to flick the seeds, your elbow remains locked but your wrist and thumb begin moving from nine o'clock to three o'clock in an upside-down U shape. You accelerate during this entire motion until the opening of the cup is facing directly toward the target, speeding up to a sudden stop, which causes the seeds to leave the cup and continue their path toward the target. Your elbow remains almost locked, moving very little to make the cast.

In this maneuver, the rod tip does not point toward the targeted seam at the end of the cast. Instead, your thumb pad points at the target while you angle the rod tip toward the opposite bank. This rod tip and line position allows for quick line control and lets you begin leading the nymphs straight down the targeted seam.

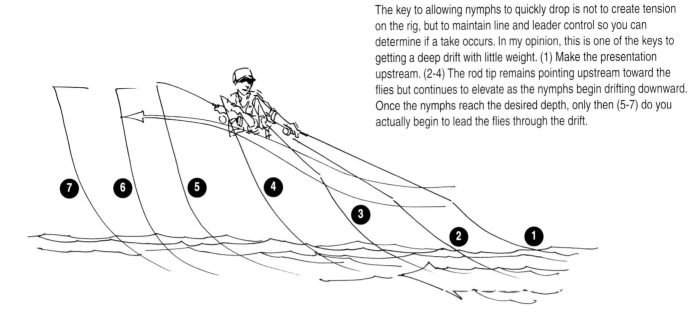

The key to allowing nymphs to quickly drop is not to create tension on the rig, but to maintain line and leader control so you can determine if a take occurs. In my opinion, this is one of the keys to getting a deep drift with little weight. (1) Make the presentation upstream. (2-4) The rod tip remains pointing upstream toward the flies but continues to elevate as the nymphs begin drifting downward. Once the nymphs reach the desired depth, only then (5-7) do you actually begin to lead the flies through the drift.

Short Drifts, Short Casts

When fishing pocketwater and riffles and runs, casts are short and you have to move closer to the target rather than work more line. To imitate a nymph or larva freely drifting in the currents, use a dead drift while maintaining enough tension to your flies to detect strikes. After delivering the flies with a simple lob and waiting for them to sink to the bottom, lead the flies with the rod; do not pull, or drag will set in. Lead them fast enough ahead of the nymphs to maintain a tight connection with them. The rod tip continues leading the nymphs until it's positioned directly across from you. At this stage, you maintain a high rod-tip angle but make a hard downstream hook set. This serves two purposes: it hooks any unobserved take from a trout, which is rare but can happen, and it positions the flies downstream of the rod tip, which creates the tension needed to make the next forward lob.

To imitate emerging insects, move your flies a little faster through the currents. As immature nymphs are swimming to the surface and beginning to emerge, trout key in on the rising insects. They also have learned to chase certain types of swimming mayfly nymphs. The former world champion Vladi Trzebunia, who was an orginal practitioner of the short-line method, has been coaching this active style of nymphing for years, when applicable. Pulling the nymphs slightly faster than the surface currents creates a tighter connection that more easily registers the soft takes of grayling and was later adapted to better imitate the movement of emerging insects. During this phase of the cast, Vladi's rule is that it's better to have a little too much drag than too much slack, and I agree, especially in pocketwater or mixed currents.

The one drawback of this tactic is that this active approach is best fished at a short distance, only as far as the leader and arm can reach. Also, because of the high degree of tension between the rod tip and nymph, there is very little slack, so you

risk breaking off fish or losing them. Some people use a softer rod to compensate for this.

The angle of the lead is based on how you want your rig to move through the column. For example, the rod tip can immediately pull level toward the bank, across the current, to imitate a stonefly emergence. This tactic worked well for me the few times I fished the Madison River during the initial salmonfly emergence. Or you can pull the flies directly downstream and begin elevating the rig with the rod tip to imitate a quickly emerging caddis. The best course of action is to understand the insect that is currently hatching and try to imitate that emergence with a natural-looking active approach.

Tight-Line Active Retrieve

You can also increase the amount of movement with an active retrieve, simultaneously stripping in line while leading with the rod tip. In September 2006, my first world championship took me to Portugal near the town of Penacova, a small village about three hours north of Lisbon. Luckily for us, Jorge Pisco, a Portuguese team member who didn't make the world championship team that year, became our guide at the last minute. Two small streams called the Alva and Ceira gave us the most trouble. They run through the Buçaco and Roxo mountain ranges, and thus the resident trout are not conditioned to seeing heavy angling traffic. Many of the sections of water were straight, wide, and shallow as a result of channelization by earlier generations, and sediment-filled dams were spread throughout the streams. The dams slowed the water upstream, so there was very little broken water, which made it almost impossible to get within 40 feet of the trout.

The bright sun and low water put the fish on high alert. As long as such conditions existed, we needed fast-moving water where we could find feeding trout and be able to get within

Give the fish a drift they're looking for. Overall, the dead drift is a productive tactic, but an active retrieve can solicit more strikes when trout are actively feeding on emerging insects. This photo shows an angler hooking a fish on an active retrieve during a caddis hatch. GEORGE DANIEL

Add a CDC collar to your favorite nymph to increase movement while using active or passive tactics. GEORGE DANIEL

casting range. When we finally got into casting position, we attempted to dead-drift small nymphs under a dry fly. After a few of us became somewhat discouraged with the lack of results, we asked Pisco to show us how he would fish the water.

Instead of using a dry-and-dropper, Pisco would cast a lightly colored Dave Whitlock Squirrel Nymph with a few turns of CDC just as we had, but instead of allowing his flies to dead-drift, he led them and retrieved them slightly faster than the current, while simultaneously swinging the rod tip and pulling the line with his left hand in one long, smooth pull. Jorge looked as if he were double-hauling in slow motion while at the same time leading his nymphs with the rod tip. For whatever reason, even when nothing was hatching, the trout responded with a take almost every time to this active retrieve.

Our group caught some fish using the dead-drift tactic, but we caught many more using Jorge's active retrieve. We never did get an explanation from him as to why the active retrieve was so effective, other than that trout like a moving fly. Pisco's lesson helped me secure a top-five finish in the Worlds, only the second time ever for a US competitor. (The first belonged to Jeff Currier, who finished with a bronze medal in Spain in 2003.) As a footnote, the following year, Pisco won the 2007 European Championships in Norway.

TIGHT-LINE ACTIVE RETRIEVE

When using the active retrieve, the presentation stage is identical to the tight-line long cast approach. That is, you identify a primary target and cast directly upstream to it. Lower the rod tip to the water's surface and fully extend it to allow maximum rod leverage during the active retrieve.

The rod tip remains low and the line hand gathers the slack as the nymphs drift downstream. The retrieve is just fast enough to gain line control but slow enough to provide the nymphs the slack needed to quickly get to the bottom. However, you may not want the nymphs to completely reach the bottom. For example, a caddis hatch may have progressed to the point that most fish are intercepting nymphs only a few inches under the surface. Trout don't look down for food—they look up. As a result, you should put the flies under tension as soon as the rig lands on the water.

Once the nymphs reach the appropriate level, begin leading the flies with the rod tip along with a long strip with your line hand. At the beginning of this phase, the rod tip is pointed at the flies to ensure that there is tension between the rod tip and fly. Now it's time to lead the flies through the drift with the rod tip.

Begin moving the rod tip perpendicular to the line to create a 90-degree angle. This means the rod tip will be pointed away from but downstream of the nymphs. This angle allows the rod to become a shock absorber during aggressive takes. Lead with your forearm and turn your body as the nymphs drift.

Even when your line hand is almost fully extended, continue to move the rod tip horizontally, parallel to the water's surface. This is an active retrieve where the flies should be moving faster than the water speed, so focus on a bubble (or something else that will provide a moving reference), and make sure the rod tip travels faster than the bubble during the retrieve.

Your shoulders continue to move downstream to provide your forearm with sufficient leeway to lead the nymphs. Essentially, your shoulders will move in a 180-degree arc from start to finish. At the end of the drift, they will be facing downstream, the rod tip will stop moving, and the tension will force the flies to swing upward toward the water's surface. The rod tip should be pointing away from the flies to provide slack in case a trout inhales them.

THE TENSION SWING

During heavy hatches when trout are actively moving up and down the water column, or when you are trying to imitate a strongly swimming nymph, the tension swing can be deadly. First you cast directly upstream, allowing the flies to drop to the stream bottom and dead-drift back to you. Then toward the end of the drift, you let the flies drift downstream from their position, while keeping the line tight, to permit them to ascend to the surface. This works really well while fishing during a caddis hatch or the beginning of the Eastern Green Drake hatch, as the nymphs are emerging.

What I like about this technique is that it incorporates two tactics in one drift: dead-drifting and swinging at the end. This is important, because all the fish are not always targeting the same insect, let alone the same insect stage. For example, in bug factories like Penns Creek, where multiple hatches can occur simultaneously, I've noticed trout in the same run taking completely different insects and insect stages. This means that both dead-drifting and actively moving your flies will produce fish. When I think that fish are keyed on both active and passive presentations, I use the tension swing after the dead drift.

Such added motions often double the time your presentation takes, however, and are not the most efficient methods. Thus if the trout are not actively chasing the naturals, don't waste your time swinging flies at the end of the drift. The tension swing covers more water than actively leading with the rod tip, and you can use it to cover water from a greater distance. I don't recommend using this dual tactic from more than 30 feet. If you are too far away, you won't be able to effectively control the line for both the dead drift and the tension swing. The one disadvantage to this tactic is that the fish often inhales the fly from a downstream position during the tension swing, which forces you to set the hook away from you, resulting in low hookup rates.

Long Drifts, Long Casts

Though it's not usually what people think of as Czech nymphing, you can also tight-line from a distance. In many ways, this technique is closely related to the Harvey/Humphreys method in the way you cast upstream with all of the leader and part of the fly line on the water. Because leader is on the water, the colored sighter material is rendered useless and the fly-line tip serves as your strike indicator. Also, because of the greater amount of line on the water, a leader under 10 feet can provide for better line and leader management.

An upstream cast is typically made in line with the targeted current. As the nymphs begin to drift back downstream, continue to elevate the rod tip, and use your line hand to retrieve the line with either a hand-twist retrieve or a short strip. This style of presentation can be effective up to 40 feet, where you can still maintain line control and detect strikes. Beyond that, it can be difficult to see movement in the fly-line tip, which you are using as the visual to set the hook. For fishing beyond 40 feet, I normally use some form of suspension device (see chapter 5).

To achieve a more active approach with a long cast, which is especially useful for slow water when trout are actively moving up and down the water column, you can use a tension loop, with or without stripping in line. The tension loop can save the day, especially when prospecting for fish on large waters. What I know about the tension loop came from my Fly Fishing Team USA captain, Anthony Naranja, who spent a week in 2007 with our Polish coach and friend Vladi Trzebunia. From what Anthony could gather, Vladi first learned this tactic from the legendary French angler Pascal Cognard, a three-time world champion, who showed it to Vladi while fishing the San River in Poland several years earlier. Vladi calls it "long lining," and the technique has been used in Eastern Europe for a number of years. The San is a large river with wide, shallow, slow-moving water that harbors healthy populations of grayling and brown trout. At that time, however, Vladi said that grayling were the dominant species. Grayling are notorious for very soft takes, and the slow-moving water of the San made it all the more difficult to register a take.

Instead of using suspension devices, which were illegal in fly-fishing competitions and not commonly used in Europe at that time, anglers used tension loops to cover large areas of water with lightweight nymphs. To use this tactic, you begin by casting upstream, and then make a small downstream mend to place the line downstream of the fly. Next, you make a small upstream mend, creating a U-shaped loop. You place the rod tip on the water, slightly facing toward the fly, which maintains the shape of the loop and the tension on the line. Once you have formed this U, drop the rod tip to the water's surface, and begin slowly stripping in line faster than the current with your line hand. The bigger the loop, the greater the tension needed. If there's not enough tension, the line will form S curves instead of being straight. Sometimes you need to make a nice long, steady pull, resembling a double haul on the backcast; other times a series of short, erratic strips is preferable. It's important to vary the speed of the retrieve based on the current hatch and what gets the best reaction from the trout. You will often register a take by either feeling the trout inhale the fly or noticing the tip of the fly line hesitating.

The greatest advantage I have noticed with this upstream active approach is the incredibly high percentage of landed fish, which is directly related to the U-shaped tension loop. The loop keeps moving downstream of the fly. When a trout decides to eat, the loop created enough tension to automatically pull

Weston Reynolds nymphing a sunken terrestrial in between weed beds on a small Czech Republic stream. Because trout normally hold deep below weed beds, hitting the fly hard on the surface helps get the fish's attention. GEORGE DANIEL

the fly downstream, setting the fly toward the trout's mouth. Most of the time, the trout hooks itself, and all you need to do is elevate the rod tip to begin controlling the line and playing the fish.

This is a great method for actively fishing your flies higher in the water column in nondescript water when searching methods are often needed to find a fish. This is one of the deadliest methods for actively fishing your nymphs, but like the other active approaches, it's effective only when the trout say so. I use a passive, dead-drift approach for more than 90 percent of

my nymphing. The tension loop also works well with suspension devices, so it is a technique worth mastering.

We used this tactic for fishing many of the long flats on the San River in Poland, where current speeds were roughly uniform across the river. The key to this tactic is using it in uniform water to allow a straight line connection to occur from the nymphing rig to the tension loop. Strong nagging currents between you and the flies can create too much belly and pull your flies downstream faster than you want. (Also see the tension loop section beginning on page 129.)

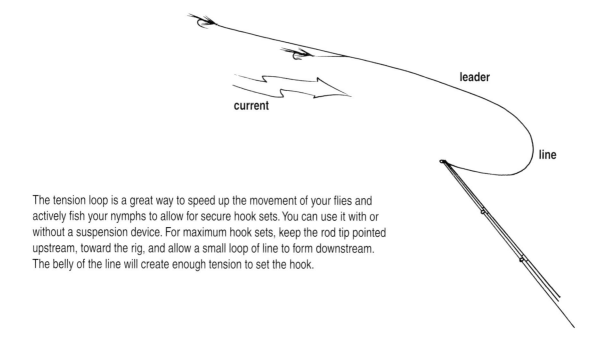

current

leader

line

The tension loop is a great way to speed up the movement of your flies and actively fish your nymphs to allow for secure hook sets. You can use it with or without a suspension device. For maximum hook sets, keep the rod tip pointed upstream, toward the rig, and allow a small loop of line to form downstream. The belly of the line will create enough tension to set the hook.

CREATING A TENSION LOOP

Cast at an upstream angle toward the opposite bank, keeping the rod tip low at first. Hold the line tightly in your rod or line hand so that no line can slip through the guides. You need a minimum of 5 feet of fly line lying on the water to create a tension loop.

At first, with a low rod hand, keep the rod tip pointed at the line after the presentation. With the line tight, begin to move the rod tip vertically, picking the belly of the line off the water. This should not be a powerful accelerated motion, but a simple raise of the rod tip. Lift until almost all the line is off the water, but allow at least the tip of the fly line to remain anchored on the water's surface.

Now use your elevated rod hand to pull the line almost directly downstream of the nymphing rig. This movement is the same as when executing a downstream reach mend. If you have done it correctly, there should be a 90-degree angle between fly line and rod tip.

With the rod tip near the water's surface, the tip will have enough leverage to create the loop.

Begin to raise the rod tip, but only high enough to lift 2 to 3 feet of line off the water.

Next, perform an upstream mend with the rod tip toward the nymphing rig, after which you drop the rod tip back to the water. Move the rod tip only a few feet upstream during this movement. The result will be a U-shaped loop off the tip.

Start to slide your rod hand upstream toward the fly. Use a stiff arm motion, actually pulling the line upstream. The U shape is beginning to form at this stage.

Continue to pull the line upstream until it has formed a complete U shape.

To maintain the tension loop, the rod tip needs to point directly toward the nymphing rig. The tension loop or belly of the line will remain under tension only if you keep the rod tip pointed at the rig. Follow the nymphing rig downstream with your rod tip, and slowly strip in slack line as it comes back to you. Any indication of the loop tightening up may signal a strike.

FRENCH AND SPANISH NYMPHING METHODS

Many of the Western European countries, including France and Spain, are known for their difficult trout fishing, which requires long casts and soft presentations. The French and Spanish styles of nymphing, which I often refer to as long-line nymphing (again, to avoid controversy), employ tight-line tactics designed for fishing at greater distances. These nymphing strategies were developed for fishing extremely shallow and clear water, where trout are on high alert for predators and easily spooked. To overcome the challenges of spooky fish and low, clear water, the French and Spanish developed a tight-line technique with leaders more than 20 feet long. With this length of leader, you can hold most of the line and leader off the water with a high rod angle, except for a short section of leader and tippet that enters the water. The lightly weighted nymph creates only a small disturbance as it enters the water, and it doesn't constantly foul on the stream bottom as a heavier fly would. Because little if any fly line is used to deliver the fly, these long leaders require a long butt section, sometimes with a sighter integrated into them.

There are slight differences between the Spanish and French techniques. According to Pete Erickson, another member of Fly Fishing Team USA, Spanish nymphing is basically Czech or Polish nymphing done from a greater distance. Here the angler presents the nymphs on a 9- to 30-foot-long leader from a side angle or slightly upstream. In French long-line nymphing, on the other hand, the angler usually presents the nymphs upstream to the fish.

Because these long-line tactics were developed to deal with spooky trout that often hold in slow and shallow water, they differ from the short-line tactics described above in the amount of weight used and the leader design. A fly that is heavily weighted will create a disturbance strong enough to spook most fish and will most likely immediately hang up. With long-line nymphing, anglers use more lightly weighted nymphs in order to create less disturbance and avoid snagging the bottom. The real difficulty with these tactics is in trying to maintain tension, as a more lightly weighted fly does not tend to become as well anchored as a more heavily weighted fly. Because of this, it's extremely important to allow the nymph to sufficiently anchor itself as described in the section on how to place and use a sighter (see page 69).

Long-line tactics usually require a longer leader to allow you to be in direct contact with the nymphs at distances greater than 25 feet. To accomplish this, anglers use exceptionally long

A long rod and leader will allow you to present to spooky bank-feeding fish from a distance. Here, I am fishing sunken terrestrials tight to the bank on Letort Spring Run. JAY NICHOLS

leaders, which can exceed 25 feet, along with rods 9 feet or longer and heavy bead-head point flies. With this combination, they present the flies up to 30 feet away while holding all line and most of the leader off the water. Usually the line does not extend out past the tip guide. The long leader has a lighter mass than the fly line and can extend beyond the guides without sagging. The angler can keep the leader tight to the flies from 30 feet away by holding the long rod higher in the air. Keeping the leader off the water in this way allows for a stealthy presentation.

My favorite moments fishing the limestone rivers and spring creeks near my home in central Pennsylvania are when I'm able to short-line big caddis and stonefly imitations during the high water of spring. At this time, trout are in prime feeding mode, inhaling the big nasties. Soon the water tables drop, however, and we are left with low, clear water and spooky fish. We can no longer get close and tight-line to fish in faster, colored water. Because of this, most anglers just fish the deeper pools and runs, which can get really crowded when the hatches are on.

By the time I get out of work at this time of year, most of the prime spots are filled, and all that remains is the skinny, shallow water that nobody wants to fish. Fortunately, just

because anglers do not want to fish this water does not mean there are no trout there, and by using long-line techniques borrowed from the French and Spanish, which allow me to present flies in the shallow water without spooking the trout, I can turn lemons into lemonade. Surprisingly, though anglers commonly refer to such sections as "frog water," meaning that only frogs and not fish would inhabit such water, they have sometimes produced the biggest fish of the season.

The French have been contenders for medals every year at the world championships, in part because they have devised techniques to provide those small winning margins, mostly through targeting trout in the skinny, marginal water that most anglers walk right past. This is the type of water most anglers don't want to be stuck fishing. I often get asked, "Why would I want to learn a technique for fishing these conditions? I never intend to be in a situation where I'm fishing skinny water with a long leader." My response it the common saying: "Hope for the best, but plan for the worst." I think this philosophy actually lends itself well to many fishing situations.

You can use the long-line style on any water, but it is especially useful for smaller streams with low and clear flows. Even

When fishing micronymphs in deeper water, it's important not to have a counterweight to the fly line. A counterweight is created when part of the fly line remains in the guides and begins to drop back toward the reel. This diagram depicts how a weighted fly line running through the guides can actually act as a counterweight to the nymphing rig. Ideally, the line should be outside the tip guide or, in some cases, still wound on the reel. When you angle the rod tip upward for line and leader management, any line within the guides has the tendency to fall back toward the reel.

In this illustration only an inch or so of fly line is out of the reel, and nothing but leader runs up through the guides. A mono leader, even one with a heavy butt section, weighs less than the same length of fly line in the guides. As a result, the lightly weighted mono leader pulls less against the weight of the nymph, creating less counterweight resistance. Also, when fishing such a long leader, it's important to use a long butt section that is knotless so it does not hang up in the guides. These days, I am beginning to lean more toward knotless manufactured leaders.

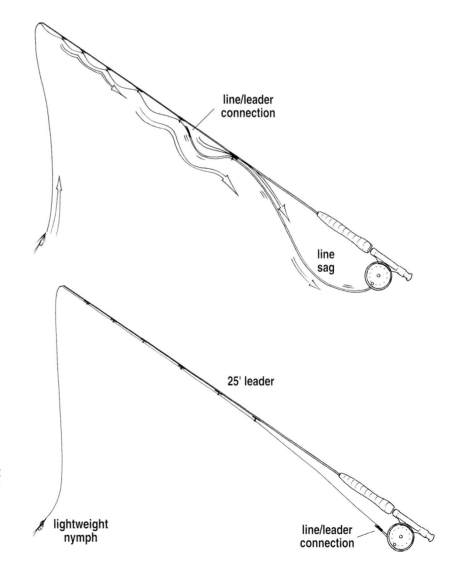

line/leader connection

line sag

25' leader

lightweight nymph

line/leader connection

Right: The Letort is known for its selective trout. I find that *not* matching the hatch often works in streams like this one that have millions of cress bugs and midges. This trout fell to a Beadhead Iron Lotus, a pattern that looks nothing like the current food supply. JAY NICHOLS

Above: Streamers can be nymphed as well. In this photo, Lance Wilt displays a beautiful fall brown trout that fell prey to a dead-drifted streamer pattern. A cold snap the night before cooled the water, and dead-drifting large streamers was the most effective tool that day. GEORGE DANIEL

Right: Fishing for New Zealand's wary brown trout is one of the only situations where I've needed to use a dull-colored fly line to avoid scaring fish. AMIDEA DANIEL

in the most demanding conditions, you can get within 20 to 30 feet of the fish with a quiet approach. With a properly designed leader, you can get the fly to the fish without having any line and leader hit the water. This nymphing style is hard work, but it may be your only option when nymphing the most extreme conditions.

For this technique, I like to use the longest rod I can; a 10-foot, 4-weight with a medium to fast action is perfect. A lightweight balanced outfit is best, as the two key movements are a full hand extension in combination with a forearm lift. The drifts are short, often lasting no more than four seconds, so fish-

ing the lightest possible rod will help reduce fatigue over the course of the day. Often the patterns are small, lightly weighted nymphs tied with a tungsten bead to keep the rig anchored in the water. While coaching in the Czech Republic during the 2009 World Youth Fly Fishing Championships, I was fortunate to have a French angler immediately downstream of me that I could watch out of the corner of my eye. It was the fourth session, and the water had been fished hard the last day and a half by three other youth competitors. The French angler beautifully fished a single lightweight nymph with a leader extended out to 20 feet and pulled four grayling out of a riffle that was no

Trout like holding tight to structure, so drift your nymph close to such holding areas. JAY NICHOLS

deeper than 4 inches. What impressed me was his ability to control such a lightweight nymph in the fast-moving water. The key to his success was giving the lightly weighted nymph a moment of slack to allow it to reach the bottom before beginning to lead the fly. This demonstrated that not much weight is actually needed for patterns to get to the bottom so long as the angler provides slack to allow the nymph to drop freely.

Because this technique is designed to present the fly from a distance in low, clear water, this often means that you have nagging currents between you and your primary target. For example, a few random boulders, creating broken pocketwater, could be between you and your targeted drift. Using a dry-and-dropper system would possibly cause the fly line and leader to land on those nagging currents while you're attempting to place the pattern in the tailout. Having the line and leader land on a current that is faster than the seam where the fly landed is a recipe for drag. Since the long leader lets you keep all the line and leader off the water except for where the nymph enters, it allows for an uninterrupted drift and a tight connection from rod tip to fly. You must also strive to keep that single weighted nymph in the same current. This is where using a leader of the proper length and design is critical.

This extremely long leader style is often debated as crossing over into spin fishing, as the long leader is held off the water's surface by a long rod. The leader mostly stays off the water current, providing a natural drift from a greater distance than with the short-line technique. However, monofilament weighs less than fly line, and keeping the fly line on the spool and allowing only monofilament to come out of the spool doesn't pull back on the fly the same way as if 5 feet of fly line were in the guides. This is why anglers often use 20- to 25-foot leaders, as they keep the leader and fly from being pulled back by the line.

The best leaders for the long-line nymphing are aggressive tapers to help ensure easier turnover of the long leader. I prefer to use a knotless or hand-tied leader with a long, smooth butt section, as this section most often stays within the guides during the drift. Knotted leaders can hang on the guides, impairing both the cast and line control. Coat your knots with Loon UV Knot Sense or similar knot dressing. This will smooth out the knotted sections and allow the leader to flow better through the guides to the rod tip. Finally, the line-leader connection should be smooth and have as slim as a diameter as possible. Dave Whitlock's Zap-A-Gap leader splice is my first choice for making this connection. I often use a 12-foot, 0X leader, attaching a 24-inch sighter along with a tippet ring. To the tippet ring, I attach a 5- to 8-foot single-diameter tippet, tying this to a single nymph. The single nymph is easier to control and makes less of an impact when entering the water, providing the stealthier delivery that is needed when employing the French technique. I have witnessed some of my teammates using two flies with this setup with great success, however, so

Long leaders are useful when fishing for educated spring creek trout. GEORGE DANIEL

keep an open mind. Some anglers prefer a medium-action fly rod because it loads easier with long leaders.

Another advantage of the long leader is that it has a thinner diameter than weight-forward or double-taper fly lines, creating less wind drag and letting it cut more easily through the air during the drift. Greater wind drag on the line applies additional drag on your nymphing rig, causing an unnatural drift. And in extreme wind, any fly line hanging out of the rod tip can act as a sail and pull your flies off the bottom, especially when you are holding the rod tip higher for line and leader control. However, even with the longer leader, there are times when holding the rod tip at a steep angle becomes detrimental to line control and drift. For example, large valleys can become wind chutes, playing havoc on any line or leader that is held off the water's surface. Anglers often lose line and leader control when the wind reaches speeds high enough to create a bow in the line or leader. This bow is a form of slack, a lost connection between the rod tip and nymph, and makes it difficult to detect strikes. In response to such conditions, I often shorten the leader a touch, maybe to 15 feet, and present the fly with the rod tip pointed at the water's surface. Wind can still affect the line even when lying on the water, but it will not have as great an effect on line control.

Dead Drift and Induced Take

As with the other methods, you can use the French style of nymphing with a dead drift or a more active presentation called the induced take. Dead-drift French or Spanish nymphing can be deadly, especially when sight-fishing for a trout. G. E. M. Skues and Frank Sawyer used a similar tactic when fishing the famed English chalkstreams. They would take a position at a down-and-across angle to the trout in order not to line the fish and then cast far enough upstream to permit the fly to settle to the exact level where the trout was feeding and slightly off to one side. As the fly drifted to either side, they paid attention to any movement of the fish toward the drift of the fly. If they saw the trout opening its mouth or moving in the direction of the nymph, they made a short, strong hook set.

The long-line leader is perfect for sight-fishing in such conditions, since only a short section of leader ever enters the water. You can make a direct upstream cast to the fish with less risk of spooking it, as no line will touch the water. Also, the long leader will not be as visible to the fish when you false-cast or present the nymphs. When you drop a fly right in front of a suspended fish while sight-fishing, the trout has only a moment to decide to take the fly and must make a split decision. The drift is short to begin with, lasting only about three or four seconds. You control the line mostly with your rod hand, so slack would likely occur if the drift lasted longer than four seconds. The rod hand can move only so far to keep tension before losing the tight connection. A normal drift begins after the presentation, when your hand is fully extended. From this point, your hand and forearm drift back to the front of your face before quickly lifting up the line to make the backcast, leading the nymphs at the same speed as the current and often faster.

A vertical raise of the rod tip lifts the fly off the bottom for the induced lift.

The induced take is a way of actively presenting the flies to the fish. The French, like many other anglers, soon figured out that quickly lifting the flies before making the backcast often produced a vertical presentation that was sometimes hard for the fish to resist. The induced lift is similar to the Leisenring lift but applied in shorter drifts. The tension lift is especially useful when a hatch is on. Trout can be as selective subsurface as they often are at the surface, and having a lifelike imitation isn't always enough. Your presentation to the fish must also behave like the naturals. Unlike long-line suspension nymphing, French nymphing is not a searching tool for big water. Instead, it's a tool used to pinpoint short but exact drifts where you believe a trout may be holding.

Long Range, Short Drift

This technique replicates the short drifts common with the Czech and Polish technique, but from at least 20 feet away. Again, your line hand is usually held off the side while your rod hand presents the flies and elevates and moves the rod tip to manage slack as the nymphs drift downstream. The drift usually lasts only three or four seconds, and as with the Czech and Polish tactic, you implement a downstream hook set when the rod tip is positioned below you to place the nymphs downstream, allowing tension for a forward casting stroke. And sometimes you will find a fish during the quick downstream hook set. Because no line is on the water, surface drag is greatly reduced, allowing you to use very little weight.

To obtain a nice dead drift, you cast (not lob as with the Czech and Polish method) the lightly weighted fly to the target. Once the fly settles to the bottom, begin to elevate the rod tip to maintain tension as the flies drift downstream. The purpose of elevating the rod and leading the flies is to maintain line and leader control and not to actively move the flies.

If you want to add movement to the flies, such as when trout are actively moving up and down the water column seeking food, you cast the same way, but with a heavier fly on the tippet to get the rig more quickly to the stream bottom. Anglers usually use a jig-style fly with tungsten bead for this technique, since this kind of fly inverts and rides with the hook point up to prevent snagging the bottom. Once the fly anchors on the stream bottom, you raise the rod tip vertically to pull the flies upward through the water column. This presentation usually lasts only three or four seconds. The long leader allows for immediate contact between rod tip and nymph so you can manually lift the flies off the bottom at the speed you want. To obtain long drifts with the French method, you need to use a low-profile suspension device like a curly Q (see page 116).

Casting Long Leaders

Casting longer leaders often requires more movement from the forearm. Because the long leader weighs less than fly line, you have to put additional energy into the casting stroke to load the rod.

CASTING LONG LEADERS

Begin with your rod hand fully extended and the rod tip pointed upward and outward. The rod handle should be slightly turned to lock the reel up against your wrist, and your fingertip should just barely touch the blank. This helps prevent breaking the wrist and allows more of the forearm, with its stronger muscles, to energize the long leader. Pinch the line under your rod hand before beginning the backcast to ensure that the leader and rod tip are under tension.

Begin lifting your elbow to start the backcast, and drift your forearm back to your face. This should be a smooth pulling motion moving the rod tip straight back.

Continue to drift the rod tip back until your hand is slightly over your head and there's a 45-degree angle between your elbow and forearm. The rod tip should be tilted slightly upward to keep it high so that the weighted rig can straighten out without ticking the ground or the water's surface.

Do not begin the forward cast until you feel the weight of the rig tug on the backcast. After the stop on the backcast, continue to hold the rod tip steady until you feel the weight pull.

Once the weight tugs on the backcast, proceed with the forward casting motion by smoothly leading with your elbow, dropping the elbow and drifting your forearm forward. Your hand tracks straight, with your forefinger or thumb pointing in the direction you want the fly to go. Do not push down on the cast, as doing so would likely collapse it to the water.

As you extend your forearm fully outward, slightly break your wrist and push down with your finger or thumb as you accelerate to the stop. Having your rod tip at an angle will keep the majority of the fly line and leader off the water, avoiding unwanted drag on the flies. The reason for beginning with your rod hand extended outward is to allow the hand to drift back as you lead the nymphs through the drift.

If applicable, you can drop the rod tip for the presentation stage. Normally, I maintain a higher rod-tip angle for better line and leader control. In some situations, however, such as in windy conditions, you may want to lay the long leader entirely on the water's surface.

AMERICAN LONG-DISTANCE TIGHT-LINING ADAPTATIONS

There are at least two American adaptations of this style of long-distance tight-lining: the greased-leader technique and small-diameter deep nymphing line.

The Greased-Leader Technique

Dave Rothrock introduced me to his greased-leader method back in the late 1990s while fishing a local stream. It was late July, and the water levels were already at their summertime low. The fish were spooky, and we needed to maintain our distance. The section we fished was almost a nonstop riffle. Dave had placed a single unweighted nymph on his rig and pinched on a single size 6 split shot 8 inches above the cress bug imitation. On the other hand, I wanted to work the same heavy

nymphing rig I had used the previous evening on a gradient freestone stream. I soon realized, however, that my short-line tactics with a heavy rig were not the best for the situation, as they were forcing me to get to close to the fish and my nymphs were constantly snagging bottom. Eventually I took off the split shot and attempted to extend my drift, but my weighted nymphs were still too heavy for a long extended drift.

After watching Dave land several fish from a distance, I decided to go see how he was fishing the long riffle. One thing I noticed was the unique way he had put together his leader. The butt section of the leader consisted of three parts fluorescent blue Stren and two parts golden Stren, the gold portions serving as two sighters spaced about 14 inches apart. A long, level section of tippet was attached between the sighter and a

Modified Rothrock Leader

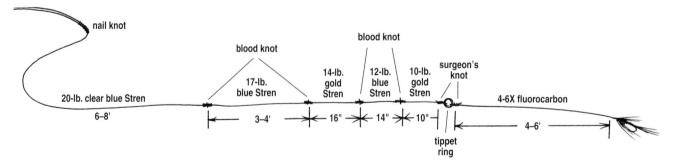

Dave Rothrock first showed me his Hi-Vis (short for high-visibility) leader more than 10 years ago. The butt section is constructed entirely of fluorescent blue and gold Stren. A tippet ring is tied off the final colored section. Dave uses this leader for all stream conditions, but I have found this setup to be especially effective when fishing lightweight nymphs in shallow water. Grease the whole butt section up to the tippet ring for best results, and allow the entire leader to lie on the water during the drift. The butt section has two gold portions about 14 inches apart, which will pull toward one another if tension occurs, signaling a potential strike. If you are tight-line nymphing in deeper water, the two separate gold pieces also serve as a depth gauge.

GETTING THE DRIFT

Two of the most challenging aspects of tight-line nymphing are determining the proper depth and drift speed of your flies. Unlike when fishing with a suspender, you have to constantly adjust depth and drift of your flies, and one of the ways that you do this is related to how long you wait before leading the flies through the drift. To fish your flies along the bottom of the stream, you must first let them sink to the bottom. To do this, elevate the rod tip as the nymphs drop to manage the slack, and begin to lead with the rod tip only after the flies are directly under the rod tip. If you do this properly, you will feel the telltale tapping that signals your nymphs are on the bottom. If you don't feel the tapping, you must wait longer before leading the flies.

Leading means keeping up with the drift to allow the nymphs to move naturally in the water and also to maintain contact so you can determine when a take occurs. It does not mean pulling the nymphs faster than the current, as some anglers tend to do. I have a tendency to begin with a suspender after any long period where I have not used tight-lining techniques, when I feel my timing is off, or if I can't concentrate well enough to tight-line effectively.

I often attach a pinch-on suspender or Thingamabobber to the bottom of my colored mono sighter, on the tip closest to the fly, and study the speed of the drift in various runs. Once the nymphing rig is anchored on the bottom, it will tighten up to the suspension device and prevent it from moving at the same speed as the surface current. As a result, the indicator moves at about the same speed as the bottom currents. Your indicator and sighter should be moving at the same speed during the drift. This gives you a general idea of how fast you need to lead your nymphs and will save you time trying to guess the correct speed.

The goal is to maintain a tight connection and not allow any of the leader, from suspender to line, to touch the water.

Basically, you are tight-lining with a suspender. Eventually I take off the suspender and attempt to lead the nymphs at a similar speed. The suspender is a great teaching tool, and I use it in many of my nymphing clinics to teach students the correct speed to lead the nymphs during the drift.

Another way to practice leading the nymphs is with colored tippet attached to your flies. When training, not fishing for fun, I use 6-pound gold Stren and fish in clear water to see how the water's currents affect the drift of my nymph. I have my sighter or suspension device where I would normally place it for the water type I am fishing. Then I take a guess at the speed at which I plan to lead my nymphs through the drift. Finally, I place the colored mono nymphing rig upstream and observe whether the line is too straight (indicating drag) or the sighter is upstream from the colored tippet (indicating slack) when leading the nymphs. This exercise will give you a good feel for how you're supposed to lead the nymphs.

Yet another idea is to use a brightly colored fly that you can watch in relation to your indicator to determine how the currents are affecting the drift of your nymphs. In central Pennsylvania in late summer, the Green Weenie is perfect for this. Not only is it incredibly effective, but the fluorescent chartreuse chenille body is easy to see from a distance. With this fly attached, I can see if I have too much slack during the drift by looking at how long it takes my indicator to hesitate after the fly gets eaten or hangs up. For example, I know I have too much slack when it takes my sighter one second or more to hesitate after I see the fly hang up on the bottom. This tells me that I need to lead the nymphs faster through the drift. On the other hand, I know I am leading my flies too fast if I don't notice the indicator fly ever bouncing on the bottom in an area where I know it should be touching bottom once every several drifts.

You can easily build a two-toned sighter to provide ultimate visibility in all light conditions. In this case, the top section is gold Stren and the bottom half is Cabela's fluorescent pink fluorocarbon.
GEORGE DANIEL

I prefer to fish weighted flies instead of using split shot because I believe they provide more direct contact with the rod tip and tangle less.
JAY NICHOLS

very lightly weighted nymph. The total leader length was about 15 feet. He had greased the entire butt section with Mucilin fly floatant, from the first sighter up to the fly line.

Dave proceeded to make long casts directly upstream, taking care to place the sighters and fly all in the same speed current. The greased leader floated high and was noticeable even when cast up to 40 feet. It actually was acting as a suspension device, since it was basically carrying the lightly weighted rig from a distance at first. In deeper runs, the rig sank deeper and pulled the leader through the column, and in these cases Dave elevated his rod tip and began executing short-line control tactics. During the drift, he focused on how his two sighters were aligned in relation to one another. When the nymphs were drifting naturally, there was a small degree of slack between the two sections of gold Stren. Opposing currents sometimes forced the two sections to point away from each other, but if the nymphs were taken by a trout or snagged on the stream bottom, the two sections immediately tightened up and realigned. This was the first time I saw how little weight you need to effectively nymph a shallow riffle. Dave had never been to France or Spain, but he had independently developed this technique out of necessity twenty years earlier to fish the pressured Pennsylvania spring creeks.

Deep Nymphing Line

Like many anglers, Joe Humphreys grew up fishing with live bait but eventually realized that he preferred fishing with artificial flies. He also understood some of the advantages that monofilament had over traditional fly line when trying to obtain a natural drift in deep water or strong currents, so he often substituted flat mono for fly line. Mono had a thinner diameter than floating line and thus allowed the flies to drop more quickly to the bottom while also being more sensitive to strikes. However, a number of fly fishers gave him grief about using mono in place of fly line, telling him this was not true fly fishing. Joe finally approached the Cortland Line Company about the idea of developing a fly line with a similar feel to mono, using fly-line backing with a fly-line coating finish over it. The company eventually began to manufacture a deep nymphing line. The line is level, with a .022-inch diameter throughout its entire length, and has several benefits for tightline nymphing.

This small-diameter fly line allows the nymphs to settle to the bottom quickly and provides excellent sensitivity. Also, whereas mono has memory coming off the reel and tends to coil, the deep nymphing line has little memory and remains fairly straight. According to Joe, "This line changed the game, especially in heavy faster water, where the larger diameter of a floating line would create additional surface drag, pulling your nymphs off the bottom."

Suspension Tactics

5

Suspension nymphing is done with the use of a flotation device to hold the nymphs at a fixed location. The depth, speed, and direction of the drift are controlled by the suspension device and its placement in the current. As explained earlier (see page 10), this book uses the term "suspension device" or "suspender" instead of the more commonly used "strike indicator." A strike indicator can be anything from a fly-line tip to section of mono to a cork bobber, but of these items, only the cork bobber is buoyant enough to actually serve as a suspension device, suspending the flies at a set distance.

You can use either manufactured suspenders or dry flies as suspension devices. Both have their pros and cons. Manufactured suspenders can be used for lightly to heavily weighted rigs. Among their advantages are that they require little if any maintenance and often can be easily put on or taken off the leader, providing greater versatility. Disadvantages are that they can be difficult to cast and often look unnatural to trout. Their most efficient use is for long drifts where a lot of mending is needed or with excessive amounts of weight.

Dry-fly suspenders can be used for lightly weighted to medium-weighted rigs. Among their advantages are that they look more natural to trout and that they can double as adult insects, often doubling your chances of catching more fish as you are covering at least two different feeding levels. Disadvantages are that they require more maintenance than manufactured suspenders, and because they are most often tied directly to the nymphing rig, they provide less versatility, as it is more difficult to remove and reattach a dry fly. Their most efficient use is for shorter drifts that require less mending, as mending will often pull the dry fly under.

Suspension nymphing is currently the most popular form of nymphing in the United States, partly because it can be easy, but also because it is deadly. Suspending the nymphs under a Thingamabobber, clump of yarn, or buoyant dry fly is a deadly technique that allows beginners to quickly catch fish, and when refined by a top-notch angler, this can be one of the deadliest nymphing systems in the right situation.

In my early twenties, often beginning in September, I would make the two-and-a-half-hour trip north from central Pennsylvania to the Great Lakes tributaries to chase lake-run steelhead, salmon, and large brown trout. When I got there, I would fish

A high-floating dry fly used as a suspension device has greater sensitivity than a waterlogged pattern. Always take the time to dry the fly, using desiccant or a dry cloth, to increase your chances of seeing the take. JAY NICHOLS

the way I did on the trout streams back home—with a 9-foot hand-tied leader and the tip of the fly line as a strike indicator.

Though this setup worked well for me on smaller streams where I could wade into position and fish with short drifts to well-defined holding areas, it didn't work so well on Cattaraugus Creek, a larger Lake Erie tributary. This stream has cloudy water that makes sight-fishing difficult, and its size and depth can often prevent even a young, aggressive wading fool like I was from reaching the best positions or getting close enough to present the fly properly with tight-line tactics.

Short drifts are good when you know where the fish are holding and can get close to your target. On certain rivers, the more water you cover, the better your odds. A suspension device allows you to achieve incredibly long drifts—even across nagging currents—while still maintaining enough tension to the nymphs to determine a strike. This long flat on the Madison River would be an ideal place for a suspension device and a long drift.
CHRIS DANIEL

Use a strike detection tool that you have confidence in. I had been tight-line nymphing on a windy day, but the wind was blowing my sighter all over the water, which gave me little confidence in strike detection. I gave up the tight-line tactics and switched to a suspension system, quickly catching this awesome rainbow on the second cast.

Short-line tactics reduced my water coverage, which greatly reduced my catch rate. As a result, I made longer casts across the currents, but the long line often caused way too much slack in my system, which did not allow me to register many takes. I was able to catch fish with tight-line tactics, but I knew I wasn't covering the water the way I needed to.

One day on the Cattaraugus, I was fishing a swift riffle that was about 25 feet wide, with steelhead holding on the opposite side. The problem was that the riffle was too deep and swift for me to get closer to the fish, so I was stuck on the opposite bank trying to get a deep drift on the bottom. For two hours, I attempted to get a take with my tight-line tactics, but I failed miserably. It was impossible to control the fly from 25 feet away, as faster currents continually pulled my line downstream. I was not able to mend the line, since I needed the tension of the fly line to indicate a strike, and I was able to achieve a natural drift of only 3 to 4 feet before drag set in. This meant that I was in touch with my system for only a short period of time, and my drifts were very short.

I eventually gave up after several hours of frustrating efforts and sat down. Eventually an older angler moved into the spot I had been fishing and caught four steelhead in twenty minutes. I had just fished that same run for two hours without touching a single fish. The other angler cast no more than 25 feet across several nagging currents with a brightly colored float and made the necessary mends. It was the farthest thing from grace I had ever seen—in fact, the man later told me he was a complete beginner—but he caught four fish and I hadn't taken any.

These anchor patterns are designed for heavy or deep water. They should not be used during low flows—a common mistake. JAY NICHOLS

The keys to his success were that his natural drifts were averaging 20 to 30 feet long, compared with my pitiful 3- to 4-foot drifts, and that he was able to control the drifts from 25 feet away. I also noticed how slowly his suspender was moving on the surface, indicating that the bottom current was almost static. My leading of the nymphing rig, on the other hand, had been twice as fast as the speed of his suspender. This told me I was unable to correctly gauge the bottom current and had been leading my flies too fast. I'd been pulling the egg patterns at an unnatural speed, and it was no wonder a steelhead wouldn't look up to eat them.

It took several more occurrences like this before I sucked in my pride and eventually started to use a suspension device. Today I kick myself when I think about all the opportunities I missed because I was so against the idea of using a "bobber." One thing is for sure: as I get older, I have a more open mind to new concepts that can help me catch more fish. The importance of keeping an open mind and implementing a wide range of techniques to meet ever-changing conditions is, in a nutshell, what I hope to convey to you in this book.

Despite how I once felt about it, and what many people still say, suspension nymphing is its own art form and takes much practice to fine-tune. Fishing a suspension rig well requires excellent line and leader placement, an uncanny ability to understand drift, and the knowledge necessary to constantly adjust your rig based on the speed and depth of the water you're fishing. This chapter goes into all of these things in detail.

A suspension device is a useful tool when searching for trout in large rivers. This Idaho steelhead was taken as a result of long drifts, compliments of a suspension device and good mending. Some anglers believe that suspenders such as these are merely "bobbers" and do not have a part to play in fly fishing. I couldn't disagree more. Used at the right time and place, they are deadly and the best means for catching fish. When nymphing, I like to have as much of an advantage as possible. CHRIS DANIEL

ADVANTAGES OF A SUSPENSION SYSTEM

Using a suspension system is often the easiest way to catch fish, because it makes it easier for you to control depth and maintain tension on the flies, telegraphs strikes so that they are more apparent, allows you to cover large portions of water with long drifts, and is not generally as physically demanding as tight-line nymphing. For these reasons, that angler on Cattaraugus Creek, though not a better or more experienced fly caster, was able to catch more fish than I did—which is the point of all this business, isn't it? Let's take a closer look at some of the advantages of fishing with a suspension system over using the tight-line method.

Easier to Control Depth and Maintain Tension on Flies

When tight-line nymphing, the angler allows the flies to drop to a certain depth before starting to lead them. Because no suspension device is involved, the depth of the drift can change from cast to cast depending on how quickly the angler creates tension, moving the flies downstream. But with a suspension system, the suspension device does all the work by keeping the nymphs at a consistent depth, set by the angler, for the entire

My wife, Amidea, uses a Thingamabobber and a sighter for strike detection. GEORGE DANIEL

length of the drift. The angler places the nymph at a fixed distance from the suspender. After the presentation, the nymph begins dropping through the water column until tension occurs, and at this point the suspender holds the nymph at a fixed depth throughout the drift. This is a major advantage when fishing in water that is relatively uniform in depth or when fish are feeding in a fixed zone.

Ability to Cover More Water with Longer Drifts

Perhaps the biggest advantage is that with the long drifts suspension systems allow, you can effectively cover much more water than you can with most tight-line nymphing techniques, which rely on very short drifts. My friend Chuck Farneth once demonstrated on a large limestoner near my home how much water you can cover by long-line suspender nymphing. An incredible caster to begin with, Chuck smoothly laid out nearly 80 feet of fly line upstream and carefully maintained good line and leader control during the retrieve. Instead of picking up the line once the flies drifted back to him, however, he kicked all the line he had retrieved back out and fed it downstream. As a result, he covered about 160 feet of water with a single cast and hooked a fish on almost every drift. Covering the water the French or Czech and Polish way, with most drifts being no more than 5 to 10 feet, takes a lot more time.

Easier to See Strikes

The farther away your suspender is, whether it's a piece of colored mono on your line or a bobber the size of a Ping-Pong ball, the harder it is to see. For fishing longer distances, I prefer suspension devices that are brightly colored and ride slightly higher off the water. A small Thingamabobber is my go-to suspension device when fishing distances greater than 30 feet because it rides high off the water's surface, allowing me to see takes from farther away. A suspension device generally is larger in diameter than a sighter and provides a better visual indication of when a strike occurs.

Not as Physically Demanding as Tight-Line Nymphing

Tight-line nymphing requires you not only to wade close to your target, which can be dangerous and exhausting, but also to extend your rod hand high and away from your body to hold the line and leader over nagging current seams in order to provide a more natural-looking drift. Tight-lining also requires that you lead the rod tip, using either your hand or your body, to maintain line and leader control. Suspension nymphing, however, by allowing you to cast from farther away, reduces the need to stand in heavy water, keep your arms at an uncomfortable level, and mend to get a good drift. This is not to say that suspension nymphing requires no participation from the angler, but that overall it is easier on the body.

A suspension device is a great tool when fishing from a moving boat. One of the rules is to "set it and forget it." That is, place the cast downstream of the boat, and just let it sit there while the person behind the oars keeps the boat moving at the same speed as the suspension device.
GEORGE DANIEL

Preferable for Fishing from a Drift Boat

For all of the above reasons, suspension nymphing is the preferred method from a drift boat. Think of a drifting boat as a never-ending downstream feed to extend a drift. One advantage of fishing from a drift boat is your ability to cover a lot of water. The use of a suspension device in conjunction with a moving boat can be downright boring, as your rig drifts along in the current while you look for any suggestion of a take. One evening, while drifting the Manistee River in Michigan with my friend Russ Madden from Traverse City, I was impatient and kept picking up my cast after only a twenty-second drift. Russ told me to "set it and forget it," meaning that I needed to leave the suspension device in the water instead of constantly picking up the line to cast again. This is bobber fishing at its core: sitting and waiting for the fish to bite.

The oarsman is really the person who determines the success of this bobber tactic, not the angler. The sole responsibility of the angler is simply to put the fly in the current, but it's the oarsman's job to keep the boat moving at a speed to allow a natural drift. In slower currents, for example, the weighted rig will eventually drop near the stream bottom, pulling back on the suspension device and ultimately slowing down the drift. This causes the suspension device to move slower than the surface currents. As a result, the oarsman is responsible for slowing down the boat so it drifts at the same speed as the suspension device. This means the boat needs to move slower than the surface current when the currents near stream bottom are slower.

CHOOSING THE RIGHT SUSPENDER

Choosing the right suspender from the many options available can be a challenge. Fly shops offer an almost overwhelming number of suspender options, and anglers often have a hard time picking the best one. I carry just a few types, which I will discuss in detail, but I suggest that you experiment with several different ones to see which suit you the best for your own needs and the type of water you like to fish.

As much as possible, I try to get within 30 feet of the fish, such as in pocketwater, riffles, low-light situations, or off-color water, so that I can fish suspenders with a short line, keeping as much line off the water as possible. However, spooky fish or water that is difficult or impossible to wade requires longer casts, which in turn require mends to manipulate the line on the water. Long casts may look pretty, but they present challenges that I prefer to avoid, such as excessive line on the water and the necessity for mending, which makes setting the hook difficult, causes a greater chance of tangles, and creates a higher risk of casting errors. At times, however, you must work a lot of line, and often the best way to do it is with a suspender.

DRY-AND-DROPPER RIGS

Known as a dry-and-dropper rig, tandem flies, or multiple-fly rig—or, as English friends across the pond refer to it, "the duo"—suspending one or two nymphs under a dry fly is an extremely effective technique. My first choice for a suspender is usually a dry fly, such as a buoyant size 4 hopper or a size 14 CDC and Elk, especially if I know there's a chance of taking a fish on top, such as in late spring through fall, when intense hatches and active terrestrial insects keep the fish interested in food on the surface. A dry fly looks more natural to fish than a manufactured suspender, which is extremely important on heavily pressured trout streams. An added bonus is that you can—and will—catch fish on the suspender dry fly, especially during a hatch or at a time of the year when trout are looking toward the surface for food.

When nothing is hatching, I most often fish a size 6-12 CDC Caddis Indicator or GD's Indicator Fly, one of my own caddis imitations. These flies look more natural than manufactured suspenders, spooking fewer fish while suspending nymphs, and because caddis are in almost every stream, they attract the occasional aggressive trout. The GD's Indicator Fly has a foam body and two-toned poly wing. The bottom layer, the side the trout sees, is darker, while the other side is fluorescent, aiding strike detection in broken water. If you treat this pattern with floatant

and allow it time to dry, it will float high and needs little maintenance to keep it floating. If insects are hatching, I choose a more realistic dry to match the hatch. As trout start to key on adults, I often switch over to a single dry fly for a more natural presentation and forget the nymphs. Nymphing during a hatch can be very effective, but sometimes drys will produce more takes than nymphs.

When choosing a suspender dry fly, I also consider the water type. Pocketwater is one of my favorite places to fish dry-and-dropper rigs, because the current disrupts the trout's vision, giving it only a split second to decide whether to take. Here I choose a foam fly such as Charlie Craven's Charlie Boy Hopper or a Foam Bullet-Head Hopper that will stay afloat in the choppy currents. In slower runs, another of my favorite kinds of water for a dry-and-dropper rig, I often switch to a CDC Caddis Indicator fly or any other pattern that will land softly on the water, be sensitive to strikes, and ride high on the water.

I use a dry fly any time during the course of the season when trout are likely to eat on the surface, especially in pocketwater where trout are less selective—in central Pennsylvania, this means about eight months of the year. When I feel that there's little chance of a trout inhaling my dry fly, I switch to a manufactured suspension device, which doesn't require floatant.

Below: This monster brown took a grasshopper imitation that I was using as a suspender fly. Whenever I come across a grass field during the summertime, I tie on a large hopper pattern to act as a suspender. I deeply enjoy the nymphing game, but I also enjoy seeing a trout crush a size 6 hopper pattern. JAY NICHOLS

A good caddis hatch is an excellent time to both dead-drift and swing your favorite emerger pattern. If too many insects are on the water and the trout are difficult to fool with an adult imitation, I switch back to nymphs. GEORGE DANIEL

If I could pick only one dry fly to fish anywhere in the world, it would be a caddis pattern. Caddis species can be prevalent in streams around the world and hatch all season long. JAY NICHOLS

DRYING A FLY

1 A high-floating dry fly telegraphs strikes much better than a poorly floating one. First rinse the fly thoroughly to remove any fish slime if necessary, and then blow on it to remove some of the water. JAY NICHOLS

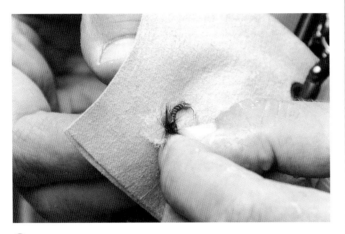

2 The Wonder Cloth is an invaluable tool for wicking moisture from a dry fly. Some anglers prefer amadou or chamois.

3 To wick moisture off the fly, fold the cloth in half so that it completely encloses the fly when squeezed. This ensures that the entire fly will be treated. Note the water droplet being pinched out of the corner of the Wonder Cloth in this photo.

4 Take the fly out of the cloth, and hold it in one hand while the other hand dips the applicator brush in the dry desiccant. I prefer to apply desiccant with an applicator rather than shake it on, because this allows me to better ensure that the desiccant gets deep into the fly.

5 Brush a generous amount of desiccant deep into the fibers of the fly. In this case, I want the entire fly to ride high, so I brush the desiccant into the entire fly.

6 A few false casts will remove any excess desiccant. To ensure your flies float high for a long time, pretreat them. I use Watershed for non-CDC flies and a CDC oil or Tiemco's Dry Magic for CDC flies.

Dapping a dry fly that's anchored with a weighted nymph is a great tactic for targeting caddis-eating fish. Lance Egan dapped a CDC Caddis to entice this grayling to the surface while fishing the upper reaches of the Simo River in Finland. GEORGE DANIEL

In pocketwater and other areas that require drifts shorter than 4 feet, you must use a heavy nymph to get to the bottom quickly so that it rides at the trout's feeding level for more than half the drift. A more buoyant dry fly is necessary to suspend the bigger load. I basically high-stick the dry fly on the water, trying to keep all the line and leader leading to the fly off the water. For this approach, it's best to use a longer leader with an aggressive butt section to turn over the wind-resistant suspender. The long leader enables you to keep more line and leader off the water, creating less surface drag and allowing you to use less weight in your rig. Any line or leader on the water creates surface tension and begins pulling your nymphs faster downstream. Having less line and leader on the water creates less tension, which translates into the need for less weight to get the flies down.

Even if the dry begins to start sinking, you can always hold the dry fly above the surface and guide it through the drift. I commonly do this when fishing size 14 and smaller dry flies. A smaller fly often looks more natural and has a better shot of raising a fish, and more important, it's small enough for the trout to inhale. Many times here in the East, when I'm fishing a larger dry fly, trout play with my suspender fly instead of actually eating it. This happens more frequently in later summer, when the water temperature rises and trout activity begins to decline.

The heavy nymph rig anchors the system near the bottom while the surface currents attempt to move it faster downstream, much like an anchored boat on a moving river. This anchoring of the dry fly can create a passive bobbing motion, similar to the

Chuck Farneth first showed me this tactic while fishing a caddis hatch on Penns Creek. This system works great with a long leader. Basically, you keep a tight connection between the rod tip and suspender dry. After tension occurs, you stiff-arm the rod tip up and down, bobbing the dry fly on and off the water. The nymph acts as an anchor, allowing you to lift the dry fly off the water and drop it back down.

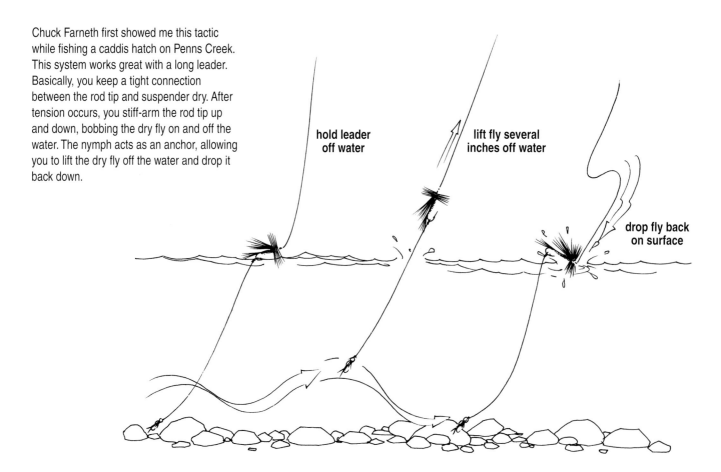

hold leader off water

lift fly several inches off water

drop fly back on surface

This New Zealand brown trout immediately became airborne after falling prey to a PMX suspender fly. The combination of the PMX dry and the nymphs allowed the angler to fish two distinct feeding levels. AMIDEA DANIEL

action of an insect on the surface trying to move upstream against the current. This is why anglers tend to catch more trout when using a dry fly as a suspension device than with just a single dry. Though this book is about nymphing, this tactic can be effective for fooling fish on the surface as well.

You can also take advantage of the anchoring nymph to fish the dry fly more actively in pocketwater. I learned this tactic from my friend Chuck Farneth while fishing a caddis hatch on a central Pennsylvania limestone stream. Chuck tied on a caddis dry-and-dropper rig and placed it in a section of pocketwater between two large boulders. The cast was only 15 feet. Once the nymph dropped and the dry fly began to drift, Chuck used the weight of the nymphs to anchor the rig and began to lift the dry fly up and down, off and on the water. The dry bobbed on the surface, resembling a female caddis depositing her eggs on the water. At the same time, the nymphs were moving vertically in the column, which is the same movement trout key on during a major hatch. Chuck's tactic resulted in a trout jumping out of the water in an attempt to inhale the bobbing dry fly.

The key is to use a long enough rod and leader so that you are high-sticking the dry fly, as well as a heavy enough nymph that will stay anchored in the current. For this tactic, I like to use my tungsten CDC Caddis Emerger. The weight of the tungsten bead ensures that the rig remains below the surface after the short lift. The tight connection from rod tip to dry allows you to pick up the nymph off the water in short movements, a deadly technique for times when insects are actively bouncing near the surface.

A jig-style *Isonychia* tied with CDC fibers is a great pattern for either dead-drifting or swinging through a fishy spot. JAY NICHOLS

When I'm going to be short-lining a dry-and-dropper, I often build a sighter into the long leader to enable me to detect strikes in and around boulders when I can't actually see the dry-fly suspender. If you create the correct amount of tension while leading the nymphs, you will be able to observe hesitation in the colored section being held above the rock's edge.

Long drifts are necessary in slow, low, or clear water, and under these conditions, when trout are skittish, the dry fly excels as a suspender. With longer drifts, you don't have to use a really heavy nymph to get a good bottom drift. Once on the bottom, a medium-weighted nymph will remain at that level but will not weigh so much as to constantly snag the bottom.

Balancing and Rigging the Dry

To increase your ability to detect strikes, the sizes of the dry and the nymphs need to be balanced. Many anglers use a dry fly that's much too large for the dry-and-dropper rig. The dry fly must be buoyant enough to suspend the weight of the rig, but not so much that the rig will not register a subtle take. On numerous occasions when fishing out West, I have seen anglers using a huge hopper, such as a size 6 Chernobyl Ant, as the suspender and dropping two lightly weighted nymphs off the bend. Though the dry fly is still able to register some aggressive takes, it will not register the softer ones because it is simply too buoyant.

Though balancing the suspender to the nymphs is an important consideration when choosing any suspension device, it is critical when choosing dry flies. Precisely matching the weight of the nymphs to the dry-fly rig had been one of my secrets to competitive fly fishing. I would tie a favorite Foam Body Stimulator in four sizes and attach a short length of leader material off the bend of each fly, adding split shot until the fly began to show signs of sinking. Then I would place that amount of split shot on a powder scale to determine how much weight it took to just keep that particular size fly floating without sinking. Finally, I would build weight into each of my competition flies using the exact amount of weight I had determined for its size, so I would end up with dry flies that were able to float the nymphs but would sink the instant the nymphs were stopped by any submerged item or the mouthing of a trout. Granted, this may be a little over the top, but my point is that experimenting with suspenders of various buoyancies will help you find the one that is most sensitive to registering takes quickly.

Premade Dry-and-Dropper Rigs

Preparing your rigs ahead of time ensures that you will enjoy more time fishing instead of wasting time rigging while on the stream. I always have the following dry-and-dropper rigs pre-

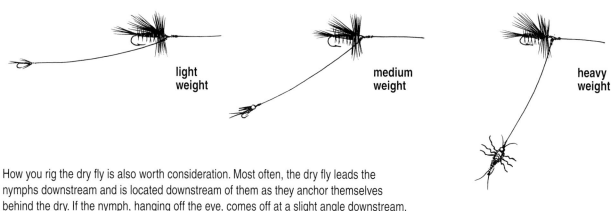

light weight   medium weight   heavy weight

How you rig the dry fly is also worth consideration. Most often, the dry fly leads the nymphs downstream and is located downstream of them as they anchor themselves behind the dry. If the nymph, hanging off the eye, comes off at a slight angle downstream, then the tippet is likely to shield the hook point and get in the way of a trout trying to inhale the fly, slightly decreasing your hookup percentage. This doesn't happen with light nymphs, where the tippet rides parallel with the floating leader, or with heavy nymphs, where the tippet rides at 90 degrees to the floating leader.

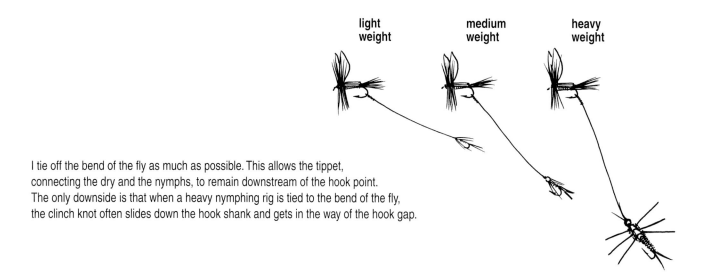

light weight   medium weight   heavy weight

I tie off the bend of the fly as much as possible. This allows the tippet, connecting the dry and the nymphs, to remain downstream of the hook point. The only downside is that when a heavy nymphing rig is tied to the bend of the fly, the clinch knot often slides down the hook shank and gets in the way of the hook gap.

made and stored in my Orvis Dropper Rig Fly Box to deal with the more common fishing conditions.

Sunken Spinner or Suspended Emerger

I like to fish sunken adults or emergers just a few inches under the water. My favorite nymphs are tied with small brass or glass beads, lightly weighted bugs that are designed to be fished only a few inches below the surface. Because these nymphs are lightly weighted, I can use a smaller dry-fly suspender to match the current hatch, which provides a greater opportunity to fool a trout with the dry fly. This is a great option for fishing during spinnerfalls, major insect emergences, and terrestrial season.

Dry Fly and Emerger or Cripple

The dropper is often a lightly weighted soft-hackle (representing a currently emerging insect or a drowned adult) 2 feet below a dry fly. The nymph rides just a few inches below the water's surface. Don't think of shallow nymphing rigs as something to use only during hatch periods; they can also result in good fishing during spinnerfalls and terrestrial season. Trico

spinnerfalls are great opportunities to use a sunken spinner pattern below a small dry fly. At times, trout are more likely to eat a drowned adult, since there's little chance of such a meal escaping their capture. Wet ants are among the most effective patterns in central Pennsylvania during the warm summer months, and fishing a lightly weighted black ant under a dry ant is an absolute must, as trout seem to have an addiction to ants. For most emerging mayflies, I use a brass-beaded Ice Dub Pheasant Tail soft-hackle trailed under an imitative dry fly. The dry doesn't need to be very buoyant, as the brass-beaded soft-hackle is lightweight. Another variation is a sunken Trico spinner, such as a size 22 black Shop Vac, under a Griffith's Gnat. For most major caddis hatches, I use a CDC and Elk dry with a lightly weighted soft-hackle trailed about 20 inches below.

Rig for Slow-Moving Water

For fishing slow-moving water, the heaviest fly or weight in the rig should be at about the same distance from the suspender as the depth of the water you're fishing. The dry fly should be buoyant enough to suspend the single- or double-nymph below. If the fish are not lifting, then drop a single nymph below the

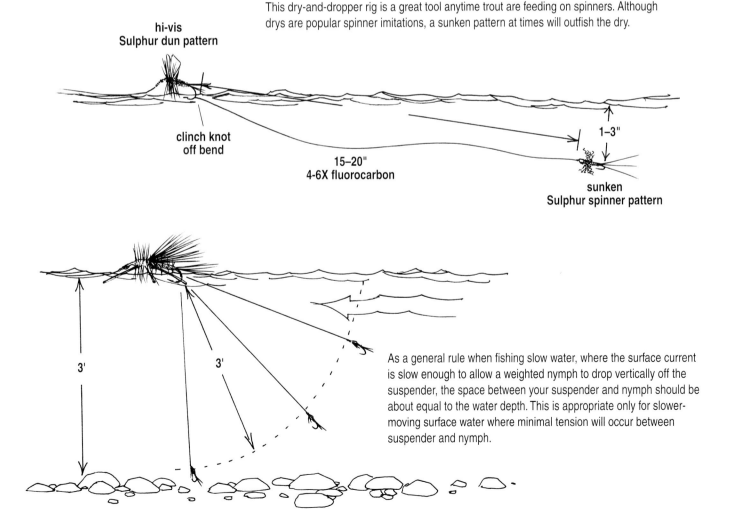

This dry-and-dropper rig is a great tool anytime trout are feeding on spinners. Although drys are popular spinner imitations, a sunken pattern at times will outfish the dry.

As a general rule when fishing slow water, where the surface current is slow enough to allow a weighted nymph to drop vertically off the suspender, the space between your suspender and nymph should be about equal to the water depth. This is appropriate only for slower-moving surface water where minimal tension will occur between suspender and nymph.

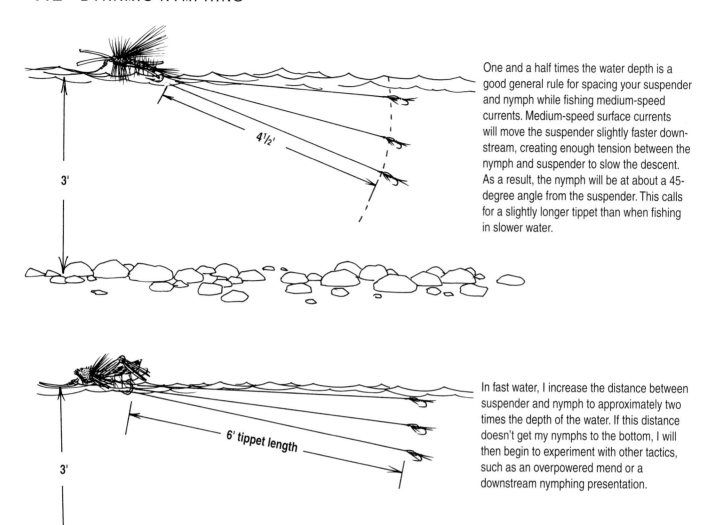

One and a half times the water depth is a good general rule for spacing your suspender and nymph while fishing medium-speed currents. Medium-speed surface currents will move the suspender slightly faster downstream, creating enough tension between the nymph and suspender to slow the descent. As a result, the nymph will be at about a 45-degree angle from the suspender. This calls for a slightly longer tippet than when fishing in slower water.

In fast water, I increase the distance between suspender and nymph to approximately two times the depth of the water. If this distance doesn't get my nymphs to the bottom, I will then begin to experiment with other tactics, such as an overpowered mend or a downstream nymphing presentation.

suspender at a distance slightly less than the depth of the water you're fishing. If the trout are lifting, attach a dropper 15 to 20 inches above the point fly. The dropper normally consists of a soft-hackle or emerger-style nymph to fish the middle level. This allows you to fish at least two levels under the surface. Most often, if the fish are feeding at two levels, I use a size 16-18 fly with a $\frac{3}{32}$-inch tungsten bead head as my point fly to anchor the rig on the bottom, with an unweighted or lightly weighted emerger as a dropper. If the trout are not suspending or moving up the column to intercept bugs, I normally fish a single weighted fly spaced about the same distance from the suspender as the depth of the water. Fly selection should be based on the current water conditions, insect activity, and what pattern styles the trout are keying on.

Rig for Medium-Speed Currents

The rig used for medium-speed currents is the same as the one for slower water, except that the length of the tippet to the heaviest fly is longer, about one and a half times the water depth. This is because the faster surface currents will create an angle

of about 45 degrees between the dry fly and nymph. Thus, to achieve a natural drift near the bottom, the tippet length needs to be about one and a half times the depth of the water. With this kind of nymphing rig, anglers often use a heavier point fly to anchor the rig on the bottom. Fly choice depends on current conditions. For medium-speed currents, a $\frac{7}{64}$-inch tungsten bead on a size 14-16 hook constitutes my anchor fly. As with the rig for slow-moving water, fly selection should be based on the current water conditions, insect activity, and what pattern styles the trout are keying on.

Rig for Fast Currents

In fast water, the distance between suspender and nymph needs to be even greater than with medium-speed currents because fast surface currents will pull downstream faster on the suspender. That places the suspender farther downstream of the nymph, decreasing the angle between the two. Here it should be about two times the depth of the water. If this distance doesn't get your nymphs to the bottom, try experimenting with other nymphing tactics.

MANUFACTURED SUSPENDERS

Though the dry fly is buoyant and has the ability to suspend considerable weight, sometimes you may want to use a more buoyant suspension device. When I need a more buoyant suspender that requires no maintenance, I use either a Thingamabobber or foam pinch-ons.

Thingamabobbers

Thingamabobbers are virtually unsinkable. With their smooth, round shape and trapped-air design, they are able to suspend a lot of weight and bob back up to the surface even after repeated mends in fast water. These hard plastic balloon-type suspenders float like corks, require no maintainence, are easy to cast, and are supersensitive to any change in your drift. In addition, they seem to resist surface drag better than some other manufactured suspenders, which allows you to use less weight to sink your flies. With one of the smallest Thingamabobbers, you can use surprisingly little weight (two size 12 or smaller tungsten beaded nymphs or unweighted flies with two size 4 shot) to achieve a natural drift in the deepest runs, if given a long enough drift. The Thingamabobber is also one of the easiest suspenders to remove or adjust, a big plus as you fish through different types of water.

Another advantage of the Thingamabobber is its rubber O-ring, which allows you to quickly put the suspender onto your leader and take it off again. This is especially important as you move from runs to pocketwater. The Thingamabobber's O-ring allows you to quickly put on and take off the suspender as you work the water, giving you the flexibility to switch between tight-line and suspension tactics as you see fit. For example, if I'm unsuccessfully nymphing a run without a suspender, I will place the Thingamabobber at the end of my sighter and nymph the same rig in the same spot, but with a suspension device. If I start catching a few trout in areas where I hadn't moved a single fish, this shows me that I wasn't in control of the fly when tight-lining.

This New Zealand spring creek flowing through a meadow is a perfect place to fish a grasshopper dry fly and nymph dropper. GEORGE DANIEL

RIGGING THE THINGAMABOBBER

The small and medium-size Thingamabobbers cover just about all my bases for trout fishing. The ½-inch size (small) has just enough buoyancy to suspend a few grams of weight, or a three-fly rig consisting of a $^5/_{32}$-inch tungsten bead-head fly; another lightly weighted tungsten bead-head nymph or a ⅛-inch tungsten bead-head fly with lead wire built in; and a $^7/_{64}$-inch tungsten bead-head fly also with lead wire. The ¾-inch size (medium) works great for the same three flies, along with additional split shot to help them reach the bottom. As when using dry flies as suspenders, you need to balance the weight of the nymphing rig with the buoyancy of the suspender to ensure it is as sensitive as possible.

I carry Thingamabobbers in all the available colors to deal with a variety of background colors and lighting conditions. For example, against muddy water, white sticks out like a sore thumb; yellow in low-light conditions; and pink when the water is brightly lit.

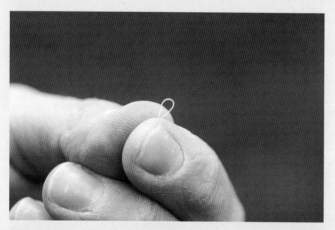

1 Double up the leader, creating a small loop where you want to place the Thingamabobber. Pinch and hold the loop in one hand.

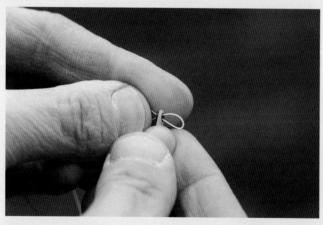

2 Next, take the loop and push it through the O-ring. Make sure there's enough of a loop to fold over one side of the Thingamabobber.

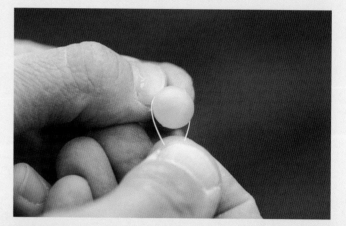

3 Pull the loop over the opposite side of the Thingamabobber, looping the leader entirely over the suspender.

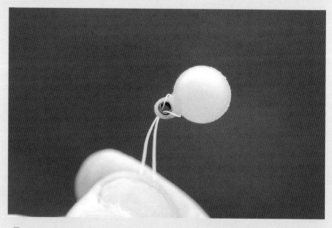

4 Pull down on the leader to secure the loop around the O-ring. To reposition or take off the suspender, push back in the opposite direction from which you attached the leader to the suspender. This will open a loop, allowing you to slide the suspension device up and down the leader or to pull the mono loop back over the device to detach it from the leader.

JAY NICHOLS

Pinch-On Suspenders

Another essential suspender in my kit is the foam pinch-on type. My good friend Chuck Farneth introduced these to me several years ago while fishing some of my home waters and hooked more trout in one hour than I would have in several days of fishing. He uses these inexpensive suspenders religiously while fishing micronymphs on his home waters, the famed Arkansas tailwaters.

This one of the most sensitive suspender styles for fishing lighter-weight rigs. I prefer to use pinch-on suspenders when fishing my lightweight systems, which may consist of two size 18 or smaller tungsten beaded nymphs or two unweighted nymphs with a small size 4 split shot. Anglers Image makes pinch-on indicators that are slightly larger than the ones from Palsa, allowing for more flexibility, as you can use a pair of scissors to cut them in half or thirds to balance a very lightweight nymphing system. I commonly do this when fishing micronymphs in the late summer and early fall, when little weight is needed for good presentations and takes are soft. Pinch-on suspenders also present themselves delicately even if your cast isn't delicate during the presentation.

I normally use small dry flies to achieve the same suspension qualities as with pinch-ons, but pinch-ons excel in the winter, when the chance of fooling a fish on the surface is limited, as well as during heavy rains when a dry fly would become waterlogged quickly.

These suspenders have several drawbacks. For one, though they are relatively easy to cast, they tend to catch on your rig when you make a bad cast. Another is that they are not adjustable or reusable. When you are done for the day or ready to switch over to a different tactic, the life of that pinch-on is over, unless you keep your rod strung up. And if you need to move the suspender, you cannot. Also, they are manufactured in just a couple of sizes, with small being the most common.

Tactics with Manufactured Suspenders

Though you can high-stick with a suspension device, Thingamabobbers really shine when you're fishing nymphs from a distance or when there is no chance of a fish eating your dry fly, such as in the dead of winter.

No matter how aggressively you wade, often you will encounter situations where the perfect run is on the other side of the river but you can't get closer than 40 feet. When this happens, you must make long casts and mend all the line on the water to maintain line control. Also, there are times during low water when you must present the flies to the fish at distances greater than 40 feet, and trying to maintain line control with a nonsuspender rig at this distance is very difficult. Finally, sometimes you don't know where the fish are holding and want to cover a vast amount of water in the shortest amount of time possible, and the long-line suspension rig, as Chuck Farneth demonstrated to me, allows you to do this. Buoyant suspenders are perfect for these situations, because they stay afloat despite repeated mending. Some masterful anglers can mend the line without moving the suspension device an inch, but I am not one of them, so I simply need a long-lasting floating device.

High-sticking a dry-and-dropper with a tight-line leader is an effective tactic when fishing around boulders. In this case, the angler is using the sighter for strike detection, as the view of the dry fly is blocked by the boulder. JAY NICHOLS

With this type of fishing, using a short, knotless leader with a powerful taper helps ensure that a heavy and often wind-resistant nymphing rig can be delivered where you want it with ease. When casting a heavy nymphing rig with a long leader, it is difficult to make accurate presentations and just as difficult to mend on the water, and therefore I recommend using a short leader when long-line suspension nymphing. The knotless leader floats higher to the suspension device, making it easier to mend.

When long-line nymphing, you will have a lot of line on the water that you need to move—either mend or pick up to cast. A clean floating line mends the easiest. One of the biggest detriments to suspension nymphing is a sinking fly line, because it takes more energy to pick up a sunken line off the water than to pick up a dry line. A sunken line needs to be lifted through the surface layers and is often the reason for poor hook sets, especially when longer lengths of line are needed to reach a more distant target. On the other hand, a high-floating line can be lifted off the water with far less effort, resulting in quicker and stronger hook sets. This is why I apply fly floatant to the butt section of my leader and the fly-line tip before each fishing trip.

THE CURLY Q

The curly Q, also called a coiled leader or Slinky, looks like the helical, springlike child's toy as it rides high on the water's surface. Because it rides so high, you can see the curly Q almost as far as you can cast when greased with a floatant; I prefer to use Mucilin, Loon Aquel, or Tiemco Dry Magic for the curly Q. During my first year coaching the US Youth Fly Fishing Team in Portugal, I watched a Spanish youth fish a curly Q from about 80 feet away.

Like the greased leader, the curly Q is meant for suspending very lightly weighted nymphs. Another advantage of the curly over a dry fly or commercial suspender is the light impact it makes when touching down on the water, and it's become one of my favorite tools for fishing over extremely spooky trout or fish suspended high in the water column. There have been times in late summer when a dry-and-dropper nymph rig would spook every fish when the dry fly touched the water. The aerodynamic nature of the curly Q allows it to make a softer landing on the water than any other suspension device I'm aware of, just as long as you deliver a soft presentation with your cast. I rely on it for the most extreme low-water conditions, when even a dry fly landing on the water would spook fish. Its soft landing may be due to the large surface areas acting as a sail, slowing the descent as the rig falls to the water. This feature works best when you make a high-trajectory cast, sending the

Left: Keep the curly Q on the water's surface for ultimate strike detection. Any movement of the curly is a sign that the nymph has moved in a different direction. Also, the long length of this suspension device makes it the best kind of indicator for determining where the fly is in relation to the sighter. The tip of the curly Q will point toward the nymphing rig. If you see your sighter begin moving downstream, this indicates one of two scenarios. Either a trout has taken your fly and is swimming downstream or your nymph just moved into a faster current than that of the curly and is beginning to move downstream of it. JAY NICHOLS

Right: The curly Q leader looks like a brightly colored Slinky lying on top of the water. When well dressed with floatant, it will ride above the water's surface, providing great visibility. You can see these indicators from up to 80 to 100 feet away. AMIDEA DANIEL

Above: Casting your fly into unlikely trout habitat can sometimes pay off. I caught this holdover rainbow during the brightest part of the day in just inches of what some anglers would refer to as "frog water." A specialized suspender such as the curly Q will allow you to effectively fish such waters.
GEORGE DANIEL

flies high above the target and allowing the surface area of the curly Q to slow the fall.

Like a Slinky toy, the curly Q's monofilament coils contract and pull apart, depending on what the nymph is doing on the bottom. The curly Q allows even the softest takes to register, so long as tension remains between the suspender and flies. Tension occurs when the curly is downstream of the nymph, pulling it downstream. The curly Q springs back and forth as it pulls the weighted nymph, and when the coils of the curly begin to slowly pull apart, you have a take.

The curly Q is the least buoyant of all my suspension devices, however, so I use it with nothing heavier than a ³⁄₃₂-inch tungsten bead with ten wraps of .020-inch lead wire on a size 14 standard nymph hook. You are using too much weight if the curly continues to sink below the surface. If this occurs, you should switch to a more buoyant suspension device.

Though originally designed for long-distance casts with longer drifts, the curly Q can be used at close range as well. It can be effective with short drifts, but usually when these occur in shallow water with lightweight nymphs or when fish are feeding in the upper levels. I prefer not to use the curly Q when fishing with standard tight-line tactics, because the wind resistance of the larger surface area creates additional drag on the line. A prime situation for using a curly is at the tailout of a pool during a mayfly spinnerfall, when the trout are eating sunken spinner patterns right under the surface.

Erickson's Dangly Indicator

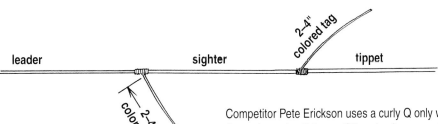

Competitor Pete Erickson uses a curly Q only when he wants to float small nymphs just below the surface at a distance. Otherwise he uses what he calls a "dangly indicator," which he creates by leaving the tag ends of the colored mono or fluoro dangling out from the blood knot. If the visibility is bad, he sometimes uses a lighter to form a coil like a pigtail with the tag end. He prefers the dangly over the curly Q because it gives him better contact with the flies and casts better.

The curly Q is an incredible tool for reading currents. Because of its length, it will bend and move, telegraphing the location of your fly. For example, the curly Q will point in the direction of the nymphs during the drift. Ideally, you want it pointing directly upstream, as that would indicate that there's a tight connection and the flies and suspension device are positioned in similar speed currents. If the curly begins to point downstream, however, this is telling you that the nymphs are in a faster current than the curly and tension is lost.

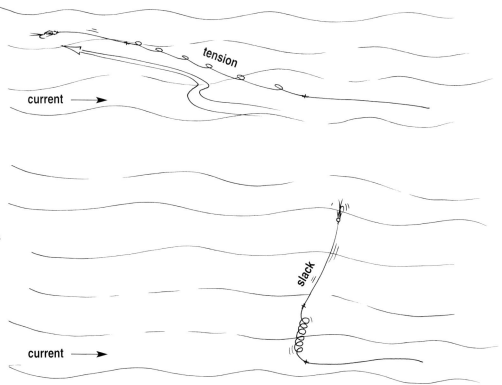

ATTACHING THE CURLY Q

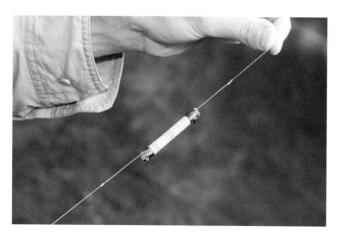

1 This photo shows the prepared curly Q being tied into the leader. Note that each tag end is straight, as this allows for easier knot connections from the curly Q to the leader and tippet. While the curly Q is still coiled around the wooden dowel, attach the two ends to both tippet and leader with blood knots. Do not take off the duct tape holding the curly in place until both ends are secured with knots.

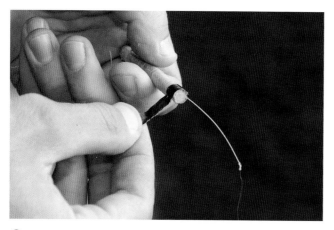

2 Now begin to unwind the duct tape off both ends.

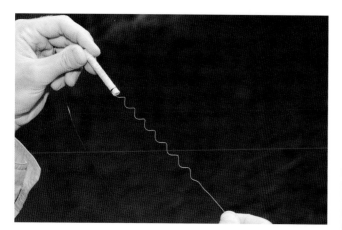

3 Once the duct tape is unwound, pull the curly Q off the wooden dowel.

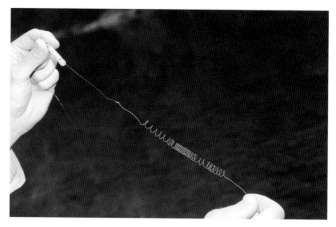

4 Place silicone floatant on the curly Q before fishing. Silicone Mucilin is thicker and tends to remain on the curly Q longer than other floatants.

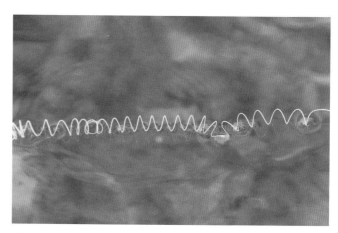

5 A greased curly Q can be seen from a long way away.

SUSPENDER STRATEGIES

Casting in Line with the Currents

When casting a suspension rig, whether it's a dry-and-dropper or a Thingamabobber with two heavy nymphs, your goal is to have tension between the suspension device and nymphing rig while the rig is drifting through the primary feeding zone of the fish. Without a slight degree of tension between the suspender and rig, strikes are difficult to register. In most situations, this means the suspension device needs to be drifting *downstream* of the nymphing rig and pulling on the rig. To ensure that this tension occurs, line and leader placement is critical.

The first thing you need to do is clearly identify a target, not just for your flies, but also for your suspension device. Look for current seams and pick one to present to. A seam is where currents join and often funnel food to trout. A foam or bubble line is a perfect example of where several currents converge into a seam, funneling insects into a concentrated area. These are the trout's conveyor belts for food. You want your flies to move on these conveyor belts like the real thing, while at the same time keeping a tight connection to them.

Just as with dry-fly fishing, where you must try to get your line, leader, and fly to land in the same current or make a corrective action, it is essential that the line, leader, fly, and suspender all fall onto the same current, or you need to mend. Placing the entire cast in the same speed current ensures that all items in the rig will move at the same speed. Casting across multiple speed currents will almost immediately cause drag, not only in the dry flies, but also in the nymphs. The only difference is that it is very easy to see the dry fly drag on the surface.

Most often, you should place the nymphs directly upstream of the suspender and in the same speed current. This requires that you not only cast accurately but that your rod tip travels straight. This is easier said than accomplished. The shape of the line that falls on the water is determined by the direction the rod travels during the casting stroke, when the rod tip is accelerating. The rod tip should travel parallel to the intended targeted seam, meaning that it should follow the flow of the intended current during the casting stroke, which will place the entire nymphing rig in the same seam.

Before attempting to mend, consider getting into a better position that allows you to make a straight cast that would result in the line, suspender, and flies landing in the same current. Also try to reposition your body before casting to a new seam. Ideally, I prefer to cast directly upstream, as this often keeps my rod tip angled with the water and not toward the bank, where there's a greater potential for snags. I also like to work from the edge of the bank out to the middle of the stream. To do this, square your shoulders upstream to the targeted seam, which allows your body to easily move the rod tip parallel to

One of the most difficult presentation scenarios is when currents are pulling at a 90-degree angle away from you. In such cases, the rod tip needs to move parallel to the flow of water, which creates a very short drift. AMIDEA DANIEL

If you are forced to cast over multiple currents, reach over as many as you can to reduce unnecessary drag. A long rod and leader will make this job easier. GEORGE DANIEL

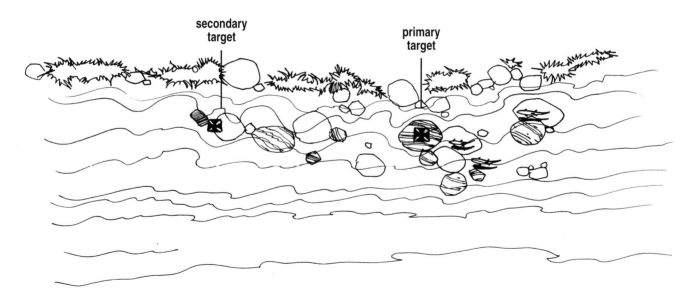

Not only do you have to make sure that your suspender lands in line with the flies, but you also must cast upstream enough to compensate for the sink rate of the nymphs, adding yet another target for you to hit. I call the place where you think the fish is, or will move to feed, the primary target and the place where your flies must enter the water the secondary target. This secondary target is often the same current pulling through the primary target, but it is a little farther upstream.

Right: Currents move in all directions and you need to study them before casting. Fish your suspension rig like a dry fly. You want a natural drift, which often means that the suspender should move at the same speed as the current, sometimes even slower. Make the same mends as you would for dry flies to accomplish a natural drift. GEORGE DANIEL

Below: In this photo, my brother Chris is showing off another Madison River brown trout that fell to a PMD emerger. CHRIS DANIEL

the current. After presenting enough times to one targeted seam, simply take as many side steps as you need to align yourself directly downstream of the next seam.

However, the direct upstream presentation isn't always possible, and it's fairly common for the suspension rig to land in currents that are faster or slower than the flies, especially when you are casting across currents. If your suspension device lands in a faster current than the nymphing rig, excessive drag will pull the flies downstream faster than the actual current speed, since the suspender is anchored in a faster current. This is often bad, except perhaps during a hatch while insects are emerging toward the surface and trout are chasing them. If the suspension device lands in a slower current than the nymphing rig, there's a good chance the rig will remain downstream of the suspender, creating slack, which makes it difficult to register a take. This is the worst possible scenario. I would rather have a little more drag than too much slack, which makes it impossible to detect takes.

When you must cast across the stream and the flies land in a different speed current than the suspender, you have to mend. If you are fishing a seam or area that's within a rod's distance away, you can use an aerial mend to place the fly line and leader in the same speed current, with the nymphing rig upstream of the suspender. I prefer this approach to mending,

because the line falls right into position from the start. This lets you focus on line control and strike detection, and you won't have to disturb the water with other forms of mending. If you are too far away to mend in the air, you need to manipulate the line on the water to achieve a good drift.

Mending

Moving the fly line to get a good drift, a technique called mending, is as much of an art form as the cast. Because it is an extra movement that introduces slack into the system, albeit controlled slack, you should try to avoid doing it as much as possible. The more slack line on the water, the more the rod tip must move to pick up the slack line to create the tension needed for a good hook set. Long-distance mends often create too much slack for the angler to overcome, which is why you should always try to get as close to the target as possible. The closer you can get before casting, the less line and leader you will have on the water. As a result, you will have better line and leader control.

However, sometimes it is not possible to get close enough for a short cast or to get directly downstream of your target, and mending is the only option. Mending, a form of developing slack in the line, is appropriate only for suspension nymphing and not for tight-line nymphing. When suspension nymphing, slack in the line and leader is okay as long as there is tension between the suspender and fly. With this technique, you do not use the line to detect movement, so slack will not impede strike detection. Tight-line nymphing, on the other hand, requires a tight line connection to detect strikes. Slack is the biggest killer of strike detection with the tight-line technique, and for this reason, you don't want to put excess slack into the leader.

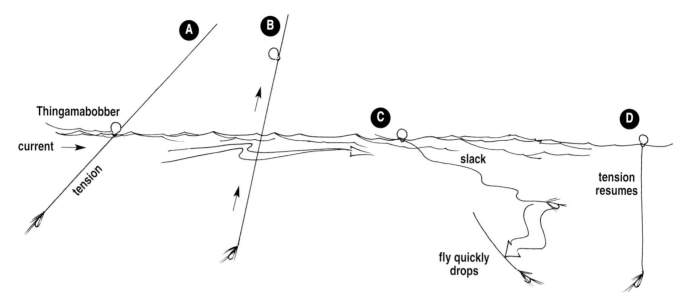

When an upstream presentation fails to sink the flies, I try a reposition mend. The idea is to reduce the tension between the suspension device and nymph by creating slack in the rig, which allows the flies to drop quickly through the water column. (A) Make a traditional upstream cast so that the nymph lands upstream of the suspension device. Tension occurs, immediately forcing the fly to sink slowly. (B) If you're fishing close enough, use a stiff arm to pull the suspension device off the water. (C) Position the suspension device directly upstream of the nymph. (You can use an overpowered upstream mend if fishing from a distance.) This creates the slack the flies need to sink rapidly to the bottom. (D) Eventually the strong surface currents pull the suspender downstream of the nymphs, creating tension again, and begin leading them deeper in the water column.

When you must make a downstream presentation, the nymphs land downstream of the suspender. (A) Since surface currents are faster than the bottom currents, the suspender moves faster downstream than the nymph, and slack allows the nymphs to drop quickly to the bottom. (B) The nymph continues to drop, resistance free. (C) The suspender eventually drifts downstream of the nymph, creates tension, and begins to lead the nymph through the drift at the desired depth.

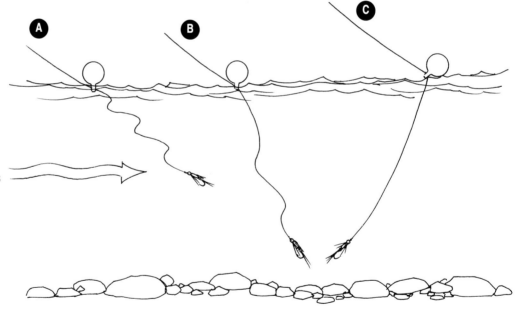

Aerial Reach Mend

Aerial mends are made during the cast, after the stop in the casting stroke. Anglers often confuse aerial mending with curve casting. A curve is a movement the rod tip takes *during* the acceleration of the cast, whereas an aerial mend is a movement *after* the acceleration. There are several different types of aerial mends, but the one I use most is the aerial reach mend, which places the entire line and nymphing rig in the same speed current when a straight upstream presentation is not possible.

Mending in the air is my first choice when attempting to position the line on the water because you have immediate line and leader control after the presentation. Mending on the water, on the other hand, requires you to throw slack in one direction, which produces a few seconds of total loss of line control. For some reason, this always seems to be when a trout decides to eat your fly, creating a missed opportunity. Therefore, you should make every effort to mend in the air and not on the water. This type of mending may be more difficult to learn initially, but it is worth learning.

AERIAL REACH MEND

In this picture, my targeted seam is on the opposite side of the stream. From this position, I will cast across the current to present the flies. Note the faster currents between me and my primary holding spot. Drag automatically sets in when the line lands in a faster current than the one in which your fly lands. Ideally, your fly line, leader, and fly should all end up in the same speed current. This is where the reach mend comes into play.

To perform an aerial reach mend, stand with your body facing the target across the current, and begin to accelerate your rod hand toward the target. Imagine drawing a straight line from your eye to the target. Your hand should travel that line toward the target.

Your hand continues to drift straight toward the target, casting across the current. It should not deviate off the straight path during the casting stroke.

Continue to accelerate as you make the casting stroke. The bend in the rod, caused by the load on the rod, is an indication of the accelerated motion.

Come to a sudden stop at the end of the casting stroke. This unloads the nymphing rig toward the target. A loop will form off the rod tip as soon as the tip stops accelerating. Continue to hold the rod tip steady in one spot.

After the loop starts to unroll past the rod tip, you begin sliding your rod hand downstream in a 90-degree angle from the path of the line. This is a very smooth sliding movement, as overpowering will create kickback in the rig. You are using too much power if your flies are being pulled away from the primary target.

Keep sliding your rod hand downstream as the loop unrolls. Do not let the rod tip drop, as this would allow line to fall on the faster currents. The tip should drift downstream along with your hand.

Continue to reach until your rod hand can drift no farther downstream. At this point, the rod tip should be parallel to your shoulders.

Now all the line should be lying in the same speed current. The rod tip is angled upward to keep as much line and leader off the water as possible. The rod is also in position to lead the flies through the drift. These small details make a world of difference when nymphing.

Here I am demonstrating a common mistake anglers make while mending—placing the line across currents of several different speeds. This will cause immediate drag. This position also makes it difficult to set the hook, as it forces the angler to pull the flies upstream and away from the fish. Ideally, you want to make a downstream hook set, which pulls the flies toward the trout's mouth. At times an upstream hook set may be the only possible method, but you should do everything you can to avoid it.

Here are a few important points to keep in mind when making an aerial reach mend: Before starting the cast, you must strip out enough line to cast as well as to shoot through the guides after the casting stroke is complete. Next, you need to identify the exact location where you want to place your patterns. Now imagine a line drawn from your eye to the target. Your rod hand should follow this path during the acceleration. At the end of the accelerated movement, drop the rod tip to a lower angle to allow slack to shoot freely through the guides. If you were to keep a high rod-tip angle, the line would have to climb a steep angle to shoot out the guides and in the process would lose energy. As the line begins to shoot, keep your rod hand fully extended and sweep the rod tip back toward one side of your body, feeding out the excess line at the same time. The fly will kick back on itself and miss the target if you don't give enough slack at this time.

Imagine your rod tip as a paintbrush, and think of where you want to lay the line on the water. The rod directs the path of the line when it falls on the water. For example, the line will fall across the currents if the rod tip is angled across-stream during the casting stroke. You need to place the line and leader all in the same speed current, so this means the rod tip must travel with the flow of water, not across, during the casting stroke. The rod tip "paints" the line as line begins to slide back. Look at the seam you want to lay the line on, and imagine drawing a line from the targeted area down the seam. This line is the path the rod tip must take during the sliding movement.

The distance you sweep the rod tip controls the size of the mend. Again, imagine the rod tip as a paintbrush, and determine how wide of a brush stroke you want to create. The greater the width of the rod tip movement during the shooting stage, the wider the mend. When mending in a larger nagging current, you need to provide more slack line to buy additional time before drag sets in.

Mending in the air disturbs the water less than does mending on the water and they are often enough to buy you a short drift, which is all you sometimes need to catch a fish. To obtain superlong drifts, however, especially on large rivers, you have to learn how to mend on the water.

On-the-Water Mends

Long drifts require more maintenance, and this is where on-the-water mends come into play. With long drifts, the rig needs to move in a longer path than with a short drift, so you need to build more slack into the line. The key is to provide enough slack while still maintaining sufficient ability to manage the line so you can securely set the hook.

If faster currents are between you and your rig, a bow will form in your fly line. One way to achieve a dead drift is to "feed" the current that is "eating the drift" by mending slack into that current. If this happens while you are casting across-stream, a common enough scenario, you must mend line upstream. You can also use on-the-water mending to extend the drift once the nymphing rig moves downstream of you and to make a downstream presentation with a nymph. My good friend Chuck Farneth gave me my first real lesson on mending while fishing Penns Creek a number of years ago. Chuck's ability to obtain dead drifts of 60 feet or longer quickly caught my attention.

There are several things to keep in mind when making an on-the-water mend. First you create slack to feed the drift, and then you kick out the slack through the rod tip and onto the water by holding your line hand above the butt of the rod handle and beginning to move the rod tip back and forth parallel to the water. Allow the line to stack off the rod tip onto the water. Kick out the amount of slack onto the water that you will need to make the mend. Accelerate and stop the rod tip during the line-stacking stage the same way you accelerate it during the casting stroke to move the line through the guides. Keep the rod tip low and the butt high to create a downward angle.

Once you have all this slack on the water, elevate and position the rod tip as you would to begin a roll cast. The idea is that you are going to roll cast the slack accurately to the nagging currents to provide additional time for a drag-free drift. The key is to roll the slack into the nagging current without disturbing the drift, and the slack off the rod tip provides that cushion. The suspender will quickly jerk if you do not provide enough slack while rolling the slack. Basically, it's an underpowered roll cast. That is, you want the line to fall short of the suspender, which creates the slack necessary for a drag-free drift. After the underpowered roll cast occurs, you then place the rod tip near the water's surface and strip in excess slack to maintain a degree of line control. For longer drifts, you may need to make additional on-the-water mends.

FEEDING SLACK

To feed slack when making an on-the-water mend, first create loops of fly line on your line hand instead of trying to pick up line off the water. Slack line from your line hand feeds through the guides a lot easier than line off the water, though there may be times when this is your only option.

Once you have enough line looped onto your line hand, hold the line hand above the rod and let gravity pull the line down through the guides. The index finger on the line hand should be angled toward the rod. This slight angle will let the loops slide off your line hand. The loops are stacked next to one another in preparation to slide off.

Now begin lifting the rod tip up and down with your forearm to kick out slack. This accelerated motion causes the rod to load and unload the loops of line onto the water. Acclerate the rod tip only a few feet upward, and then bring it to a sudden stop to unload the loops. A short stroke is all you need to move the line coils off your hand. Do not pinch the line or hold it in place during this upward movement. The coils begin to fall off your hand one loop at a time during each movement with the rod tip.

Now quickly drop your elbow, accelerating the rod tip toward the water and bringing it to a sudden stop immediately above the surface. The next loop will fall off your line hand and land on the water in the form of slack off the rod tip. The rod tip points directly down because that's where you want the slack for mending or feeding a drift.

Continue this up-and-down motion until all the coils of line are off your line hand. The result should be a pile of slack off the rod tip.

This slack is necessary for the rod tip to begin elevating in preparation for the mending movement. That is, the rod tip needs to move without pulling the line and suspension device, which you can accomplish when slack accumulates off the rod tip.

Tension Loop

Many writers have advocated mending fly line upstream of the suspender to achieve a dead drift, which eliminates drag and helps the flies sink faster. But, in many situations, I think a little bit of drag is beneficial and I prefer to mend my line so that a small amount of leader and fly line is downstream of the suspension device, creating a tension loop. I usually do this only in very slow water where I think a little more tension is needed in order to register a take. It doesn't take much, just a small, bow-shaped portion of line and leader—often 3 feet or less—downstream of your suspension device. Seldom do I use a tension loop when fishing faster waters with a suspension rig, as the faster surface currents are already moving the suspension device downstream of the nymphing rig.

Having slack line directly upstream of your suspension device is also a disadvantage during the hook set. When you set the hook, the rod tip puts the line under tension and begins pulling it upstream toward the rod tip. As a result, the line also pulls the suspension device upstream, away from the trout's mouth, reducing the chances of a secure hook set. A downstream tension loop has the exact opposite result. When the tension loop is formed downstream of the suspension device during a hook set, the downstream position of the loop first pulls the suspender downstream, toward the trout's mouth, before straightening out and eventually pulling it upstream.

Though I use the tension loop most often in slow-moving water, I sometimes use it in faster water when trout are looking for more movement in the flies. In fast water, this may

Unlike dry-fly fishing, your fly is below the surface here, and it's rare that you will get the chance to see the trout inhale your sunken pattern. Instead, you look for the sighter or suspension device to move, but it will only do that if there is tension between it and the fly or flies. The tension loop ensures that tension occurs between the suspender and flies. To create a tension loop, position a foot or less of line or leader downstream of the suspender. The small loop that forms will pull the suspender along slightly faster than it would travel without the loop. With a suspension device, I use no more than 3 feet of leader and line to create the loop, and often it consists of only 12 inches of the leader butt section.

current →

line

imply having only a few inches of line or leader on the water. The more line and leader you have on the water, the greater amount of tension will occur on the suspension device, moving it faster downstream, and vice versa. This is a great tool to micromanage the speed of your nymphs.

The dead-drift tactic isn't always the best form of drift for your nymph. For example, take the famed salmonfly hatch on many Western waters. Before the dry-fly action picks up, a massive migration occurs as the immature nymphs start heading to the streamside banks, where they will crawl out of the water early in the morning and find a piece of vegetation or substrate to lie on before breaking out of their shucks and becoming winged adults. Trout become aware of this movement and begin taking nymphs, which may at times be moving across or against the current as they seek the banks. A tension loop or similar type of tension applied to the fly at the end of a dead drift, so that it moves toward the streambank, can be an effective tool.

Effective nymph fishing is all about imitating the natural movement of the trout food. If dead drifting were the only effective tool for subsurface flies, then wet flies would never have been developed. My few experiences snorkeling in trout streams have revealed that insects swim both with and against the currents. For example, freshwater shrimp are fast swimmers and can move significantly faster than the current speed on the bottom. As a result, I dead-drift my scud patterns and also pull them slightly faster than the current, as both are natural drifts.

Sometimes a fly moving faster than the current is exactly what you need to trigger a take from a trout. This often occurs during heavy hatch periods, when the immature insects are moving quickly through the water column to make the transition to the winged adult stage. The trout soon recognize this movement and may begin feeding only on patterns that follow their exact path. To create this accelerated movement of the fly, you need to create surface tension with the line on the water. Therefore, you will do the exact opposite of what it takes to create a drag-free drift. That is, you will throw a mend downstream of the suspension rig to create surface drag. The fly will begin to accelerate as soon as the line is under tension from the current. It's similar to a tuber being pulled by a jet boat. The tuber rises to the surface as soon as the boat begins pulling the rope and quickly drops through the water column as soon as the boat stops.

I use a downstream mend only when I know the trout are looking up through the water column for food. The downstream mend can also be used in combination with the upstream mend. For example, during a hatch, I often make long upstream casts to achieve long dead drifts with my nymphs. I manage line as the nymphs come back to me and immediately throw a large downstream mend when the nymphs begin to pass me to create a quick ascending drift.

STACK MEND

Stack mending is a technique to quickly and smoothly move excessive amounts of fly line off the rod tip. This slack is essential when the angler needs to execute normal mending techniques. It's the first step before actually making the mend.

After delivering a cast upstream, kick out excess line with stack mends. This photo shows the first stage of the stack mend, as the rod tip accelerates downward toward the water and begins to pull the excess coils off my line hand.

To kick several more coils of line onto the water, elevate the rod tip into a vertical position by simply lifting the rod tip upward toward the sky.

After the rod tip is elevated high enough, begin a downward accelerated movement as you aim the rod tip toward the water's surface. Come to a sudden stop, as this will unload the rod tip and rip the coils of line off your line hand and onto the water.

Once enough slack is on the water's surface, begin to elevate the rod tip again, but position the rod as if preparing to roll cast. Angle the rod tip behind you, with line hanging off the tip to load the rod.

As you begin the forward casting stroke, your target should be a point off to the side of the line lying on the water. To avoid throwing the line onto itself, you need to aim off to either side so you can create a loop of line on the water.

Accelerate the rod tip and then bring it to a stop, allowing it to unload to move the slack line upstream. You don't want to unroll all the line off the water. All you want to accomplish is to create a loop off to the side of the line already lying on the water. Therefore, you should use an underpowered casting stroke so you don't lift the entire line off the water. You just want to move the slack you created using the stack mend.

The loop continues off to the side of the main line but only halfway up. The underpowered stroke creates just enough energy to turn over the slack line to create a small loop on the water's surface.

If the initial loop is too small, you can make a second underpowered cast upstream to create a larger loop on the water's surface.

Now the loop is large enough to create enough surface drag to pull the rig faster downstream. The larger the loop, the greater the surface drag and the faster your flies will be pulled downstream. If the rig is moving too fast, you can use a smaller tension loop. This is an effective tool for both tight-line and suspension nymphing tactics.

READING THE DRIFT

Once the nymphs drop to the appropriate level in the water column, which you determine by the distance between the nymphs and the suspension device, the suspender maintains tension by holding the nymphing rig through the drift and pulls the nymphs through the drift at the correct speed. This eliminates the need to guess the current speed, as you have to do with tight-line nymphing, and maintains a tight connection from the suspender to the flies. Because the trout can spit out a fly in a split second, any slack in the system works to your disadvantage in setting the hook.

The direction and speed of your suspension device on the water's surface are good indicators of what your nymphs are doing below the surface. Make it a habit to compare the drift speed of the suspension device with floating bubbles or foam. This will tell you the speed at which your nymphs are moving along the bottom.

First you need to understand the hydraulics of the piece of water you're fishing. For example, is the water speed stratified from top to bottom? That is, do you think the speed near the surface is faster than at the the bottom? A good pair of optics will allow you to see through the surface to gauge the currents near the bottom. If the water is relatively shallow, there's a good chance the speed is the same at both the surface and bottom. In this case, the suspension device should float at about the same speed as the current. However, in deeper water of 3 feet or more, with substrate near the bottom or drop-offs, currents will be slower. As a result, your suspension device should move slower than the surface speed.

The key is to allow your nymphs time to settle to the stream bottom. Once they reach the bottom, the nymphs will anchor themselves in the bottom current and actually slow down the speed of the suspension device. In fact, in such cases, I often see that my suspender is moving slower on the stream surface than a line of bubbles or anything else that is floating naturally in the surface currents. This tension between your flies and the suspension device enables you to notice the slightest change in movement in your drift.

Left: Once experienced anglers dial in their suspender nymphing systems, they develop "nymphing eyes"—the ability to notice extremely subtle changes in movement during the drift and develop a sixth sense that tells them to strike, for no other reason than that something felt different. GEORGE DANIEL

Right: A high-floating dry fly allowed me to suspend a lightweight nymph and maintain tension in the slack-water section of this run. AMIDEA DANIEL

Adjusting the Distance between Flies and Suspender

When changing the distance between suspender and flies, I prefer to change the length of the tippet rather than slide the suspender up and down the leader. This is because I use tapered leader for a butt section, and if I move the suspender too far up the leader, the thicker butt material will be between my sighter and flies. The tapered section will not sink all at the same rate. A level tippet not only sinks uniformly, but also provides better contact between suspender and flies.

Specific water conditions ultimately determine the optimal distance between suspender and flies, since most rivers and streams have a mix of riffle, runs, glides, and pools, all of which differ in speed and depth. Before rigging up your suspender, you need to consider several variables, including the speed and depth of the water, the level at which the fish are feeding, and, when fishing pocketwater, the length of the drift.

Water Speed and Depth

The suspender on the surface, where current speeds are normally the fastest, will pull your bottom-bouncing nymphing rig, where current speeds are slower, downstream. This difference in current speed between the suspender and flies creates an angle. For fast water, I often rig the suspender two to two and a half times the depth of the water. This allows the nymphs time to get to the bottom before the suspender starts dragging them.

In medium to medium-fast currents, as a rule, it's best to place your suspender at a distance from your nymphs that is one and a half to two times the depth of the water. I ordinarily start off at two times the depth, because shortening the tippet section is easier than adding tippet. Since these faster surface currents move the suspender downstream more rapidly than the nymphs, your suspender will create a roughly 45-degree angle to the flies and weight. If you used a distance equal to the depth of the water, then the flies would be suspended midway in the water column. This may be a desired result if the trout are feeding at this level, but it is ineffective when targeting bottom-feeding fish.

When fishing in slow water, you want the rig to fish at a true 90-degree angle from suspender to nymph, which means directly under the suspender. Thus the length between nymph and suspender should be slightly less than the depth of the water. A dry is my first choice during the hatch season, when I believe there's a chance of catching a fish on the dry or anytime little weight is needed to obtain a 90-degree angle. However, I use a buoyant manufactured suspender when significant weight is needed to reach the bottom.

Time on the water is the best teacher, and making the proper adjustments is a must. However, most anglers fail to take the time to do so.
GEORGE DANIEL

Level at Which the Fish Are Feeding

One of the first rules I learned when competing in lake venues is that trout look up for their food and you are simply wasting your time if you are presenting your flies below their feeding zone. And this rule applies to river fishing as well. First, you need to know the level at which the fish are feeding. If trout are actively taking emerging insects right below the surface, then it makes sense to have at least one pattern at that level. If, on the other hand, you're fishing at a time when trout activity is slow and the fish are hugging the bottom, such as during the winter months, then all your subsurface patterns should be bouncing on the bottom and not being suspended below the surface. A three-fly rig with a dry fly and two droppers (the heavier fly on the point) allows you to fishing at three different levels. This rigging setup should be your first choice if you're unsure about the level at which the fish are feeding. In order to fish all three levels, you should still follow the guidelines above regarding the water speed—slow, medium, or fast—when attaching the suspender and point fly to ensure that the point fly gets down near the stream bottom. Then place the dropper at about the halfway point between the suspender and point nymph to ensure that this fly drifts near midlevel.

Length of Drift in Pocketwater

In high-gradient Western rivers with lots of pocketwater, the length of the drift is usually short between boulders. For maximum control, the distance between your suspender and point fly should be shorter when fishing short drifts and vice versa. Also, for short drifts, it's often a good idea to increase the weight in the rig. Keep in mind that the suspender and nymphing rig all need to lie in the same drift line. If, for instance, the average length of drift between boulders is 4 feet, it makes no sense to place your nymph 5 feet from the suspender, as this would already create a foot of slack between the suspender and nymph.

Trout holding in pocketwater are often more eager to move up and down the water column to chase a fly. While nymphing pocketwater, I normally fish a single nymph about 2 feet under the suspender, as this length permits me to place the entire rig, with suspender and nymph, in the same drift line for most pocketwater scenarios. This often goes against the general rule that the distance between suspender and nymph should be one and a half times the depth of the water for medium-fast currents. Following that guideline, if the water is 3 feet deep, the suspender and nymph should be $4\frac{1}{2}$ feet apart (3 feet x $1\frac{1}{2}$ = $4\frac{1}{2}$ feet), but it's not a hard-and-fast rule, and there will be exceptions. It would be difficult to control a $4\frac{1}{2}$-foot nymphing rig in a pocket that's only 3 feet long. In this example, $1\frac{1}{2}$ feet of slack would occur, as you are attempting to place a $4\frac{1}{2}$-foot rig in a 3-foot-long drift line, giving you an excess of $1\frac{1}{2}$ feet. Also, in pocketwater, trout will likely move up a foot through the water column to eat.

This is a typical scene where the angler picks up all the line and the suspension device off the water at once to either set the hook or begin the backcast. Often a section of the fly line will sink, and it can pull the suspension device underwater when the angler lifts the line off the water. When the suspender is pulled under, it will quickly reemerge, and the tension of the line being lifted off the water creates a popping sound and a splash. This is likely to spook fish, especially in low-water conditions. To solve this problem, I use the corkscrew pickup, or voodoo cast.

CORKSCREW PICKUP

Suspension nymphing often requires you to pick up an excessive amount of line off the water for setting the hook or preparing for a backcast. Either way, more line lying on the water means that you will have to expend more energy picking it up. As an example, have you ever tried picking up 70 feet of fly line off the water all at once, with a 4-weight rod, to make a backcast and had the power to completely turn over the rig? There are some who can accomplish this, but they are very few in number and do not include me. As a result, you have two options to pick up that much line off the water. One is to continue stripping in line until you have 25 to 30 feet lying on the water. At this point, you should have enough power in your cast to energize the rod to turn over the entire 30-foot length. A good backcast sets you up for a good forward cast, but the one disadvantage of picking up the entire line off the water is the disturbance it makes when the line lifts off the water. This is especially critical when you're fishing in low water where a line being ripped off the water can put all the fish down.

Recently, I have begun experimenting with a different cast that enables me to quietly pick up the line off the water. I learned this cast from Mike Mauri, a top-notch casting instructor from Germany, while we were both working the fly-fishing show circuit. He calls it the voodoo cast; others have called it the corkscrew pickup. The cast has several applications, especially for dry-fly fishing, but the one I've found the most important for long-line nymphing is its ability to easily and quietly pick up excess line off the water. Instead of lifting all the line off the water at once, the voodoo cast lets you start picking line off the water before beginning the backcast. The nymphing rig is anchored in the water, which allows you to use a circular motion with the rod tip to begin lifting line off the water before executing a backcast. This motion picks up all the line and leader off the water and requires less energy for you to execute the backcast, since little if any line remains on the water, enabling you to pick up a fairly long portion of line. It also creates a lot less disturbance on the water's surface. I often use this cast with the curly Q in slow, shallow water where any disturbance on the water would spook fish.

Point your rod tip at the suspension device and line lying on the water. No slack should occur in the line or leader anywhere between the suspension device and reel. Begin elevating the rod tip to about a 45-degree angle, keeping your hand fully extended away from your body to provide a full range of motion for the backcast.

Once the rod tip is in position, your elbow should be at about chest level. Now begin lifting your elbow upward toward the sky, keeping the rod tip at the same angle. Continue to elevate the rod tip until your hand is close to full extension, and let the rod and line come to a stop.

With the remaining room for the rod tip to travel, begin to accelerate (not just lift) the rod tip upward as if you were stabbing the sky, and then come to a sudden stop. The belly of the line will begin to lift off the water, and a section will lift up to the same height as the rod tip.

After a split-second pause, accelerate your rod hand downward in a half-circle arc, but with the rod tip still pointed upward at a 45-degree angle, and speed up to a stop. Your rod hand will travel in a sideways U shape. The key in both of these steps is to accelerate and stop the rod tip in the same manner you would when making a standard forward cast or backcast.

The loop of line that will create the corkscrew continues its path downward toward the nymph.

The accelerated half-circle movement forms a loop off the rod tip that travels down the belly of the line in a circular motion, hence the name corkscrew. The key here is to wait until the corkscrew loop travels all the way to the suspension device and begins to lift it off the water.

If you wait long enough, the circular loop will lift the suspender off the water in an upward manner. The wider the arc the rod tip travels during the accelerated half-circle movement, the higher the fly will lift off the water.

With your hand still fully extended forward, begin making the backcast as the suspension device is hovering above the water. The goal is to do this in the air, where no disturbance will be created, and avoid having to pick up the suspension device off the water.

The backcast here is like any other—make a smooth acceleration to a stop, and then wait for the line to begin unrolling before making the forward casting stroke.

Fly Patterns

I have had the great privilege to meet and fish against some of the best anglers in the world, and after competitions, we always love talking about fly patterns. One common theme among top-notch competitive fly anglers is that they frequently use suggestive-looking patterns. These anglers train to catch fish on unfamiliar waters on a regular basis. As a result, their fly boxes must contain a wide range of suggestive patterns that could approximate the naturals on streams anywhere around the globe. Having exact imitations would limit them to the waters that hold those particular species. Most anglers would be surprised, if they could look into these world-class competitors' boxes, to find many variations of Hare's Ears and Pheasant Tails and not a lot of the super-realistic-looking patterns. Why? Because these anglers believe that great technique along with a good pattern is far more productive than just okay technique using a great pattern. Though it's important to devote great time and attention to pattern selection, you should spend even more on refining your nymphing techniques.

At times, I do favor the more imitative-looking patterns. As an example, many Pennsylvania streams have great Eastern Green Drake and *Isonychia* mayfly hatches. The nymphs of both species are long and slender, with prominent gills, and have a unique appearance that differs from other mayfly nymphs. Fishing these hatches are among the few times when

If you are fishing multiple flies, try to use at least one attractor pattern to get the trout's interest. A Rainbow Warrior fished as a point fly fooled this wild brown trout during the Sulphur hatch, whereas the imitating nymph produced few hookups. JAY NICHOLS

141

Patterns are often designed to catch anglers, not fish, and the most intricate patterns are not always the most successful. I much prefer a suggestive pattern that closely resembles the natural, but not an exact imitation. After I won back-to-back national championships, more anglers asked me what pattern I was using rather than how I was using it. It's a common misconception that it's the pattern that makes an angler successful. It's more important to focus on your technique than on the patterns. JAY NICHOLS

a traditional-looking Hare's Ear or Pheasant Tail just can't correctly imitate the natural. This doesn't mean you won't catch fish using a black Hare's Ear just before an *Isonychia* hatch, but you may find it more productive to use an imitation with a longer, narrower body and prominent gills. I normally use imitative patterns only when the trout are keying on insects with unique physical characteristics. For example, while fishing the *Isonychia* nymph, I use a jig hook with a tungsten bead to enhance the undulating movement of the pattern, along with CDC to imitate the prominent gills. This pattern not only moves up and down in the currents like the natural, but also appears to breathe like the natural. My pattern isn't an exact imitation of the natural, but it's close enough to give me confidence in its effectiveness.

For the purposes of this book, I have divided nymphing patterns into three categories: imitative, suggestive, and wild. Imitative patterns are designed to replicate, as closely as possible, the colors, body parts, and movements of the naturals. Suggestive patterns, on the other hand, resemble the naturals but emphasize general shape and movement over exact replication. Wild patterns are not imitative and are essentially attractor patterns. Anglers use these often gaudy constructions in an attempt to trigger the trout's aggressive side or in extreme fishing conditions when nothing else seems to work. This chapter focuses on imitative and suggestive patterns; I talk more about wilds on page 206.

Thread-bodied flies treated with epoxy or nail polish will quickly drop through the water column. The Iron Lotus, designed by Lance Egan, is a small mayfly imitation that drops like a rock. GEORGE DANIEL

THE POWER OF SUGGESTION

The biggest problem I have when fishing Pennsylvania's nutrient-rich streams is the abundance of aquatics. Our local streams possess a vastness of mayflies, stoneflies, caddis, freshwater crustaceans, and other naturals such that it would be almost physically impossible to carry all possible presentations at one time. Instead, we simplify and carry a smaller selection of suggestive patterns that can imitate the naturals for the waters we fish. I love to sample as many different waters as I can throughout the year, and I have a tough time fishing one river for an extended period of time. This is why I prefer the suggestive approach, as my selection should allow me to effectively fish any trout water around.

One of my standbys is the Pheasant Tail, one of the most widely used nymphs in the world. Whenever I've used a Pheasant Tail or modified Pheasant Tail during a fishing trip, it has invariably produced a fish. If you're fishing foreign water, you should use a suggestive pattern for your first attempt. The Frenchie, a modified Pheasant Tail, is usually one of the first patterns I place on my rig when fishing unknown waters, especially if mayflies are known to live in the stream. For whatever reason, this pattern has consistently produced fish for me on rivers containing mayfly nymphs. As a result, I find that carrying this fly in a number of sizes is more efficient than trying to match every single mayfly nymph to its exact specs.

Most of my patterns are not pretty, but they do have a few qualities that I believe is essential for a nymph imitation. First, the pattern has to have movement tied into it. My mentor Joe Humphreys figured this out years ago, when he began experimenting with emu and ostrich herl for imitating gills, especially for his Slate Drake and Green Drake Nymphs. He was the first one to tell me the importance of movement being tied into the fly. Besides ostrich and emu, I tend to favor dubbings with heavy guard hairs. For example, Wapsi's Squirrel SLF dubbing is a perfect combination of a shaggy natural fur with just the right amount of synthetic flash. You can brush out the guard hairs with a piece of Velcro to create a nymph with lots of natural movement. CDC is another great material that adds lifelike movement to the nymph; you can mix it in with dubbing or use it for color on a nymph. Finally, unlike traditional nymph hooks, jig-style hooks provide movement, especially when the rod tip twitches the fly. These are just a few examples of materials that can add a little spice to your presentation.

Though there are exceptions, an overwhelming majority of my go-to nymphs have contrast. I've found that most of my successful nymphs are ones that feature contrast, so I tend to stay away from monochromatic flies and usually use imitations with multiple color schemes. Have you ever rolled over a few rocks and taken a good look at the naturals underneath? You don't have to be an entomologist to notice that just about all the aquatic insects you see have distinct segmentation, and many have multiple color schemes. This is why the Zebra Midge is so effective for such a simple fly. This pattern basically consists of a thread body, wire counter-rib, and bead. It's one of my top three patterns for a midge larva, and I know it would not be as effective without the wire counter-rib. The Prince Nymph is

another great example: its white biots create a distinct contrast that has allowed it to fool trout for many years in both East and West, although it doesn't imitate any exact nymph.

Keep your pattern selection fairly simple. Carry a good variety of patterns, but not in every possible shade. Do not complicate things any more than you have to. The more patterns you carry, the more complicated your fishing becomes, and this takes away from the true nature of fly fishing. Far too many anglers refuse to fish when they don't have a particular color nymph in their box. But once you have mastered a higher level of angling skill and gained confidence, you will have learned to fish with what you have and not to focus on what you do not have. The successful French youth team did not mind showing other angling teams their patterns because they

Though I usually prefer to use suggestive-looking patterns, imitative patterns such as this GD's UV Sow Bug can be a good option for fish keying on specific naturals. JAY NICHOLS

The Frenchie scores again. This simple fly has caught trout in almost every conceivable set of water conditions. It has become one of my top three nymphs, and what's more, it takes only a few minutes to tie. JAY NICHOLS

knew that the patterns had little to do with their victories. They knew they would still beat the other teams with solid fly-fishing techniques. Though you should have a good selection in your fly box, focus more on how you plan to use your flies on the water.

Simplicity in pattern design also means that your patterns take less time to tie. In my teens, I was more focused on tying realistic nymphs, believing that the closer a fly looked to the natural, the more likely it was to fool fish. I thought success was a fifty-fifty split of presentation and pattern. Some of the more common mayfly nymphs, including several of my favorites, took me ten to fifteen minutes to tie. This stage lasted until I joined the US team, where I soon learned that many of the top competitors spent more time focusing on their presentation skills than on how natural their flies looked. My first real introduction to efficiency came in the form of the Frenchie. Unlike many other mayfly nymph imitations, this fly had no legs or moving gill sections. It was basically just a beadhead Pheasant Tail Nymph with an orange dubbing hot spot, and it took me only three minutes to tie. This fly proved to be deadly and is still one of my favorite patterns to this day. And the fact that it took much less time to tie than some of my old favorites gave me more time to tie additional flies or be on the water sharpening my skills. I do enjoy tying flies, but I'd rather spend my free time fishing.

Give some thought to what is essential in your flies and what is not. For instance, don't build beautiful wing pads on top of the fly if it is going to ride upside down. If you feel that you must add this extra step of realism, then go for it, but at least tie them on the underside of the hook shank. After careful consideration, you may decide to forgo tying in the wing pads, as I have, since you've already caught a number of trout on a pattern that had its wing pads hidden from the fish. With suggestive patterns, you won't cringe as much when you have to break off a Hare's Ear that took three minutes to tie rather than a fifteen-minute Woven Stone. This lets you be more aggressive when casting around cover, areas that many anglers pass over to avoid lost flies.

Left: Czech-style caddis nymphs are easy to tie, look great in the water, sink quickly, and are great representations of the larvae. You can tie this style on a scud hook, with beads, lead wire, or both for additional weight. The body is often dubbed with a mixture of natural fur and synthetics with a shellback to create a two-toned effect.

Below: Never leave home without a Zebra Midge. This simple but effective nymph will take fish anywhere the trout are feeding on midge larvae. Its slim profile allows this nymph to quickly drop to the bottom. GEORGE DANIEL

Left: Thread-bodied nymphs with a glossy coating of nail polish sink like a rock and have a translucent look that trout find hard to refuse. A variety of Iron Lotus patterns make up this style in my box. Slim Pheasant Tail Nymphs will also drop quickly through the water column. JAY NICHOLS

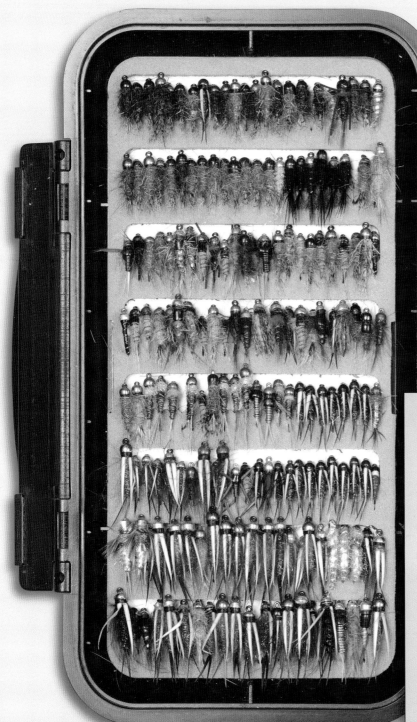

I use these patterns in spring in Pennsylvania or any time the depth is 3 feet or greater and the water is flowing strong. All these patterns are on the suggestive side, imitating a wide range of aquatic insects. The bottom two rows consist of heavy tungsten Prince Nymphs along with a few miscellaneous nymphs with $5/32$-inch tungsten beads. The fifth and sixth rows are mostly size 12 and smaller Prince Nymphs with $1/8$-inch tungsten beads. The last four rows comprise size 12 and smaller nymphs (mostly Hare and Copper modifications) with $1/8$-inch tungsten beads.

FLY BOX ORGANIZATION

I store my weighted nymphs in large, waterproof C&F fly boxes, organized into three categories: heavy, medium weight, and lightweight. These boxes contain several thousand flies, and I keep them in an out-of-the-way compartment in my pack or vest. From these boxes, I choose the flies I plan to use for the day's fishing and put them into my working fly box.

For most of my mayfly nymph patterns, I use slight variations of Pheasant Tails and Hare's Ear Nymphs. I tie the Pheasant Tail Nymphs in natural, olive, chocolate brown, and black in sizes 12 to 20. Often I tie in a natural-looking thorax or a hot spot in fluorescent orange or pink. These patterns cover many of the darker mayfly species and even some smaller stoneflies. I tie the Hare's Ear Nymphs in natural and dark hare's ear in sizes 12 to 20. The original Hare's Ear Nymph best imitates many of the lighter-colored mayfly nymphs, and a paler version may resemble the stage when nymphs shed their exoskeletons and become almost white. I prefer dubbings that contain a good number of guard hairs, which provide additional movement in the water. Sometimes I substitute SLF Squirrel Dubbing when I want a shaggier look with a bit more flash.

Medium Weight (Center)

The first seven rows are mostly general mayfly nymphs, including Whitlock's Squirrel Nymphs, Walt Young's Sulphur Nymphs, Hare and Coppers, Egan's Rainbow Warriors, and a flashy Hare's Ear. Green Weenies occupy the last row. All of these flies are between size 12 and 14 and have $1/8$-inch tungsten beads.

Medium Weight (Right)

The third page of my medium-weight box holds a variety of fly styles, but all range from size 12 to 14. They include Copper Johns, Hare and Coppers, Frenchies, and a handful of other general nymphs capable of fooling fish around the globe.

Heavy Weight (Left)

These flies usually range from size 4 to 8 and have $^5/_{32}$-inch tungsten beads along with lead wire. On this side, caddis dominate, since I find that I can add serious amounts of weight and still maintain the natural appearance of the caddis. Usually reserved for extremely deep and fast flows, these patterns are normally used early in spring in the East, when streamflows are running above average. As little as I use them in the East, these heavy anchor patterns become mainstays when fishing many of the fast-moving Western waters. These patterns also have slim bodies, allowing them to quickly drop through the water column.

The middle section of my heavyweight box contains patterns that are lighter in weight, averaging size 8 to 10, with $\frac{1}{8}$-inch tungsten beads. Here, too, caddis dominate the fly type, as I find I can place more weight in the patterns yet still maintain the appearance of the natural caddis nymphs.

Heavy Weight (Right)

On the right side of my anchor box, the flies again average from size 4 to 8, with $^5/_{32}$-inch tungsten beads, but there's a mix of stonefly, caddis, and worm imitations.

Light Weight (Left)

I fish from this box more than 70 percent of the time in average to low-water conditions, usually with a handful of patterns in a number of different sizes. These patterns range from size 14 to 18 and most have $7/64$-inch tungsten beads with additional lead wire. The bottom three rows are all caddis larvae and pupae patterns. The remaining rows consist mostly of mayfly nymphs, with a heavy dose of Frenchie Pheasant Tails.

Light Weight (Center)

The flip page of the lightweight box has an emphasis on shrimp and sow bug patterns.

The right side of my lightweight box holds flies that are slightly smaller than those on the two previous pages, averaging size 16 to 18, with $3/32$-inch tungsten beads. Mayflies, caddis, and general attractor flies make up my lightweight selection.

153

Light or No Weight (Left)

Beginning at the top, the flies are the Walt's Worm in various sizes, several Bird of Prey Caddis, a variety of midge larvae, and flashy Lightning Bugs.

Light or No Weight (Right)

These flies are, beginning at the top, a variety of caddis, several small mayfly emergers, a good variety of shrimp and sow bugs, and a variety of soft-hackles.

GETTING DOWN WITH WEIGHT

I prefer a nymph pattern that has weight built into the body for the majority of the conditions I face. Nymphing is all about having a good connection to your nymphs, and weight built into the fly may provide a more direct connection. A weighted fly anchors itself better, which results in a great connection from rod tip to nymph. This is especially useful when fishing fast currents with various seams.

Making minor adjustments to the weight when nymphing is absolutely critical, but anglers often neglect to do this. One of the biggest reasons anglers fail to fine-tune their flies' weight is the hassle of putting on and taking off split shot. Instead of using split shot, however, I usually adjust the weight simply by changing flies. On average, it takes me two minutes to add or remove shot, but only thirty seconds to change flies. Also, removing shot often leaves a small nick in the leader that can weaken the tippet. Another benefit of adjusting the weight by changing flies instead of using split shot is that you don't have to carry a huge assortment of lead. Most of the time, I carry just two pots of shot, in sizes 4 and 6, to make microadjustments to my rig, and I use the shot only when I can't make the proper adjustment by changing flies. In these cases, I use split shot without ears, as they have less of a tendency to hang up.

Unweighted flies drift very naturally, and during hatches I often use split shot to sink an unweighted or lightly weighted fly. First, an unweighted fly with shot moves more naturally through the water column than a heavily weighted fly and better imitates the emerging insects. Natural movement is one of the key triggers for trout when feeding during heavy hatch periods. Second, an unweighted fly rides slightly higher in the water column than a heavily weighted pattern. One of my favorite tactics is to place a split shot 10 inches in front of an unweighted Sulphur nymph just as the natural nymphs are preparing to hatch. The unweighted fly rides several inches above the bottom, nicely imitating a nymph that is just beginning its emergence.

Top: Devin Olsen weighing each fly before inserting into his box. Devin is a fanatic when it comes to organizing his weighted flies. **Bottom:** Olsen organizes his flies according to specific weight, weighing them in grams with a powder scale and then inserting them at the appropriate place in his fly box. He then labels each row with a black permanent marker. GEORGE DANIEL

FINE-TUNING WEIGHT

You can fine-tune the weight in your nymphing rig by changing flies or by adding or removing split shot. To fine-tune by changing flies, which is my preferred method, you first need to tie a variety of flies with different sizes and types of beads. I tie flies with both brass and tungsten beads, but I use the flies with tungsten beads for most conditions, as the tungsten weighs twice as much as brass. In order to distinguish between the two types, I darken the eyes of all my brass flies with a black permanent marker, since I have fewer flies with brass eyes than with tungsten. Thus a black head tells me the fly has a brass bead, and an undarkened eye means it has a tungsten bead. When fine-tuning the weight, you can use beads of different weight on the same hook size or add lead or lead-free wire to the fly along with a bead. For example, a size 14 nymph hook can accommodate a $7/64$- or $3/32$-inch bead along with lead wire. These kinds of adjustments allow you to fine-tune the weight without having to use split shot most of the time. To fine-tune with split shot, I usually use size 4 or 6 shot, as these smaller weights allow me to make microadjustments to the rig. So between carrying a couple pots of small split shot and a variety of flies with beads of different sizes and materials, you can easily fine-tune your rig to get the nymphs to the exact depth you need to fish.

However you organize your flies, you need a system that enables you to easily find the flies you want and quickly adjust the weight for various stream conditions. I darken all the eyes on my brass bead-head nymphs with a black permanent marker so I can readily see if a particular nymph has a brass or tungsten bead. Since I also add lead wire to some of my brass- and tungsten-beaded flies, I create a hot spot with thread on those with wire and dubbing on those without. For example, one of my favorites, the Frenchie, has an orange hot spot right behind the bead. I make the hot spot from fluorescent orange thread if I tie additional lead wire onto the hook shank and from fluorescent orange dubbing if I do not add weight. JAY NICHOLS

Another situation where I prefer unweighted flies is when fishing over mossy stream bottoms, as weighted flies will constantly snag on the bottom. For example, in late summer, when the bottom of one of my favorite spring creeks is covered with vegetation, I like to use an unweighted shrimp or cress bug pattern in combination with split shot placed 8 to 10 inches away from the fly. The shot will bounce along the bottom and allow the nymph to drift freely over the vegetation and rarely snag.

Anglers who stop into the fly shop where I work often ask me for suggestions on Czech nymph patterns and are often surprised—and at times incredulous—when I suggest more lightly weighted Copper Johns for the lower-gradient streams in the area. Several, after hearing this, have told me I need to read up on European nymphing, because Czech patterns should be heavily weighted and tied on a Gammarus hook. For a long time, I too was of the mindset that large, heavily weighted flies were the only patterns appropriate for Czech nymphing. During my four years of international travel with the United States team, however, I noticed that the top-notch Czech competitors were using not only much more lightly weighted nymphs, but also many forms of mayfly and stonefly imitations. For deep or fast-moving water or when large caddis are present, heavy flies have their place, but even with Czech nymphing, it's important to match the weight of the pattern to the water type you are fishing.

In the Bohemian region of the Czech Republic, many of the rivers are smaller freestone streams, no wider than 20 feet, with a slight gradient, similar to what I fish in central Pennsylvania. The streams were running full of water and in certain stretches aquatic vegetation covered much of the bottom. Any fly resembling a heavy Czech nymph would have hung up on the bottom almost immediately. When the US Youth Fly Fishing Team traveled to the Czech Republic to fish in the 2009 World Youth Fly Fishing Championships, our team fished lightly weighted

Right: Fly floatant, including Frog's Fanny, can help keep a nymph floating above the weeds. Such floatant also produces additional bubbles on the nymph as it rides underwater. GEORGE DANIEL

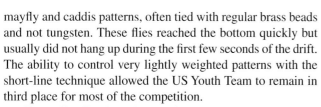

Above: Ryan Furtak holds a solid brown trout that he caught on an unweighted Sulphur nymph fished in the film. GEORGE DANIEL

Right: Ian Colin James, creator of the Brass Ass and other epoxy-style nymphs, holds a fresh Grand River steelhead that fell to one of his many innovative patterns. IAN COLIN JAMES

mayfly and caddis patterns, often tied with regular brass beads and not tungsten. These flies reached the bottom quickly but usually did not hang up during the first few seconds of the drift. The ability to control very lightly weighted patterns with the short-line technique allowed the US Youth Team to remain in third place for most of the competition.

Since slim flies have less surface area, they sink quickly, unlike thick-body patterns that have lots of materials which slow the flies descent due to drag. Many of the European patterns, especially those for Czech and Polish nymphing, have a slender profile, which I also prefer. Slender flies sink faster and require little weight to reach the bottom. This is critical when fishing in pockets where drifts are so short that they may last only three seconds, not giving a buoyant pattern enough time to reach the target zone. You can add split shot to increase the sink rate, but I would rather have most of the weight built into the fly. Movement should be tied into your pattern, but not to the point where excess material seriously affects its sink rate.

The slim and weighted characteristics of Czech and Polish nymphs can be applied to any subsurface pattern, including mayflies, stoneflies, and midge larvae.

I like to tie my own flies, as do many other anglers. However, as much as I enjoy tying flies, I enjoy fishing even more, so I choose to tie patterns that are effective but simple. Nymphing accounts for more lost flies than dry-fly, wet-fly, or streamer fishing, so I know I'm going to lose flies almost every time I fish. That being the case, I would rather lose flies that took me less than five minutes to tie instead of fifteen minutes or more.

The following patterns are those that I think are particularly good for tight-line and suspension nymphing. Listed below are patterns I would never leave home without. I feel they will take trout in just about any stream condition around the world. After all, the origin of these patterns comes from fellow anglers across the globe and I have witnessed their effectiveness during my time traveling with Fly Fishing Team USA.

Use a rod as long as you can get away with. Here, Stephen Salwocki fishes with a 9-foot rod on a small stream in the Czech Republic.
ROBERT MILLER

MARCH BROWN NYMPH

(Bob Jacklin)

Hook:	#12-14 Dai-Riki 275
Weight:	.015-inch lead wire
Thread:	Rusty brown UTC
Body:	Amber Australian opossum dubbing
Rib:	Rusty brown UTC Vinyl D Rib
Legs:	Natural or dyed brown Hungarian partridge
Wing case:	Brown or rusty Scud Back over turkey tail feather strip
Head:	Same as body

GD'S CZECH CAT NIP (OLIVE)

(George Daniel)

Hook:	#6-12 Tiemco 2499 SP-BL
Bead:	Black tungsten
Weight:	.020- to .035-inch lead wire
Thread:	Black 8/0 Uni-Thread
Body:	Olive Hareline Micro Polar Chenille
Thorax:	Black Hareline Micro Polar Chenille
Shellback:	Olive Mottled Oak Thin Skin

GD'S CZECH CAT NIP (CHARTREUSE)

(George Daniel)

Hook:	#6-12 Tiemco 2499 SP-BL
Bead:	Black tungsten
Weight:	.020- to .035-inch lead wire
Thread:	Black 8/0 Uni-Thread
Body:	Chartreuse Hareline Micro Polar Chenille
Thorax:	Black Hareline Micro Polar Chenille
Shellback:	Olive Mottled Oak Thin Skin

BRASS ASS BUZZER

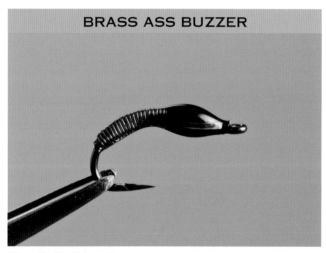

(Ian Colin James)

Hook:	#8-20 Tiemco 2457
Thread:	Black 8/0 Uni-Thread
Body:	Copper wire
Thorax:	Black 8/0 Uni-Thread
Cheeks:	Orange (#4067) Hedron Holographic Fly Fiber
Epoxy:	Devcon 5-Minute

EPOXY CZECH NYMPH

(Ian Colin James)

Hook:	#6-16 Tiemco 2457
Thread:	Brown 8/0 Uni-Thread
Rib:	Clear mono 5X nylon tippet
Body:	White Glo Yarn
Back:	Pheasant tail
Epoxy:	Devcon 5-Minute

TUNGSTEN RAINBOW WARRIOR

(Lance Egan)

Hook:	#12-22 Tiemco 2457
Bead:	Silver tungsten
Thread:	Red 70-denier UTC
Tail:	Ring-necked pheasant center tail fibers
Body:	UTC Pearl Tinsel (large)
Thorax:	Rainbow Sow-Scud Dubbing
Wing case:	UTC Pearl Tinsel (large)

TAILWATER SOW BUG

(Lance Egan)

Hook: #12-18 Tiemco 3769
Thread: Red 70-denier UTC
Tail: Medium pardo Coq de Leon
Rib: Silver wire (fine)
Body: Mix of half rainbow Sow-Scud and half natural dark hare's ear dubbing
Back: Sepia Prismacolor marker

TUNGSTEN TAILWATER SOW BUG

(Lance Egan)

Hook: #12-18 Tiemco 3769
Bead: Silver tungsten
Thread: Red 70-denier UTC
Tail: Medium pardo Coq de Leon
Rib: Silver wire (fine)
Body: Mix of half rainbow Sow-Scud and half natural dark hare's ear dubbing
Back: Sepia Prismacolor marker

IRON LOTUS (OLIVE)

(Lance Egan)

Hook: #12-20 Tiemco 3769
Bead: Gold tungsten
Thread: Olive 70- or 140-denier UTC
Tail: Medium pardo Coq de Leon
Body: Tying thread
Rib: White 6/0 Uni-Thread
Thorax: Arizona Synthetic Peacock Dubbing (natural peacock)
Wing case: Black UTC Flashback Tinsel

Note: Finish the fly with red 70-denier UTC thread, and then lacquer the body and rib (not the thorax) with Gudebrod rod finish.

EGAN'S FRENCHIE

(Lance Egan)

Hook: #12-18 Tiemco 3769
Bead: Gold tungsten
Thread: Olive 70-denier UTC
Tail: Medium pardo Coq de Leon
Rib: Copper wire (fine)
Body: Dun ring-necked pheasant center tail fibers
Hot spot: UV shrimp pink Ice Dub

Note: Finish the fly with red 70-denier UTC.

BARON

(Loren Williams)

Hook:	#10-18 Mustad C49S
Bead:	Gold tungsten
Weight:	Eight wraps .010-inch lead wire
Thread:	Brown 6/0 Danville
Tail:	Male wood-duck flank fibers
Abdomen:	Rusty brown turkey biot
Thorax:	Jan Siman Peacock Dubbing (Eye)

RED DEVIL

(Loren Williams)

Hook:	#16-18 Mustad C49S
Bead:	Gold tungsten
Weight:	Eight wraps .010-inch lead wire
Thread:	Fluorescent red 6/0 Danville
Tail:	Male wood-duck flank fibers
Abdomen:	Rusty brown turkey biot
Wing case:	Gold holographic tinsel
Thorax:	Fluorescent red 6/0 Danville

GD'S DARK AND DEEP SQUIRREL NYMPH

(George Daniel)

Hook:	#10-16 Knapek nymph
Weight:	Copper Tungsten Tear Drop
Thread:	Black 8/0 Uni-Thread
Tail:	Dark pardo Coq de Leon
Body:	Dark brown SLF Squirrel Dubbing
Rib:	Copper UTC Ultra Wire (small)
Wing case:	Black Thin Skin
Wings:	Natural partridge

GD'S PINK PANTHER

(George Daniel)

Hook:	#12-18 Tiemco 3769
Bead:	Black tungsten
Thread:	Black 8/0 Uni-Thread
Tail:	Black Coq de Leon
Rib:	Copper UTC Ultra Wire (small)
Hot spot:	Fluorescent pink Antron

VLADI WORM

(Vladi Trzebunia)

Hook: #2-12 Tiemco 8089
Weight: .020- to .035-inch tapered lead wire
Thread: Red 6/0 Uni-Thread
Body: Red latex
Rib: 3X nylon tippet

Note: Bend the hook to shape. Taper both ends of the lead wire with a pair of flat-nosed pliers, decreasing the tension as you move inward, so that the wire gradually tapers to be flattest at the ends. For the worm, only a ¹/₂-inch taper is needed at each end.

TURD STONE (GOLDEN)

Hook: #2-8 Daiichi 4660
Bead: Black tungsten slotted
Weight: .020- to .035-inch lead wire
Thread: Black 8/0 Uni-Thread
Body: SLF Kaufmann Golden Stone Dubbing
Legs: Barred orange/orange-black Sili Legs

PEEKING CADDIS

Hook: #10-14 Tiemco 5262
Bead: Black tungsten
Weight: .025- to .020-inch lead wire
Thread: Black 8/0 Uni-Thread
Tail: Chartreuse Sparkle Yarn (tip burned with flame)
Legs: Natural partridge
Rib: Copper UTC Ultra Wire (small)
Body: Hare's Ear Plus #7

WALT'S SULPHUR NYMPH

(Walt Young)

Hook: #14-16 Tiemco 3671
Weight: .025- to .020-inch lead wire
Thread: Camel 8/0 Uni-Thread
Tail: Natural partridge
Body: Cinamon caddis TCO East Coast Dubbing
Rib: Brown V-Rib (Midge)
Wing case: Black Thin Skin
Legs: Natural partridge

GD'S MICRO QUILL BODY NYMPH

(George Daniel)

Hook:	#14-18 Dohiku dry fly
Bead:	Gold tungsten
Thread:	Olive dun 8/0 Uni-Thread
Tail:	Dark pardo Coq de Leon
Body:	Hends Body Quill (#32)
Thorax:	Dark olive SLF Squirrel Dubbing

GD'S UV SOW BUG

(George Daniel)

Hook:	#12-16 Tiemco 2457
Weight:	.020- to .025-inch lead wire
Thread:	Tan 8/0 Uni-Thread
Body:	Scud gray Micro Polar Chenille
Shellback:	Loon UV Wader Repair

GD'S BLACK DEATH

(George Daniel)

Hook:	#12-16 Hanak jig
Bead:	Black tungsten
Thread:	Black 8/0 Uni-Thread
Tail:	Black Coq de Leon
Body:	Black SLF Squirrel Dubbing
Rib:	Red UTC Ultra Wire (small)
Hackle:	Black CDC

WILT'S GREEN DRAKE NYMPH

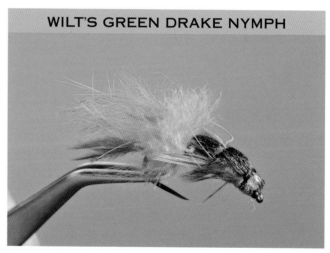

(Lance Wilt)

Hook:	#6-8 Knapek grub
Thread:	Yellow Roman Moser 10/0 Power Silk
Weight:	.015-inch lead wire
Tail:	Four to six ginger ostrich herls
Body:	Ginger or cream rabbit zonker marked with golden brown Prisma Marker
Gills:	Two natural gray CDC feathers (clipped)
Wing cases:	Dark brown Antron coated with Sally Hansen Hard as Nails
Head:	Brown Magic Shrimp Foil
Legs:	Tan speckled hen
Thorax:	Pale olive UTC Wee Wool
Eyes:	Black mono eyes (extra small)

BUBBLE PUPA

(tied by John Stoyanoff)

Hook:	#16 Mustad R70
Thread:	Dark brown 8/0 Uni-Thread
Body:	Gold Quick Descent Dubbing and tan Antron
Wing pads:	Dark tan hen hackle
Head:	Dark brown SLF Squirrel Dubbing

DRONE STONE

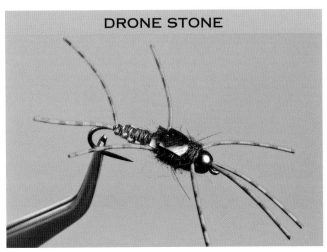

(Aaron Jasper)

Hook:	#6-10 Skalka streamer
Bead:	Matte black tungsten
Weight:	Twelve turns .020-inch lead wire
Thread:	Dark brown 140-denier UTC
Legs:	Brown/black Centipede Legs (medium)
Rib:	Copper UTC Ultra Wire (Brassie)
Body:	Weave of brown (898) and yellow (726) DMC embroidery floss
Thorax:	Dark brown SLF Squirrel Spiky Dubbing
Wing case:	Natural mottled Thin Skin

ANTOLOSKY'S STONE

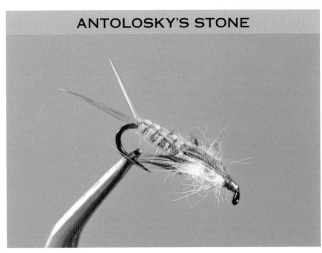

(Mark Antolosky)

Hook:	#6-10 Tiemco 5262
Weight:	.020-inch lead wire tied to each side and flattened
Thread:	Orange 8/0 Uni-Thread
Tail:	Tan goose biot
Body and thorax:	Bleached Australian opossum
Wing case:	Mottled turkey wing
Rib:	Gold UTC Ultra Wire (extra small)
Legs:	Ruffed grouse

TRAVIS MARCH BROWN NYMPH

(Will Travis)

Hook:	#10-16 Knapek Scud/Czech Nymph
Bead:	Copper tungsten
Thread:	Fire orange 8/0 Uni-Thread
Tail:	Pheasant tail fibers
Abdomen:	Pheasant tail fibers
Rib:	Copper UTC Ultra Wire (small)
Wing case:	Brown Thin Skin
Thorax:	SLF Kaufmann Brown Stone Dubbing
Collar:	Rusty brown Ice Dub

MOTTLED GOLDEN RUBBER LEG STONEFLY

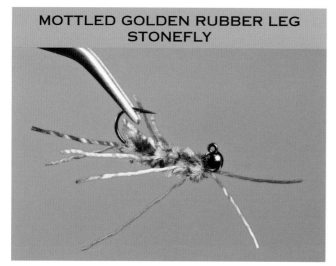

Hook:	#6-8 Daiichi 4660
Bead:	Black slotted tungsten
Thread:	Black 6/0 Uni-Thread
Body:	Brown/yellow Wapsi Variegated Chenille (medium)
Legs:	Amber Beartooth Super Floss

RED TAG PT

(Peter Scott)

Hook:	#12-16 Dohiku jig
Bead:	Copper tungsten
Thread:	Brown 6/0 Uni-Thread
Tail:	Medium pardo Coq de Leon
Body:	Pheasant tail fibers
Collar:	Brown TCO Super Select CDC
Tag:	Red SLF Hank dubbing

Note: This fly was inspired by a series of nymphs with fluorescent tags that our guide, Peter Scott, showed us on a January 2010 trip to New Zealand's North Island.

HARE'S EAR JIGGY

Hook:	#12-16 Dohiku jig
Bead:	Copper tungsten
Thread:	Black 8/0 Uni-Thread
Tail:	Hare's mask fibers
Rib:	Gold UTC Ultra Wire (extra small)
Body:	Natural hare's ear
Thorax:	Pink Sow-Scud Dubbing
Legs:	Natural brown TCO Super Select CDC

JARKKO'S CZECH NYMPH

(Jarkko Suominen)

Hook:	#8-14 Dohiku Gammarus
Bead:	Copper tungsten
Thread:	Black 8/0 Uni-Thread
Shellback:	Clear Thin Skin
Body:	Olive Antron dubbing
Hot spot:	Red Antron dubbing
Thorax:	Black SLF Squirrel Dubbing

JARKKO'S STONEFLY

(Jarkko Suominen)

Hook:	#6-8 Dohiku streamer
Bead:	Black tungsten
Thread:	Black 8/0 Uni-Thread
Tail:	Black hen fibers
Body:	Black peacock Ice Dub
Collar:	Red Antron dubbing
Legs:	Black round rubber (medium)

SAN JUAN WORM (RED)

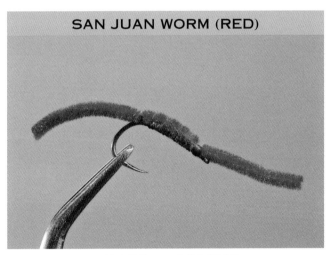

Hook:	#10-16 Tiemco 2499 SP-BL
Weight:	.020-inch lead wire
Thread:	Red 8/0 Uni-Thread
Body:	Red Ultra Chenille

TUNGSTEN TORPEDO (OLIVE)

(Kevin Compton)

Hook:	#12-18 Dohiku barbless nymph
Bead:	Gold tungsten
Thread:	Olive 12/0 Giorgio Benecchi
Tail:	Pardo Coq de Leon fibers
Rib:	Black flat synthetic ribbon and gold wire (extra fine)
Body:	Olive 12/0 Giorgio Benecchi thread
Thorax:	Peacock bronze Jan Siman Synthetic Peacock Dubbing

PEARL BRAIDBACK PT

(Kevin Compton)

Hook:	#12-16 Dohiku special nymph hook for beadheads
Bead:	Copper tungsten
Thread:	Sandy dun 12/0 Giorgio Benecchi
Tail:	Bronze mallard fibers
Rib:	Pearl Fly DK Synthetic Quill Body and copper wire (extra fine)
Body:	Pheasant tail fibers
Wing case:	UV purple Pearl Braidback
Thorax:	Natural pine squirrel guard hairs

JUJUBEE MIDGE (BROWN)

(Charlie Craven)

Hook:	#20 Tiemco 2488
Thread:	Off white 10/0 Giorgio Benecchi Ultrastrong
Abdomen:	Dark brown and white Super Hair
Thorax:	Camel 8/0 Uni-Thread
Wing case:	White Fluoro Fibre
Wing buds:	White Fluoro Fibre

ZEBRA TWO-TONE (BLACK/RED)

Hook:	#18 Tiemco 2487
Bead:	Copper tungsten
Thread:	Red and olive 8/0 Uni-Thread
Rib:	Copper UTC Ultra Wire (small)
Body:	Thread coated with head cement

MERCURY *BAETIS*

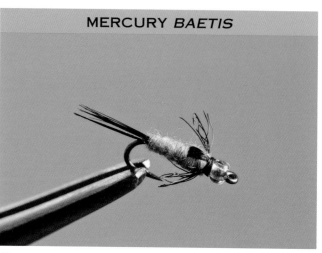

(Pat Dorsey)

Hook:	#18 Tiemco 101
Bead:	Silver-lined glass
Thread:	Black 8/0 Uni-Thread
Tail:	Black hackle fibers
Abdomen:	BWO Superfine Dubbing
Thorax:	BWO Superfine Dubbing
Wing case:	Black Z-Lon
Legs:	Black Z-Lon

BARR'S PURE MIDGE (FIRE RED)

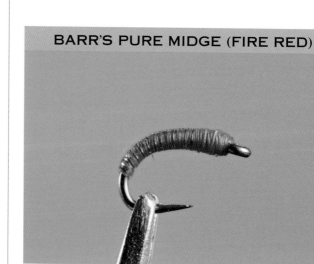

(John Barr)

Hook:	#18 Tiemco 2488H
Thread:	Red 70-denier UTC
Body:	Clear Pro Micro Tube coated with Sally Hansen Hard as Nails
Head:	Black 8/0 Uni-Thread

TOP SECRET MIDGE

(Pat Dorsey)

Hook:	#18 Tiemco 2488
Thread:	Brown 8/0 Uni-Thread
Abdomen:	Brown 6/0 Uni-Thread
Thorax:	Brown Superfine Dubbing
Rib:	White 6/0 Uni-Thread
Wing:	White poly yarn or Glamour Madera

SHRIMP

(Vladi Trzebunia)

Hook:	#6-12 Tiemco 2457
Bead:	Gold tungsten
Thread:	White 6/0 Uni-Thread
Body:	Shrimp and white Uni-Stretch
Rib:	Copper UTC Ultra Wire (small)
Collar:	Light hare's mask

CRANE

(Vladi Trzebunia)

Hook:	#6-12 Tiemco 2457
Bead:	Gold tungsten
Thread:	White 6/0 Uni-Thread
Body:	Light gray and white Uni-Stretch
Rib:	3X mono tippet
Collar:	Light hare's mask

JOSEF

(Vladi Trzebunia)

Hook:	#6-12 Tiemco 2457
Bead:	Gold tungsten
Thread:	Brown 6/0 Uni-Thread
Body:	Woven brown and pumpkin Uni-Stretch
Rib:	Copper UTC Ultra Wire (small)
Collar:	Light hare's mask

KRIVA

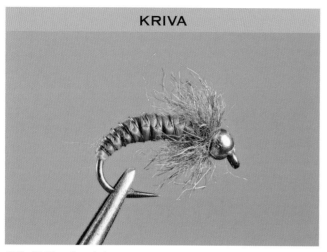

(Vladi Trzebunia)

Hook:	#6-12 Tiemco 2457
Bead:	Gold tungsten
Thread:	Olive 6/0 Uni-Thread
Body:	Woven olive and pumpkin Uni-Stretch
Rib:	Copper UTC Ultra Wire (small)
Collar:	Light hare's mask

VISTULA

(Vladi Trzebunia)

Hook:	#6-12 Tiemco 2575
Bead:	Gold tungsten
Thread:	Chartreuse 6/0 Uni-Thread
Body:	Green and chartreuse Uni-Stretch
Rib:	4X mono tippet
Collar:	Light hare's mask

COTTER'S SOFT-HACKLE JIGGY (NATURAL PHEASANT TAIL)

(Riley Cotter)

Hook:	#12-16 Tiemco 108 SP-BL or Dohiku 302
Bead:	Slotted tungsten
Thread:	Black 6/0 Uni-Thread
Tail:	Medium pardo Coq de Leon
Rib:	Lagartun Varnished Wire (fine)
Body:	Natural Pheasant Tail
Thorax:	Peacock bronze Jan Siman Synthetic Peacock Dubbing
Hackle:	Brown CDC

COTTER'S SOFT-HACKLE JIGGY (EL DIABLO)

(Riley Cotter)

Hook:	#12-16 Tiemco 108 SP-BL or Dohiku 302
Bead:	Slotted tungsten
Thread:	Black 6/0 Uni-Thread
Tail:	Medium pardo Coq de Leon
Rib:	Lagartun Varnished Wire (fine)
Thorax:	Peacock bronze Jan Siman Synthetic Peacock Dubbing
Hackle:	Dark dun CDC

BEARD OF ZEUS

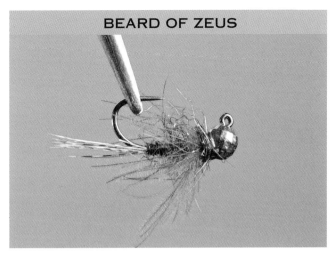

(Brett Bishop)

Hook:	#12-16 Tiemco 108 SP-BL or Dohiku 302
Bead:	Slotted tungsten
Thread:	Camel 6/0 Uni-Thread
Hot spot:	Fl. red SLF Hank
Tail:	Medium pardo Coq de Leon
Rib:	Copper UTC Ultra Wire (small)
Collar:	Gold Waspi Stonefly Lifecycle Dubbing
Hackle:	Brown CDC

ERICKSON'S SPANISH FLY (THE SPANIARD)

(Pete Erickson)

Hook:	#10-14 Tiemco 108 SP-BL or Dohiku 302
Bead:	Slotted tungsten
Thread:	Creme 6/0 Danville
Underbelly:	Gray natural squirrel SLF Davy Wotton
Body:	Natural Nymph Skin

ERICKSON'S BLUE STEEL

(Pete Erickson)

Hook:	#10-16 Tiemco 108 SP-BL or Dohiku 302
Bead:	Slotted tungsten
Thread:	Fire fl. orange or fl. red 70-denier UTC Thread
Body:	Dun UV Ice Dub
Thorax:	Pink UV Ice Dub

BALTZ'S CDC EMERGER

(Tom Baltz)

Hook:	#12-16 Tiemco 3761
Bead:	Tungsten
Thread:	Black 6/0 Uni-Thread
Tail:	Natural Wood Duck
Rib:	Copper Ultra Wire (small)
Body:	Natural Pheasant Tail
Wing:	Natural CDC
Collar:	Natural CDC

GD'S PURPLE CZECH

(George Daniel)

Hook:	#6-14 Tiemco 2499 SP-BL
Bead:	Fl. pink tungsten
Thread:	Black 6/0 Uni-Thread
Rib:	Black Ultra Wire (small)
Body:	Purple Ice Dub
Thorax:	Black Peacock Ice Dub
Shellback:	Gator Thin Skin

SPRING CREEK MIDGE

(John Stoyanoff)

Hook:	#18 Tiemco 2488
Bead:	15/0 glass
Thread:	Gray 8/0 Uni-Thread
Body:	Gray 8/0 Uni-Thread coated with superglue
Rib:	Copper UTC Ultra Wire (extra small)
Wing bud/post:	White Neer Hair
Collar:	Gray Sow-Scud Dubbing

SOFT-HACKLE (OLIVE)

Hook:	#12-18 Dohiku nymph
Thread:	Black 8/0 Uni-Thread
Body:	Olive Uni-Yarn
Hackle:	Brown partridge

ICE DUB SOFT-HACKLE

Hook:	#12-18 Dohiku nymph
Thread:	Black 8/0 Uni-Thread
Bead:	Black brass
Body:	Rust Ice Dub
Rib:	Gold UTC Ultra Wire (extra small)
Hackle:	Brown partridge

WET ANT

Hook: #12-18 Dohiku nymph
Thread: Black 3/0 Uni-Thread
Body: Black 3/0 Uni-Thread coated with Sally Hansen Hard as Nails
Legs: Black hen fibers

TRANSPARANT (BLACK AND RED)

Hook: #14 Tiemco 101
Thread: Black and red 3/0 Uni-Thread
Hackle: Black rooster
Body: Thread coated with epoxy

GREEN WEENIE

Hook: #12-14 Tiemco 5262
Thread: Chartreuse 6/0 Uni-Thread
Bead: Tungsten or brass
Body: Chartreuse Furry Foam

MAC ATTACK

(John Maciejczyk)

Hook: #4-8 Skalka streamer
Cone: Gold tungsten
Weight: .020-inch lead wire
Thread: Dark brown 6/0 Uni-Thread
Tail: Rusty brown marabou
Flash: Gold holographic Flashabou
Body: Root beer Pearl Chenille
Legs: Black rubber

GD'S INDICATOR FLY (POLY)

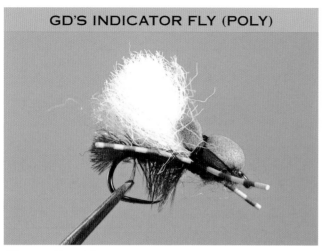

(George Daniel)

Hook:	#4-10 Tiemco 5262
Thread:	Dark brown 6/0 Uni-Thread
Tail:	Red Antron
Body:	Chestnut Antron dubbing
Hackle:	Coachman brown saddle
Wing:	White over tan poly
Head:	Tan foam (3 mm)
Legs:	Tan Centipede Legs (medium)

GD'S INDICATOR FLY (CDC)

(George Daniel)

Hook:	#10-14 Knapek dry fly
Thread:	Dark brown 8/0 Uni-Thread
Body:	Chestnut Antron dubbing
Wing:	Fluorescent pink over tan CDC
Hackle:	Coachman brown saddle

CRAVEN'S CHARLIE BOY HOPPER (OLIVE)

(Charlie Craven)

Hook:	#8 Tiemco 5212
Thread:	Olive 6/0 Uni-Thread
Body:	2 mm Olive Fly Foam
Wing:	Deer hair
Legs:	Olive round rubber (medium)

PARACHUTE MADAM X (ROYAL)

(Doug Swisher)

Hook:	#8 Tiemco 5212
Thread:	Black 6/0 Uni-Thread
Tail:	Elk
Body:	Peacock herl and red floss
Post:	White poly yarn
Hackle:	Brown rooster
Legs:	Brown round rubber (medium)

Fishing Pocketwater, Riffles and Runs, and Pools

7

O nce while pointing out a fishing hot spot to me, Russ Madden, an innovative fly tier and a master of reading the streams, referred to it as "prime real estate." And just as with real estate, when fishing, you have to think location, location, location—not only in order to find where the fish are, but also to put your fly in front of them with an accurate cast and good drift.

The most basic needs of trout are food and protection, and they will hold where food is present, hide from predators, and try to accomplish both simultaneously when possible. Because feeding trout are most likely to take our flies, we can make the best use of our time and increase our odds of success by fishing in locations where trout are feeding. In theory, this may sound ridiculously simple, but it's not. A feeding trout will hold

A slow pocket behind a boulder is great spot to drop a lightweight nymph. Because surface currents are slowed, a lightly weighted nymph will drop quickly to the bottom. In such locations, I usually fish a fly with only a brass bead or an unweighted nymph with a single size 4 to 6 split shot.
JAY NICHOLS

175

near current—its meal ticket. Current is the conveyor belt that brings the food to the trout, and knowing where the greatest food concentrations are located will help you find the greatest trout densities. Humans know that a family diner is a better feeding spot than a gas station minimarket, which sells food but not the type that can sustain a healthy person for long. Similarly, although food is available to the trout just about everywhere within the stream, some areas offer more feeding opportunities than others, and these are the areas you should target. You need to find the trout's local diner.

TROUT LIES

Anglers refer to different spots where fish hold as "lies." Trout lies fall into three basic categories: feeding, sheltering, and prime lies.

Feeding Lies

Feeding lies are locations that offer foraging opportunities but typically little protection from predators in the form of overhead cover. Shallow water and shallow riffles are great examples of feeding lies. Riffles are the breeding grounds for many stream invertebrates and offer abundant food to the trout. However, trout are exposed to predators when holding in shallow water, especially during daylight hours, when they are easy targets for herons and eagles. Therefore, trout need to strategically pick times to feed when they are afforded the greatest amount of protection and will move into these feeding lies when certain variables such as low light or off-color water permit them to feed with more security. Trout holding in feeding lies are often more vulnerable, and therefore wary, but they are preoccupied with eating and that improves your chances of catching them.

Josh Day holds a healthy brown that he caught on the West Branch of the Delaware River while fishing a sunken terrestrial along a shaded bank in the late morning. The trout was holding in just 6 inches of water but felt protected by the distinct shade line. We caught several more fish before the sun moved directly overhead, eliminating the shade line. GEORGE DANIEL

Sheltering Lies

Trout have to balance their needs for shelter and food. Sometimes they are more focused on hiding from predators than feeding, and sheltering lies provide trout with more defensive features than foraging opportunities.

When water temperatures exceed 70 degrees, trout will seek the deepest lie in a river. Less light is able to penetrate the deeper water, and as a result, cooler temperatures are found at these depths. A deep sheltering lie provides trout with a comfort zone during the daylight hours, and the fish may not move out of this spot until later in the evening, when water temperatures drop as a result of cooler air temperatures. Eventually these fish will move into the riffles, banks, or tailouts when conditions are right. This is especially true of large trout, which are known for their nocturnal feeding habits, and trying to catch big fish when they are holding in their daytime sheltering lies can be a waste of time.

Trout in sheltering lies are often the most difficult to catch, because they are not always in a feeding mode. When fishing a sheltering lie, I frequently use a wild pattern with some motion added to the fly in the form of rubber legs or a CDC collar to provoke a strike. Just like humans, sometimes trout need a little encouragement.

A deep sheltering lie does occasionally give up trout, but I prefer to spend most of my time fishing through feeding and prime lies. However, at times trout holding in sheltering lies aggressively seek food such as in low-light conditions or during a heavy hatch. The deepest part of a pool is usually a sheltering lie, and it does pay to work this area while fishing. Nevertheless, it's preferable to spend more time in the tailout, drop-offs, and run area of a pool, as these are prime and feeding lies during typical fishing conditions. The goal is to spend the majority of your time fishing the most productive river sections.

Prime Lies

The prime lies provide both shelter and feeding opportunities simultaneously, and the strongest and biggest trout end up here. Experienced anglers coming across such an area think to themselves, "There's got to be a big one in there." Unfortunately for the fly fisher, a prime lie is sometimes the most difficult spot to properly place a fly. As an example, a fallen tree may lie horizontally in a great-looking run. The fallen tree provides the fish with overhead cover from predators, but it also provides the angler with an unwanted obstacle to presenting the fly. A downstream approach with a suspension device is a great tool in such a situation. Sometimes you catch a fish, and other times you lose a fly. But as Joe Humphreys says, "Don't be afraid to cast

During a heavy rain, trout come out from their sheltering lies and feed in relatively shallow water. Pictured is Matt Rose fishing a shallow riffle in heavy rain during the 2009 World Youth Fly Fishing Championships in the Czech Republic. Matt ended up with more than a dozen fish, all caught in water less than 10 inches deep. GEORGE DANIEL

into the most inaccessible areas. The worst thing that can happen is that you lose a fly. And that isn't life-threatening."

Undercut banks with the current pulling toward the bank are also favorite prime lies. Not only does the undercut bank provide cover, but the current also brings the food right to the trout. Wherever you find an undercut bank with current, there's a good chance a big fish is there. A large rubberleg stonefly tied on a jig hook is one of my favorite nymphs when attempting to pull a big fish from its cover. The jig action on this stonefly is seductive.

Prime lies can also occur in the runs, the transitions from riffles to pools. Runs provide sufficient depth to comfort the trout while the currents continue to serve as food lanes. If I had to pick one water type to fish year-round, a good run would be my first choice. The currents under the runs are often slow enough to hold fish during the winter months, when a trout's metabolism is low, but there's still enough flow to create distinct feeding channels on a year-round basis. This type of prime lie is a fish magnet.

This hefty brown fell to a jig-style stonefly at the head of a fast run. Brian Wilt carries the same stonefly pattern in three different weights that vary by bead-head size. It took Brian two attempts before he figured out the correct amount of weight to effectively cover the heavy run. GEORGE DANIEL

FISHING THE POCKETWATER

Pocketwater is common in higher-gradient stream sections, where fast, turbid water is broken up by random boulders, such as many of the Rocky Mountain, Sierra, and southern Appalachian streams. Fishing pocketwater offers several advantages. First, trout are less prone to spook in this type of broken water, which allows you to fish under the rod tip. The broken water helps conceal your presence and the crashing sound of water around pockets muffles other noise. Because you can get so close, 10 to 15 feet of leader, along with a 10-foot rod, is all you should need. Second, identifying where trout hold in pocketwater is usually straightforward, because in-stream obstructions create well-defined seams. It's usually easier and quicker to find the fish in pocketwater or riffle water than in large flats that need to be methodically covered, so I target these areas when I have limited time to fish, such as when squeezing in a little fishing before work.

In my experience, however, pocketwater offers a hit-or-miss angling experience, with some good fishing days and others bad. For example, I catch fewer fish in pocketwater after a quick drop in water temperature. This can slow any trout fishing to standstill, but I feel it has a greater effect in pocketwater. Trout holding in this water are like high-performance athletes who need every ounce of awareness and energy to perform. A sudden temperature drop can cause a level of discomfort such that the trout do not have enough motivation to weave in and out of the strong currents to feed. This may not be the case everywhere, but this has been my experience on many central Pennsylvania limestone streams. On the other hand, highly oxygenated water in late summer may provide your best chance of finding an actively feeding fish, since pocketwater can produce more dissolved oxygen than other water types during warm-water conditions.

Pocketwater is technical not so much because the trout are hard to catch—in fact, they often take flies more aggressively—but because the varying speed, depth, and direction of the current make it more difficult to stay in touch with the nymph. For example, a midstream boulder that creates a pocket may have two distinct currents flowing at different speeds on either side. As a result, you will have to adjust the speed at which you lead your nymphs as you proceed to work the pocket.

When fishing pocketwater or any other water type with tricky currents, make more than two casts in an area. It may take several efforts to obtain a drift where the fly moves naturally in the water column while you're in control of it. Ozzie Ozefovich's videos demonstrate that "changing cross currents" sometimes occur without any warning from the view above the water's surface. This means that you may not get a good drift if you present only once or twice to a specific area. How many times have you hooked a fish while making your "last cast," especially in area you believe is superfishy, even though you have already thoroughly presented your flies to it? It may be that it took a number of casts to get a natural drift.

My good friend Lance Egan is stubborn in this regard, and this is what makes him such an exceptional fly angler. Rarely will Lance move from an area until he catches a fish. Before moving on to the next run, he will exhaust all possibilities, changing patterns, weights, tippet lengths, and so on until he figures out a solution. Too often, anglers just give up on a piece of water and don't take the time to work on problem solving. Sticking with it and making several casts to an area before moving is almost certain to increase your angling success.

You can often get close to trout in pocketwater, but conditions sometimes prohibit that. Some pocketwater is just too powerful. To overcome this, you need a long rod and leader to deliver a 30-foot controlled drift in rapid water. For example, on the Slide Inn section of the Madison River in Montana, taking

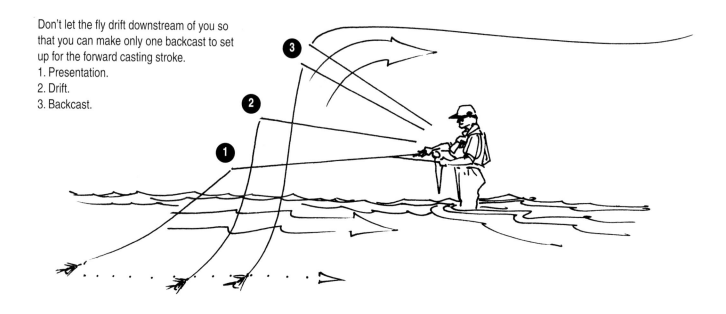

Don't let the fly drift downstream of you so that you can make only one backcast to set up for the forward casting stroke.
1. Presentation.
2. Drift.
3. Backcast.

Currents can be fast and furious in some sections of pocketwater. Fast, mixed currents require that your line and leader placement be spot on, and in these conditions, I would rather have drag than slack. Such currents at times can pull your rig downstream faster than you expect. One way to ensure that no slack occurs is to move your lead nymphs at approximately the same speed as the current. This type of lead may not be a true dead drift, but at least you will be able to register a take. I also like to use a single nymph or at least concentrate the weight of the nymphing rig into a smaller area to reduce drag.

When trying to catch fish in pocketwater, you can't have an idle mind. Your brain has to be as active as the water you are fishing. In pocketwater, your biggest challenge is getting into position to make the cast. Here you must do everything you can to keep as much line and leader off the water as possible, to ensure that fewer nagging currents interrupt the drift. The more drag-free your drift, the quicker the rig will reach the bottom. JAY NICHOLS

Above: Here I'm bobbing a suspender dry on the water while fishing the South Platte River during the 2006 US Nationals. Though the dry didn't catch many fish, the bobbing tactic was critical in gaining the trout's attention before it ate the nymph. In pocketwater, I like to use a dry fly instead of another type of suspender whenever possible, since fish in the fast currents are often eager to hit a dry. AMIDEA DANIEL

Left: Where you find a midstream boulder residing in a strong current, the most visible holding area is the pocket directly behind the boulder. However, a pocket often forms directly in front of the boulder as well, and this can be one of the most successful areas to fish. Basically, the boulder obstructs the current and slows it down, creating just enough of a cushion to hold a fish. Anglers rarely fish this upstream pocket, since it's not as easily distinguishable and often appears to be moving too fast for holding water. Nevertheless, this upstream pocket is usually just as fishy as its downstream counterpart and should always be in your crosshairs. You can catch more fish by targeting areas that others don't. GEORGE DANIEL

one step off the bank during runoff is suicide, but pocketwater within this reach still offers decent fishing possibilities if you can reach it with a long rod and leader.

Whether tight-lining or fishing a suspension rig, eliminate any unnecessary drag by keeping as much line and leader off the water as possible. Even the slightest amount of leader on the water creates surface drag and can hinder a natural drift, and this is why you should strive to keep all the leader off the water except for the section that's anchored in the water by the nymphing rig.

Rigs and Tactics for Pocketwater

Primary targets in pocketwater include the slack water behind and in front of boulders. However, these areas are often small so that they dictate short drifts, and short drifts in fast water require weight or modifying your cast. Before adding more weight, which takes time, try adjusting the angle of your nymphing cast (see the section on the tuck cast on page 53) and stopping your rod tip as high as possible, perhaps even using the downer-and-upper variation. It takes only a few seconds to adjust the casting angle, saving you time over reaching

When fishing in varying current speeds, I like a single, heavily weighted fly tied with a tungsten bead on a jig hook. Not only does the weight anchor the fly and create a tight connection, but the jig hook snags the bottom less often because it rides hook point up. Today several European companies produce jig-style nymph hooks in size 12 to 16.
JAY NICHOLS

into the fly box and tying on a new fly or adding split shot. And at times, this may be the only adjustment you need to get a deep drift. The second solution is to try to sink your fly deeper by making a longer cast, which still doesn't require changing the fly or weight. The longer the drift, the more time the nymph has to settle to the bottom. However, in pocketwater, this is not always an option because the drifts are so short. A steep tuck combined with a longer drift is another possibility.

After you have exhausted all the casting possibilities, if you still are having no success, it's time to change to a pattern that sinks faster—one that is heavier, has a thinner profile, or both. First try switching from a brass- to a tungsten-beaded fly in the same size. Tungsten weighs twice as much as brass, and often this change is all you need to get a deeper drift. In pocketwater, I believe a little extra flash helps get the trout's attention, and seldom do I fish it without a gold, silver, copper, or other brightly colored bead on my fly.

In preparation for the 2007 World Championships in Finland, our team was fishing dual dry flies for grayling, and I decided to cast to a run that appeared to have a uniform current pulling through it. I placed both dry flies in the same seam, 40 inches apart. The flies drifted naturally for about two seconds and then quickly pulled away from each other as if they were moving in separate currents. Drag set in, creating an unnatural presentation. I never would have guessed that a uniform-looking seam could have that many microcurrents. That experience got me thinking about subsurface drag with multiple currents and how a varied weighting system could decrease drag with nymphs.

Eventually I decided that the best way to deal with water types that have extreme variance in speeds is to concentrate the weight. There are several ways to do this. One is to use a heavily weighted fly, which I think of as a "sacrificial pattern," on the point as an anchor, and drop the unweighted rig off a tag

Weight that is spread throughout the tippet does not sink as fast as weight that is concentrated into a smaller area. A larger surface creates more drag and does not allow the flies to drop as quickly.

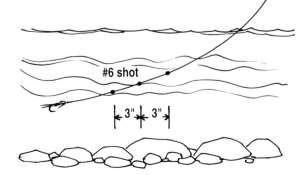

Concentrated weight sinks faster due to a smaller surface area, which creates less drag.

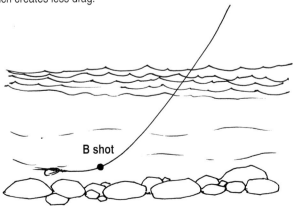

about 20 inches above. If drag sets in and pulls the nymph, the anchor fly acts like a pivot leg does for a basketball player, keeping your presentation tight and limiting the amount of drag as both flies drift in the same direction, not different directions as they would if you were using a system with two nymphs of equal weight. In that case, with no anchor to keep the rig tight, flies of equal weight could be pulled in two opposite directions, creating drag. I like to use this anchor fly tactic, for example, when fishing in the canyon section of the Thompson River in Colorado, where several areas have a high gradient with random boulders naturally scattered about. It's almost impossible to avoid having microdrag set in when fishing multiple-fly rigs because of the high variance in current speeds, and in this situation, the rig with the anchor fly works well.

In extreme pocketwater, I may even fish with just a single nymph to reduce drag. Similar to having shot spread out along your tippet, multiple flies create extra drag and can slow the descent of your rig. To really get a sense of this, tie on two dry flies 20 inches apart, and place a cast into a pocket with multiple-speed currents. The flies will be pulled in opposite directions. Now think about that same kind of drag happening with your nymphs underwater and how that will prevent them from sinking quickly to the bottom. This is why I often prefer to fish with a single weighted nymph in pocketwater. With only one

nymph, you avoid the potential for additional drag from another fly being pulled in a different direction by a nagging current. If you choose to fish multiple flies in pocketwater, don't use two of the same weight. Instead, use an anchor fly with an unweighted or lightly weighted nymph. Tying the flies closer together, about 6 to 10 inches apart, helps center the weight on the leader. Because the drifts are short in pocketwater, this concentration of weight is critical to reduce surface drag and allow the nymphing rig to drop more quickly to the bottom. Sometimes the drift length is less than 5 feet, so you want your flies to drop within the first foot of drift, which still allows you to effectively cover nearly 4 feet.

When you do use split shot in pocketwater, which is often necessary when fishing small flies that can't accommodate lots of weight without ruining their proportions, you can help your rig sink faster by concentrating the weight rather than spreading out the shot as some recommend. Think about diving off a bridge to reach the bottom of a deep pool. If you enter the water hands first with a straight torso, you will reach the bottom more quickly than if you perform a belly flop. When using split shot along with a lightly weighted nymph, place the shot 5 to 6 inches away from the point fly, as this will prevent slack from occurring between the two.

During nonhatch periods, when insects are less active, I prefer to tie off the bend rather than off a dropper. Tying off the bend results in fewer tangles, and though droppers provide more natural movement during the drift, this is not as necessary at times of reduced bug activity. I also use this method when I want to fish my nymphs close to one another. For example, I keep my nymphs within 10 inches of each other when fishing pocketwater in an effort to concentrate the weight into a smaller area, which allows the nymphs to drop through the water column more quickly.

#14 tungsten nymph

8–12" 3-5X fluorocarbon

clinch knot

tippet

#6 tungsten stonefly

Though droppers are prone to tangles, they give flies additional movement and can be effective during insect emergences. For example, during the salmonfly hatch on Montana's Madison River, many of these robust creatures begin migrating to streambanks, rocking back and forth through the current. Droppers allow more interplay between the current and the nymphs, letting the nymphs move more naturally through the water. Dropper length should be 4 to 7 inches, as this provides wiggle room for the nymphs, permitting them to move more freely, and allows you to make several fly changes before having to tie another dropper. If you decide to fish two lightly weighted flies, place split shot at the halfway point between them to pull the entire rig down to the stream bottom. If fast currents hold the flies near the surface, change to a heavier fly or split shot. Remember, the closer the shot is to the fly, the deeper the fly will drift.

unweighted or lightweight flies with shot

heavyweight flies without shot

Josh Stephens working a single nymph in a heavy pocket on the Simo River in Finland. Fishing multiple flies around multiple-speed currents increases the risk of drag and slows the drop rate. Another tip to get your fly down is to use a tippet with as small a diameter as possible. It's amazing how much faster a 5X tippet will cut through the current than a 4X tippet. Very seldom do I go below 5X in fast pocketwater.

ANTHONY NARANJA

Fishing a single nymph in pocketwater reduces the chances of subsurface drag. A two-fly rig increases the chances of excessive drag in short pockets.

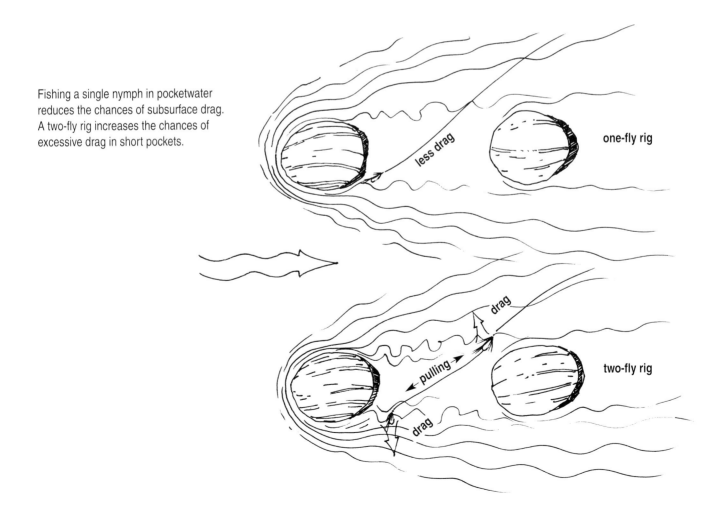

FISHING THE RIFFLES AND RUNS

Riffles and runs harbor an overwhelming majority of a stream's bug life. The shallow nature of the riffles permits sunlight to penetrate to the stream bottom, enabling aquatic vegetation to grow here. Soon many aquatic creatures migrate to these vegetated, oxygenated areas to thrive and build populations. These creatures include mayflies, caddis, stoneflies, midges, sow bugs, freshwater shrimp, and many others that provide a steady diet to the trout. Some of the densest bug life can be found in the riffle sections, creating some of the best foraging opportunities for trout. And trout spend lots of time feeding in riffles. If you find a stable food source, you'll find the trout. The riffles are the local diner that I mentioned earlier.

In turn, the riffles and runs provide you with some of the best angling opportunities. The broken water is a boon to anglers, as it allows us to get close to our targets and forgives the light splash of nymphs or small suspension devices. Yet riffles are mostly overlooked by anglers, perhaps because it's more difficult to wade in the fast water and to cast accurately so that the line, leader, and flies all land in the same seam.

During the summer months, when the water temperatures rise, riffles and runs stay cooler and thus can offer greater oxygen concentrations than pools and flats. The hot summer sun doesn't have as much time to warm the moving water found in riffle sections as it does in slower and shallower areas. At this time of year, a riffle and run section is almost a sure bet to find trout, as the fish need the colder water for its higher dissolved oxygen content. However, fish become very vulnerable in water temperatures over 70 degrees, and riffles provide refuge for the trout under these conditions. Though they are likely to eat your fly, hooking and playing them in this situation can spell immediate death for the fish. Please avoid these areas when trout are holding there for refuge and not food—do not take advantage of their vulnerability.

The intersections of riffles and runs provide trout with all of the above advantages along with water depth, which gives them overhead protection and a sense of added security. The shallow section of a riffle produces best on low-light, overcast days and during hatches. In sunny condition, however, trout are not as likely to actively feed in shallow riffles and will drop back into the depths of the run for protection and feeding.

A riffle is the ultimate conveyor belt, providing nonstop foraging opportunities to the trout, and trout holding in riffles are often feeding trout. During the regular spring and summer seasons, a riffle or run would be my first choice for one of my nymphing students to fish, because trout here are probably feeding, and a feeding trout is far more likely to eat an imitation nymph than a nonfeeding trout. Also, trout in these moving waters don't have as much time to decide whether to eat the imitation. The takes are more sudden and easily recognizable than in pools, where trout have far more time to examine your fly.

Once you've learned how to fish riffles and runs, you will have many more opportunities on the water. You'll also find your fishing areas to be less crowded, as many anglers pass up the opportunity to fish prime riffles because they don't know how to fish them or don't want to learn.

Runs are the transitions between riffles and pools. They often occur where the gradient of the stream starts to level out and water begins to slow down. Identifiable surface currents in the form of visible seams are still recognizable in the runs before flattening out into the pool section. If I were a trout, runs would be my number-one choice as a year-round residence. At the beginning of a run, there is typically a drop-off where the current on the stream bottom is almost nonexistent, and the trout can leisurely hold in position here while looking overhead for any food item being pulled downstream by the stronger current above.

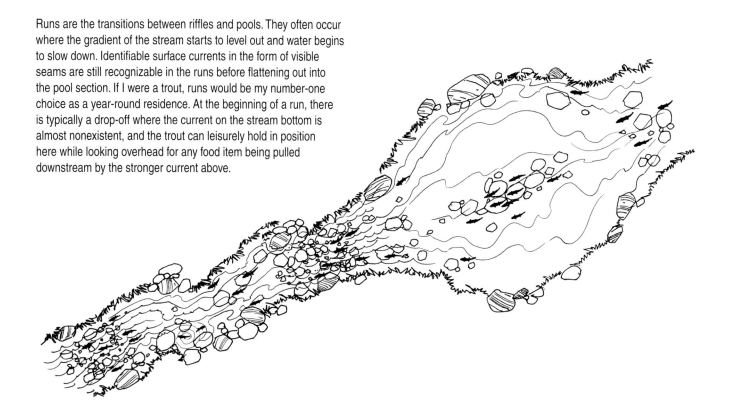

Left: Brian Keen reaches out over nagging currents with a 10-foot rod to get a natural drift in a fast run. A longer rod permits you to wade in safer water conditions but still allows for good line and leader control from a distance. GEORGE DANIEL

Below: Big trout leave their sheltering lies in low-light conditions to feed in riffled waters. This healthy brown trout moved up into a shallow riffle to feed during a heavily overcast day in central Pennsylvania. LANCE WILT

Left: Riffles are prime feeding grounds for trout, especially when it's overcast. In this photo, Brett Bishop holds a healthy New Zealand brown trout that he caught in a shallow riffle while quickly wading up to a deep run. Never hesitate to wet a line in a shallow riffle at any time. GEORGE DANIEL

Rigs and Tactics for Riffles and Runs

Shallow riffles have more uniform current speed than pocketwater. Because the speed at the surface is similar to that at the bottom, very little guesswork is involved in determining how fast to lead your flies. These uniform currents also create less drag on your flies, which means that you can use less weight to get to the bottom and that both tight-line and suspension nymphing are equally effective.

A good drift in a fast pocket may last only two or three seconds, which is why I recommend using heavier rigs while fishing pocketwater. The longer drift associated with riffles and runs, on the other hand, allows you to use a lighter-weight rig, which will hang up less and afford longer, more productive drifts. The key to using lightweight nymphing rigs is finding a drift long enough to enable the rig to slowly drop to the stream bottom and remain in the killing zone for a sufficient amount of time before reaching the end of the drift.

Trout are opportunistic and often feed on the surface, especially in riffles and runs, where they don't have to expend too much energy moving from the stream bottom to the surface. This is very true during the hatch seasons, which, for mayflies, can begin as early as mid-February and continue through the fall. While fishing riffles and runs during the hatches, I almost exclusively use a dry fly as a suspension device. I do my best to try to match the dry fly with the current hatches in order to take more fish. For example, a buoyant yellow Wulff used during the Eastern Green Drake hatch not only will suspend a heavy Green Drake Nymph, but also is likely to fool several

When fishing riffles and runs, use as long of a rod as you can get away with. Here Brian Wilt fishes an 11-foot, 5-weight rod on a medium-size stream with overhanging vegetation. GEORGE DANIEL

Anthony Naranja landing a trout in front of a nesting pair of eagles on a small Colorado spring creek. *Baetis* nymphs were active, and an induced lift with a #18 Iron Lotus was just the ticket. GEORGE DANIEL

surface feeders. A dry fly that matches the hatch looks more natural to the trout and increases your chances of taking a fish on the surface. I switch to a traditional suspender later in the winter months, when surface feeding becomes more limited due to the colder weather and ice begins sinking my dry fly. Also at this time, trout start moving into the slower reaches of the streams, where you may need additional weight.

Riffles and runs are often the starting points for various hatches, and trout hold and lift in the column, eating nymphs that are dead-drifting and emerging. You can imitate this ascending movement in at least two ways. First, stop the rod tip at the end of the drift but permit the nymphs to drift downstream. Eventually drag creates enough tension to force the flies toward the surface, imitating emerging insects. This is a good strategy when you are searching for trout.

Second, if you know exactly where the trout are holding, you can use an induced lift. When looking upstream, you may see trout breaking the surface while taking emerging insects just under the surface. Make the same kind of cast you use for a dead-drift presentation, and allow the flies to settle to the bottom. However, instead of allowing the flies to crawl on the bottom for the entire drift, quickly elevate the rod tip fast enough to pull them toward the surface. The sudden movement of the flies drifting toward the surface can trigger a response from the

When you know exactly where the trout are holding, try an induced lift. After the cast, instead of allowing the flies to crawl on the bottom for the entire drift, quickly elevate the rod tip fast enough to pull them toward the surface. This can sometimes trigger fish to take. Move the rod tip about one and a half times faster than is necessary just to maintain line control. Experiment with different speeds based on the insects' movements or the trout's reactions to them.

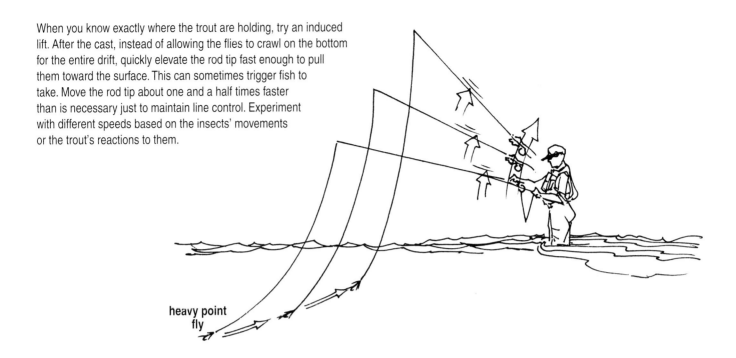

Sometimes it pays to fish at three levels, especially when trout are eating at multiple levels or when you are uncertain about the level at which they are feeding. On a stream like my home waters of Penns Creek, which is a bug factory where multiple hatches sometimes occur simultaneously, covering all three levels can be an effective tool. I often place the heaviest fly in the point position, on the end of the leader, as an anchor fly to keep the entire rig tight. A fly tied on a jig hook makes a good anchor, as it will hang up less on the bottom.

fish. This is what Frank Sawyer discovered many years ago while fishing the English chalkstreams. Move the rod tip at least one and a half times the speed necessary just to maintain line control. Some insects are faster than others when ascending to the surface to hatch, and you may need to vary the speed at which you lift the rod tip depending on the current hatch.

When fishing riffles and runs, make multiple casts for each drift, especially in bug-rich environments. One of my favorite streams is a little spring creek near my home, where even small sections are home to hordes of cress bugs and freshwater shrimp. I have snorkeled some of these reaches and was amazed to see the incredible numbers of drifting insects near the bottom. There simply are too many insects moving through for a single trout to notice them all. As a result, it may take multiple casts before a trout finds your nymph among all the naturals.

FISHING THE POOLS

Pools often form where the streambed's gradient levels outs and slows the water. A slow body of deep water soon appears and has a tendency to widen out. This deep-water environment offers trout the best of all worlds. Trout seek pools at all times of the year, and therefore pools provide angling opportunities 365 days a year. The deepest sections of the river serve as sheltering lies, where trout hold during the warmest and coldest times of the year, more to rest than to feed. In summer, these depths are not warmed as much by the sun as the riffles and flats, and they provide a cold refuge. In winter, the trout's metabolism slows in the colder weather, leading the fish to seek slower currents where they expend less energy.

Drop-offs and edges often serve as prime lies where both food and shelter are located together. Drop-offs are the transition areas between shallow water where insects live and deep water where trout hold. To avoid exposing themselves to predators, trout take up positions right off the edges in the protection of the deeper water. Trout here feed in a more comfortable manner and are less likely to be spooked by poor casts than fish feeding in shallow riffles.

If water temperatures are greater than 70 degrees, I will not even wet a line. Trout do not need the additional stress of being hooked and played by an angler. However, pools are one of my primary targets in the summer months when water temperatures are less than 70 degrees, especially during periods of bright sun when fish—especially light-sensitive browns—find cover in the depth of the water.

I also prefer to target pools during the coldest weather. Trout are cold-blooded creatures, and their metabolism slows down as water temperatures drop. As a result, they become almost lethargic and are less likely to feed in heavy current, where they have to expend additional energy to hold close to the conveyor belt. The velocity in a riffle or run may force the trout to expend too much energy, making them likely to drop back into the pools. However, this is a general concept and not always the rule, and I've had great success nymphing riffles in the winter for trout, but the best spots are most often the slower-moving pools. As an example, the few times I have spent on the Roaring Fork have been in the winter months, and the best bet to find fish was to find the pools. This tends to hold true on most trout streams and for most trout species.

The colder the water, the slower the trout's metabolism and the slower the current the fish seek. Not only do they seek the slowest water, but they also are less likely to move up and down the water column chasing food. Instead, they will hold and feed at a certain level, and it's your job to adjust the rig until you find that level. For this reason, I believe that making adjustments to your pool nymphing rig is more critical than with a rig for a riffle or pocketwater. I spend more time adjusting my nymphing rig for pools than for any other water type. There's no question that you can find some of the best fish in pools, and there appears to be a correlation between size and eagerness.

Trout that reach a certain length are known to forage more on other baitfish, and many of these large fish seek the pools for

Trout are attracted to foam, as this provides a sense of overhead protection. Find foam in a back eddy and you will find trout. GEORGE DANIEL

Unlike pocketwater, riffles, and runs, which all have distinct surface currents that provide clues as to where trout are likely to hold, pools can seem a bit intimidating to many beginning nymph fishers, especially when no rising trout are visible on the featureless flat water. Fishing a pool requires a bit more detective work. Drop-offs and edges often serve as prime lies where both food and shelter are located together. Drop-offs are the transition areas between shallow water where bugs thrive and deep water where trout can intercept them.

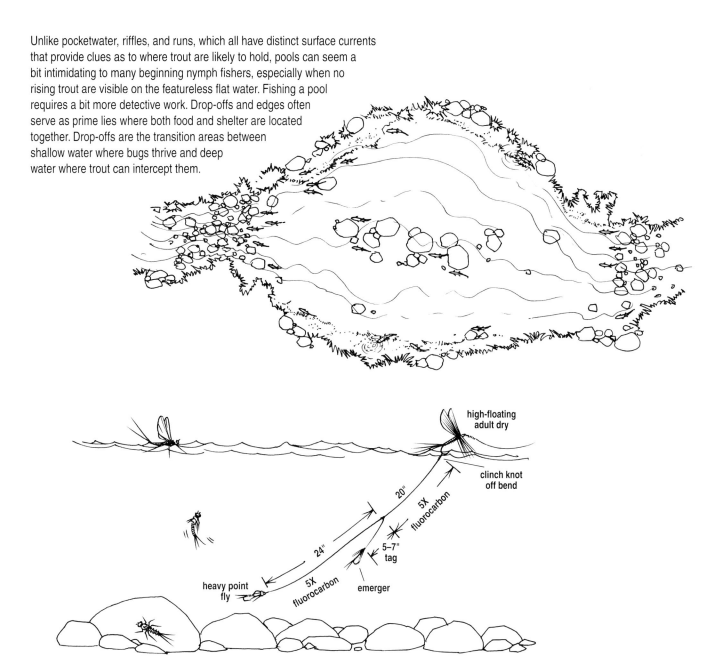

Fish all possible feeding levels, imitating the adult, emerger, and nymph, during a hatch or whenever you are unsure about the exact feeding levels of the trout. Trout not only key on a specific insect, but also feed at a certain level in the water column based on conditions. There's a short period during the Eastern Green Drake hatch when I have witnessed trout ascending 10 feet up the water column to inhale both nymphs and adults. It's one of the few times when the larger, well-educated trout feed like juveniles—that is, without much hesitation. A three-fly rig with a weighted Green Drake Nymph on the point and two soft-hackle emergers on the droppers works perfectly (but check the local regulations before using such a rig, as they are not legal in some areas). Though dead-drifting the rig can be fruitful at times, most takes come at the end of the drift when the flies begin to swing upward. The Green Drake Nymph is a strong swimmer, and trout are conditioned to seeing this movement.

cover. However, my good friends Chuck Farneth and John Wilson, who fish for monster trout in the famed Arkansas waters, both catch exceptionally large fish with smaller nymphs in pools. Their rationale is based on the theory of snacking. They compare large trout to human adults. Most humans eat three square meals a day but often snack on junk between meals.

Similarly, large trout may forage on other fish for their main meals, but they snack on smaller food items throughout the day. Also, when snacking between meals, larger trout in pools are less likely to chase their food items. Instead, their snacks must come directly to them.

Above: A rig that is too lightweight will not drop directly under the suspender in slow water. It's up to you to determine how much weight to use in the rig. Catching on the bottom 20 percent of the time is a good start. If you are not catching on the bottom 20 percent of the time, you need to add weight. CHRIS DANIEL

Right: Lance Wilt demonstrates that drifting a nymph beside a submerged log can provide a nice reward. Though anglers risk losing several flies attempting such tactics, I'm willing to lose several dozen flies for a fish of this quality. GEORGE DANIEL

Rigs and Tactics for Pools

Pools often require long drifts with a suspender, so I use my standard suspension leader and adjust the tippet length based on the current speed and depth of the pool. I usually use 5X tippet. In slow water, which allows time for the nymphs to drop at almost a 90-degree angle below the suspender, I use a tippet that is slightly shorter than the distance from the surface to the stream bottom. This keeps my nymphs off the bottom and provides a bottom roll. In medium-speed currents, I generally change the tippet length to one and a half times the depth and adjust the weight based on how frequently the fly hangs up on bottom.

I use a suspension system when fishing an unknown pool or when I don't know where trout are holding because I can cover large areas of water in a few casts. But when fishing a lot of line, you have some challenges to overcome when setting the hook. You need to keep the rod tip low to the water to allow a full range of motion during the hook set. The lower the rod tip is to the water, the more leverage you have to pick up the line. In addition to using the rod tip, you must also strip in line with your line hand at the same time to help gather slack.

After I locate fish with a suspension system, sometimes I tight-line nymph for them. For example, in 2007 I was part of the US team competing in the World Fly Fishing Championships in Finland. We practiced on the lower reaches of the Simo River, a massive body of water that had no clear-cut areas to find trout. The Simo harbored an okay grayling population, at best, and finding one grayling was the first step to any success. Grayling are typically schooling fish, meaning that if you catch one, chances are good that you'll catch another in the same area. As a result, some team members made 80-foot-long drifts with a suspension system to search for grayling over a large area. Once one fish was caught, my teammates switched to a tight-line system and thoroughly covered that area with the confidence that more grayling were holding there.

When tight-lining a pool, I use my standard tight-line leader but increase the length of the tippet from the sighter to the rig by estimating the depth of the water and adding about 2 feet to the length of the tippet. This ensures that my sighter will remain above the water level so I can more easily detect any takes. The length of the tippet also allows my sighter to be close to the surface as the nymphs are descending to the bot-

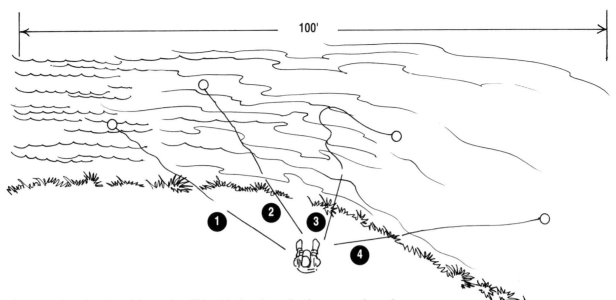

Ideally, I prefer to stand on the edge of the pool and bisect its length, so that I can cover the entire pool with a cast that reaches its head, and feed out enough line as the flies drift below me to reach the water downstream. Not only does this reduce the length of my cast, but it also gives me less line on the water to manage, which results in better hook sets. This tactic allows me to cover the entire length of the pool with just one cast. Casting a heavy, wind-resistant suspension rig 100 feet is not the most desirable and is not likely to be well executed by 99 percent of anglers, including me. When a middle position isn't possible, try to get into a position that allows for the shortest cast and the longest drifts.

In slow water, a weighted nymph will drop to almost a 90-degree angle below the indicator. As a result, the tippet length should be slightly shorter than the distance from the surface to the stream bottom. This keeps your nymphs off the bottom and provides a bottom roll.

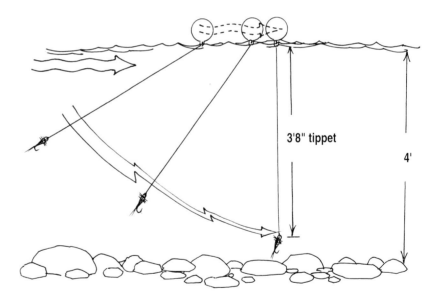

tom at close to a 45-degree angle. As the nymphs begin to drop, the sighter is too deep in the water column to see at first. However, it will come back into sight near the surface when the flies are directly under the rod tip before you begin leading the nymphs.

A tip I learned from John Horsey, one of England's most decorated competitive anglers, is that trout normally look up for food and not down. During the hatch season, when water temperatures are warmer, there's a lot of food, and fish are moving to take insects, my rig often consists of only one heavier fly along with one or two lightweight or unweighted patterns to attract fish suspended higher in the water column.

When the hatch is on, you can catch some trout by fishing deep, but you'll catch more by fishing higher in the water column as they tune in to emerging nymphs and insects. A trilevel rig allows you to fish all three levels at once and quickly pinpoint the level where the trout are feeding.

For instance, in May, when the sulphurs are hatching, I use a heavy anchor Sulphur nymph on the point to imitate the immature nymph, a Pheasant Tail Soft-Hackle 2 feet above that to represent the emerging insect, and another emerging nymph with a trailing shuck another 2 feet up to mimic a stillborn. This rig lets me fish multiple levels and, with luck, discover where the fish are actively feeding. Controlling multiple flies

When you're fishing larger bodies of water and are not sure where trout are holding, look for foam lines that indicate merging currents. Trout know that food concentrates in these areas. JAY NICHOLS

can be difficult, and placing the heaviest fly on the end of the leader creates a tighter connection. Some anglers prefer to place their heaviest fly on the top dropper and trail two more lightly weighted nymphs below it, but this arrangement permits more slack between the flies.

I may change the rig to keep all the flies at the same level if I find the trout are consistently feeding at only one level. For example, early in the morning before the Sulphur hatch, I often fish two or three Sulphur nymphs with equal amounts of weight. The naturals are just becoming active and are not yet moving up and down the water column, so I want all three of my patterns where the naturals are, which is the level where the trout are most likely to take my offering. Once the Sulphurs become active and start emerging, I may switch to a #16 Sulphur dry and a #16 BH Pheasant Tail Soft-Hackle, to fish the same level as the emerging insect.

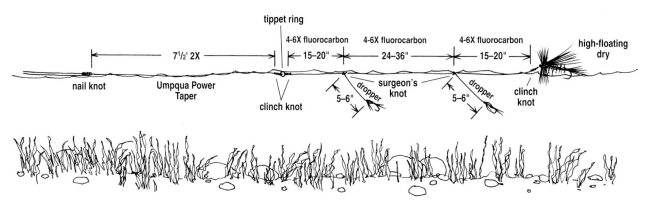

When fishing over shallow, mossy bottoms, I use a washing line rig. This rig was originally designed to hold a nymph at a specific height when fishing lakes and can also be used to fish over weedy spring creek bottoms choked with aquatic vegetation. The point fly is a buoyant pattern, such as a foam-eyed nymph or a dry fly. (You can tie in a round foam cylinder to imitate eyes and convert any nymph into a buoyant point fly.) The middle fly is weighted and tied approximately 20 inches (for most stream conditions) from the buoyant point fly, and the third fly (closest to angler) is also spaced approximately 20 inches away from the weighted middle fly. Essentially, you are fishing a weighted nymph between a higher floating dry fly (fly closest to angler) and the point fly, a floating nymph pattern. Looking at the rig in cross section, it is shaped like a V. The idea of this rig shape is to keep the middle nymph just off the stream bottom. The longer the distance from the buoyant point fly to the middle weighted fly, the deeper the fly will ride.

DIFFERENT WATER TYPES

Conditions like this heavy riffle on the Roaring Fork in Colorado dictate a heavy tight-line rig designed for short drifts. The strong surface currents could create too much surface drag on a suspension device and not allow your rig to naturally drift along the bottom. GEORGE DANIEL

The tailout of a flat, as seen here, between the flat and the riffle of the next run is a transition area that attracts fish, as food from the flat is funneled and concentrated into a smaller area here. These relatively shallow areas usually require a low, stealthy approach. GEORGE DANIEL

Reading the water provides clues to locating trout as well as to the best rigging and presentation methods. Joe Humphreys found this nice brook trout by locating a prominent foam line and drifting his nymph through it.

If you find foam, you will also likely find trout. Foam captures floating insects, providing an easy meal for trout, and it also offers overhead protection from predators. GEORGE DANIEL

When fishing pocketwater containing a number of different currents, a direct upstream presentation is a good approach to ensure that all the line and leader falls into the same current. Casting across-stream would place the line and leader in a number of different speed currents, a recipe for instant drag. GEORGE DANIEL

Always target the dark water edges on any trout stream. Such contrast indicates a transition area from shallow to deeper water, a prime holding spot. GEORGE DANIEL

When fishing short pocketwater like this, shorten the distance between flies. In such water, I often use only one nymph to reduce the chance of two flies landing in two separate speed currents, a common cause for drag. Flies that land in separate speed currents are likely to pull against one another, which creates tension and slows their descent to the bottom. GEORGE DANIEL

In a shallow pocket, fish will hold in the soft water behind the boulder, just off to the side of the currents pulling away from the boulder. Trout need to expend little energy to hold here and have a constant food supply drifting past them on either side. Use a lightweight nymph to reduce hang-ups when fishing these pockets. GEORGE DANIEL

A back eddy is a great spot to drop a lightly weighted nymph off a dry fly. Back eddies often fish like stillwaters, with trout cruising about in search of food. A suspension device will keep your nymph at a fixed level for an extended period, giving the trout an opportunity to find your offering. GEORGE DANIEL

A plunge pool can scour deep into the ground and is a great location for a heavy anchor pattern. GEORGE DANIEL

Nymphing the Extremes

Some anglers fish rivers only when flows and conditions are ideal. Fishing is relatively easy, and that creates a lot of confidence to return under similar conditions. But since flows and conditions are not always ideal, and I want to learn how to catch fish 365 days a year, I'll still go out and fish when the rivers are high, or shallow, or the air temperature is cold.

Knowing how to fish in tough conditions can not only provide some of your best days of fishing, in relative solitude since the fair-weather fishermen are home, but it can also be a trip saver. Anglers plan vacations long in advance to a favorite river or a new body of water we want to explore. Sometimes we find mud flowing within the streambanks as a result of excessive rain or extremely shallow water because of a lack of rain. Most anglers would view either situation as a lost cause and head back to the cabin to call it an early day, because such conditions never yield trout, right? Well, not exactly. We can't control Mother Nature, but we can decide whether to fish or head home. And I choose to fish 90 percent of the time.

Sometimes when foul weather appears and most anglers leave the streams, the big boys come out and play. This monster brown ate a Vladi Worm five minutes after a fierce thunderstorm left the area and the scene was safe to fish. JAY NICHOLS

Though you may not achieve the same level of success when fishing in extreme conditions as you would in the most ideal conditions—perfect water levels where a close approach is possible and lots of eager fish are ready and willing to take your fly—fish still feed in exceptionally high water and hold in shallow water less than several inches deep. Any seasoned guide will tell you that you can catch trout in even the most extreme situations.

Above: Riley Cotter fishing high-water conditions during the 2009 US Nationals in Pennsylvania. In such conditions, use lightly weighted nymphs, as the fish will be holding tight to the bank, where there's little current and the water is often relatively shallow. The biggest mistake anglers make while fishing such conditions is using too much weight. You're not fishing the high water itself; you're fishing the shallow water near the bank. AMIDEA DANIEL

Left: It may not be the most desirable method, but a good strategy for fishing high water is to stand near the center and fish toward the banks. This is especially true when fishing vegetated banks, where access is limited. AMIDEA DANIEL

SHALLOW WATER

During low-light conditions, predatory trout forage in the shallows, and shallow flats that are vacant during the middle of the day can be feeding grounds in the low light of early morning or evening for larger trout as they search for prey. Even on heavily overcast days, I have seen trout feed regularly in the shallow reaches of a local spring creek. These waters are only 3 to 5 inches deep, with a gravel bottom and little overhead protection. Yet before work every morning, I walk these shallows during low light, sight-fishing with nymphs, and it's rare that I don't find trout actively feeding in the shallows with their backs out of the water.

Other conditions, such as high water or low light, may encourage trout to feed in shallow water to avoid stronger currents or for clearer visibility. For example, when a flood occurred during the 2009 US Nationals, the floodplains became trout feeding grounds, similarly to bonefish on a flat.

Approach

Shallow waters dictate a slow, careful approach. Trout holding in shallow waters are more skittish than trout holding in more protected lies. This means darker clothing, more lightly weighted nymphs, cautious wading, and a more careful presentation cast. Use quality optics to thoroughly survey the water before stepping in. Good optics will allow you to notice small depressions or any obstacle worthy of holding a trout. Think like a heron. Do you see these birds running up and down the river? No, they spend time surveying and getting into position before they attack. I try to spend at least thirty seconds looking over the area before making my first cast.

Never step into the water without making a cast. This has been said for years, but how many anglers actually follow this advice? So often a spooked fish will bolt and send warning signals to others, which can quickly clear an area. Place a cast anywhere along the bank that provides cover, into a depression where a trout could be holding, or alongside a small boulder

that a fish could be wedged against. A shallow-water fish will spook as soon as any line or leader lands over its back, so to reduce your chance of lining fish, start short and gradually add distance. Make your first cast from about 15 to 20 feet away, and gradually increase the length of the casts by 5-foot intervals. An upstream approach keeps you downstream of the fish and out of sight.

Tactics

Close-range presentations are possible when you can get to within 30 feet of the fish. In shallow water, this occurs most often when trout are feeding on emerging insects in a shallow riffle so intently that they let their guard down and don't notice a carefully wading angler getting close to them.

For making short, quiet casts at close range, I prefer a longer leader (with a sighter), and depending on how close I can get to my target, I try to fish only the leader. I often grease the fly line tip, the entire leader butt, and the sighter. Not only does this help suspend lightly weighted nymphs, but the higher floating line tip and leader butt are easier to pick up without disturbing the water. Shallow water does not require a lot of weight, so most of my patterns are brass bead-head nymphs, slim in profile (I love epoxy body flies such as Egan's Iron Lotus, James' Brass Ass, Epoxy Czech, as well as the Frenchie, and other similar slim flies) to drop quickly to the bottom but not too heavy to avoid hanging on the bottom. If your sighter continues to get pulled under the surface, you need to lessen the amount of weight. Focus on the tip section of the sighter, watching for any hesitation or movement, and strike as soon the drift changes.

For casts exceeding 30 feet, I shorten my leader so that the tapered fly line does the work of carrying the rig to the target. To provide a visual at this longer distance, I use the curly Q, which rides higher on the water than the flush-floating sighter.

Shallow water and sight fishing go hand in hand. One of my favorite tactics is to approach the fish from downstream and cast

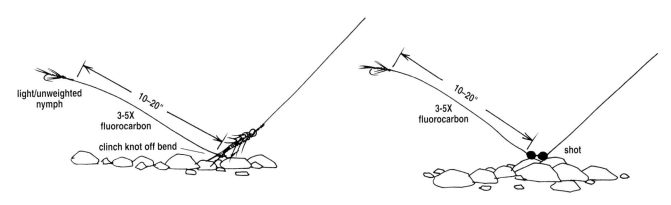

A bottom-bouncing rig is not always the most effective, as trout often prefer a nymph that is lifting off the bottom. When this is the case, try a lifting rig, which allows your pattern to ride higher in the water column. Ideally, I prefer to fish two flies, as this allows me to cover two possible feeding levels. However, regulations may dictate the use of only one fly or the stream bottom may be choked with aquatic vegetation, which could snag a heavy anchor fly. If so, I use a single unweighted or lightly weighted nymph, with the correct amount of shot to effectively roll the nymph on the bottom placed 10 to 20 inches away. The fly will ride higher in the column with this kind of rig, as the shot is placed farther from the nymph than usual.

my fly so that it plops just downstream of the trout. A trout's lateral line can sense even the most lightly weighted nymph dropping below it, and the fish will sometimes react by turning around and searching for the fallen morsel. The trout will see the fly first, not the leader. A lightweight fly is a must (brass bead or several wraps of lead wire only), as a fly that is too heavily weighted will drop too quickly and will be out of the trout's view by the time it turns around to search for the fallen fly.

Casting in Shallow Water

Casting a lightweight nymph to trout holding in shallow water requires a quiet presentation. The two key elements to a quiet presentation are the fly line's trajectory and your application of power during the cast. If you aim directly toward the target, the downward trajectory can collapse the cast, causing the line and leader to land hard on the water and create excessive slack, an undesired result when fishing shallow water. A better tactic is to aim toward an imaginary secondary target, a spot 3 to 5 feet above your primary target. The fly will unroll above your primary target and fall gently onto the water. If you're using a curly Q, which has a greater surface area, it will act as a parachute and aid in a gentle landing.

One of the biggest mistakes anglers make when casting is an overapplication of power. Rarely does shallow water require a cast of 50 feet or more, and with today's high-quality fly rods, it takes very little power to cast a lightweight nymph 40 feet. The greater the power during rod acceleration, the greater the force with which the fly lands on the water. Therefore, when casting in shallow water, you need to adjust so that your fly lands gently. The rod tip should still speed up to a stop during the acceleration phase, but with less power and speed.

Above: Mike Sexton makes a long cast to a grayling he spotted upstream while fishing the San River in Poland. You may need a shortened leader and a longer length of line out of the rod tip when casts exceed 40 feet, as additional force is necessary to deliver the cast. GEORGE DANIEL

Left: A curly Q is a great tool for suspending a lightweight nymph over aquatic vegetation. I use one frequently when fishing spring creeks or in water shallower than knee height. AMIDEA DANIEL

MUDDY WATER

Heavy rains, excessive dam releases, or spring runoff can turn a great stream into a muddy mess. Some anglers mistakenly think that trout won't feed at this time, but they do; you just need to know where to look for them and how to get them to see your fly. In high, muddy water, the trout's ability to see a fly is limited, and the key to fishing in these conditions is to find a feeding zone and hold your fly there long enough for a fish to take notice. You may not achieve the same rate of success as in clear water, but you can still catch decent numbers of fish.

The first step is to find feeding fish. After my second national championship in 2009, when other anglers asked how I caught fish in the flooded conditions, they would get frustrated with my simple response: "I found feeding fish." During high water, there might be only a few select locations where trout are likely to feed. In my case, the key was finding a dead spot in the raging water, and it didn't have to be large. In fact, during my final session on Fishing Creek, the few spots where I caught my four fish were maybe 6 by 6 inches at best. (The

forty-nine other anglers caught a total of only eleven fish on Fishing Creek during the three-day event.) These dead spots were the only possible feeding areas in such conditions, and putting my fly in these areas increased the odds that I was covering feeding fish.

When visibility is less than 18 inches, begin to focus along the slow shallows, near the bank. Because you are targeting slow currents that are no more than 2 feet deep, use a lighter-weight nymphing rig. My thinking is that though many fish likely do hunker down in their midstream spots, since you can't get your flies to them through the raging water effectively, you might as well target the fish you *can* reach.

In muddy water, it's a good idea to drift your nymphs several inches off the bottom. Trout tend to look up for food, and by presenting your fly several inches above a fish holding tight to the stream bottom, you give it the opportunity to see the fly's silhouette against the sunlit sky, which is much easier to see than against a dark bottom.

Even in flooded conditions, there are feeding fish to be caught. Trout often move up into the floodplains to feed in the grass like carp. This trout is cruising the flooded grasses in search of its next meal. GEORGE DANIEL

During high water, some trout move to the bank and begin to feed. Often anglers use flies that are too heavy to fish the shallow water along the banks. A larger but more lightly weighted nymph, such as a large San Juan or Vladi Worm, is a great choice for such conditions. In muddy water, dead-drifting or slowly jigging a streamer is another good approach when fish move tighter to the bank to feed. Patterns should have flash and lots of movement tied in. This approach allowed my team and me to win both gold medals during the 2009 US Nationals when the rivers were close to flood stage. My good friend John Maciejczyk shared with me one of his favorite streamers, a size 8 Rubberleg Root Beer Bugger a few weeks before the competition. A combination of erratic jigging and dead-drifting with the Root Beer Bugger produced fish in pure mud. Streamers are not designed to only be stripped.

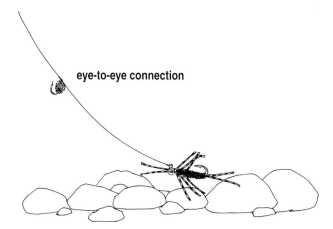

This bottom-bouncing rig with a stone as an anchor and a Glo Bug riding higher is useful for off-color water. Trout look up in muddy water, and bright eggs will stand out against the off-color water surface.

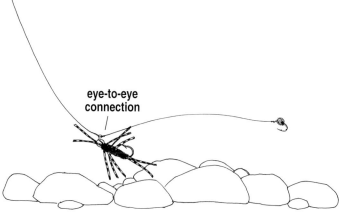

The position of the two nymphs is reversed in this rig, which has the same effect as the bottom-bouncing rig on the left.

Short-line nymphing sometimes requires aggressive wading. Here I am crossing the Simo River in Finland to get to the opposite side.

When I am tight-lining, one of my favorite rigs for murky shallows consists of two unweighted nymphs, an orange egg and a red San Juan Worm, spaced 10 to 12 inches apart with a small shot in between. Allowing the unweighted patterns to ride several inches above the shallows also prevents hang-ups. Often, high water rises high enough to create fishable shallows on vegetated banks, where additional debris occurs. A fly that rides low along a flooded streambank would snag more frequently than a pair of unweighted flies anchored by shot. This rig is appropriate mostly for fishing shallows with a strong enough current to move the nymphs downstream.

For suspension nymphing, I use the same unweighted nymph and split-shot rig along with a small Thingamabobber. In this case, the flies are positioned at a fixed location from the suspension device, about 4 inches less than the water depth, so that the nymphs will ride several inches off the stream bottom. Because of the slow surface currents, the rig should drop directly under the suspension device. This setup is most effective where there is very little current. The suspension device is able to hold the flies at a constant depth, maintaining tension even in the slowest currents.

Another method that I like to use is to dead-drift a lightly weighted streamer such as a deer-hair-head sculpin pattern or a booby-eye streamer in the shallows. The slow speed of the dead-drifting streamer provides more time for the trout to find it in the murky water. Don't use a heavy fly that hangs on the bottom.

One last key to success in muddy conditions is to fish slowly, remembering that the trout's vision is reduced. The ability to hold the fly within the trout's feeding zone for extended periods is the key to fishing high, murky water. Be patient, stick with the slow shallows, and you may become a fan of murky waters.

COLD WEATHER

Cabin fever is only an option. The extreme cold winter months are one of my favorite times to be on the river in central Pennsylvania. Few anglers are willing to deal with extremely cold temperatures, but trout must, as they need to feed all year round. Some of my best moments have come from fishing the winter season—times when my hands were frozen but the fish were hungry.

I find that it's easier to locate fish in many freestone and limestone streams and spring creeks during extreme cold weather. As water temperatures drop and the trout's metabolism kicks down a notch, the fish migrate to deeper, slower moving water. Pocketwater and the faster riffles that produced fish several months earlier become almost vacant as the trout's metabolism slows down. Trout will continue to feed, but their foraging grounds change.

Just as the trout's metabolism slows in the winter, so must your approach become slower and more methodic. Trout can become lethargic in the cold and feeding slows, which means they may need some encouragement to eat your offering. Unlike the spring and summer months, when a trout is likely to eat your offering during your first several attempts, in cold weather it has taken me as many as thirty drifts before soliciting a strike. Because trout become more lethargic about feeding at this time of year, they seem less willing to move up and down the water column to intercept nymphs and you need to place your fly directly in front of the fish. However, winter hatches do take place, including midges, and can create a feeding frenzy where trout begin to feed throughout the water column.

In the cold, I also prefer to fish slightly larger and flashier patterns. Though smaller patterns can still be productive, I opt for larger-than-average patterns with a bit of flash to provide additional encouragement for the trout to eat. When trout metabolism slows down, I believe that they are more readily triggered by larger food items, as this allows them to consume more calories while expending less effort. An orange egg fished with split shot is one of my favorite winter patterns. This egg doesn't represent a natural egg of any species, but the brightly colored pattern produces more strikes than any natural-looking nymph. Other larger and flashier patterns I like to use at this time include the Turd, Rainbow Warrior, Frenchie, and GD's Czech Cat Nip. These patterns have worked well for me throughout the Northeast and in the West, but experiment for yourself and see what works best where you are fishing.

In the winter, takes are soft, so a sensitive, well-balanced suspender is a must if you are suspension nymphing, and weighted flies win out over unweighted flies and split shot because of the straight connection between indicator and fly that telegraphs softer strikes better. A long leader will provide even greater sensitivity. Make sure all line is located within the reel and nothing but monofilament is coming off the reel. Next, create a mono loop around one of the fingers of your line hand. The back of your finger is more sensitive than the inside, and creating that loop around it provides you with a direct link to the flies. An added benefit to a long leader such as Loren Williams' tight-line leader is that it also eliminates the need to constantly cast out fly line and strip it back in, which causes a lot of problems with ice buildup, which not only makes casting nearly impossible but also ice can scratch the finish off a fly line.

Above: A lob is all you need when fishing close to the bank, especially during high water. Feeding fish move to the slower water, tight to the bank. A long rod allows you to pick up the fly and drop it into the correct location without actually casting. GEORGE DANIEL

Right: Midges hatch throughout the year and carrying a selection of midge larvae and pupae is a good idea when nymphing during the winter. GEORGE DANIEL

WIND

Wind is the fly fisher's nemesis, especially when tight-line nymphing where a strong wind can blow the leader back and forth, ruining your ability to detect a strike. Sometimes I just switch over to a suspension device and keep my rod tip low to the water's surface so that the wind can't blow it around. However, there are conditions where a tight-line tactic will outproduce a suspension rig, such as in short pocketwater, and here you need to maintain a higher rod-tip angle to manage slack and lead the flies.

There are at least four tactics you can implement so that wind will have less effect on a tight-line nymphing rig. The first is to use the elevation and lead techniques to make sure the rig actually anchors itself on the stream bottom where the wind will have less effect on the drift. As you elevate the rod tip during strong winds, you will see the line getting pushed back and forth by the wind and moving in all directions. However, once the rig anchors, the leader becomes tight again and will no longer swish back and forth.

Second is to switch to a long leader. A long leader is smaller in diameter than most manufactured fly lines, and the smaller surface area creates less wind resistance so that your nymphs quickly reach the bottom and anchor there.

The third tactic is to add weight. At times, elevation and a long leader still will not allow the rig to properly anchor. If this is the case, add more split shot or use a heavier fly to assist the flies in anchoring to the stream bottom faster. During extreme winds, I may add one or two size 4 lead shot to counter the surface drag created by the wind.

A fourth way to deal with the wind is to keep the rod tip low to the water. Occasionally there are times when the winds become so strong that even changing to a longer leader and adding split shot cannot give you enough line control. The best method during the most extreme wind conditions—when the wind is strong enough to blow a tight-fitting hat right off your head—is to completely avoid it by keeping the rod tip close to the water. Holding the rod tip up in the air allows the wind to push against the leader and line, which creates surface drag. Often this surface drag is strong enough to pull a heavy nymphing rig right off the bottom. I learned this trick while fishing with Dave Rothrock in a canyon section of a local river. Because of the low, clear water, Dave was tight-lining with a lightweight nymphing rig while keeping a high rod tip for line and leader control. However, the wind picked up and blew his leader all around, creating enough tension to pull the lightweight rig completely out of the water. To counter the wind, Dave lowered his rod tip to stream level. Because the leader and line were now lying flush on the water's surface, the wind no longer had much of an effect on his drift.

Anchor patterns are designed to drop quickly to the bottom and stay there. JAY NICHOLS

We can't force-feed trout; we simply must provide imitations they seek, and an egg imitation is sometimes the best choice, especially during periods when trout and suckers are spawning or in high and off-color water year-round. JAY NICHOLS

GOING WILD

Wild patterns are gaudy attractor-type flies that anglers often turn to in extreme fishing conditions when nothing else is successful. An example of a wild pattern would be a fluorescent orange flashback scud, a favorite pattern of mine when fishing off-color conditions. I would not consider this a suggestive pattern, because the fluorescent orange is not even close to the color of a dying scud, but the bright color really appeals to the trout.

When water clarity is low, I like to have at least one wild pattern on my rig, and in muddy water, I will often fish with two, but poor visibility is not the only condition for which I use these gaudy patterns. Wild patterns will also take fish in low water and on highly pressured water. Lance Egan's Rainbow Warrior has been my most productive wild pattern on Pennsylvania's hard-fished spring creeks and limestone streams, even during the late-summer months, when the water

is low and gin clear. Sometimes it may take a little flash to get the fish to eat—and don't believe anyone who says that flashy flies don't work on hard-fished waters. I consider the Pennsylvania limestoners and spring creeks to have some of the most demanding fishing in the country, and I wouldn't even attempt to fish them without a few wilds.

And, sometimes standing out from the crowd is actually a good thing. For example, sow bugs and freshwater shrimp are two fairly common species in many tailwaters and spring creeks. As a result, anglers commonly use imitative-looking cress bugs and shrimp, which can and do catch fish. However, the trout in these waters see thousands, if not millions, of these tiny crustaceans drifting in the currents, and an imitative pattern can get lost among the naturals. Therefore, a wild, something a touch different, is a great choice when imitative bugs are not productive.

Above: The Frenchie, a Pheasant Tail with a hot spot, has become a standard in my fly box. It's simple to tie, has contrast, sinks rapidly to the bottom, and has caught trout and grayling around the globe. JAY NICHOLS

Left: My GD's Czech Cat Nip is a favorite pattern when fishing in exceptionally cold water conditions, as I believe the UV qualities help trigger trout to bite. Trout can be sluggish in cold water, and sometimes a gaudy pattern can entice a few more grabs. JAY NICHOLS

Nymphing
Small Streams

I grew up in north-central Pennsylvania just south of the New York border. A tributary to Kettle Creek named Germania Branch flowed past my doorstep, and it was a child's dream come true. The stream was designated as a kids' only section for fishing, and luckily my brother and I were the only two kids who fished in our small village. Some of my favorite fishing memories took place during those eight wonderful years with my 7½-foot Fenwick fiberglass rod when, from age six to fourteen, I terrorized the native brook trout population, along with the few resident wild browns, with my rough tactical approach. Luckily for me, it required less presentation finesse to catch the native brook trout than the wary wild browns.

Summer vacation ran from June through August, providing splendid dry-fly fishing with large attractor patterns including my favorite, the yellow Adams. Most kids have a short attention span, and I was no different. If trout were not willing to come up for a dry fly, then I was off on other non-fishing-related adventures. At that time, my father was strictly a dry-fly

I prefer to fish dry flies when chasing native brook trout on small streams. However, variables such as water and air temperatures can put these fish down, and the ability to cast a weighted nymph rig in tight brush may be your only hope for success when they are not eating flies at the surface. JAY NICHOLS

You can use a bow-and-arrow cast to "plop" a sunken terrestrial around highly vegetated streambanks where trout are hiding, looking to ambush food. JAY NICHOLS

fisherman, and without saying, so was I. I never really understood that nymphing small streams could be as fun and productive as dry-fly fishing until several years down the road.

When I was fourteen, my family relocated to central Pennsylvania, and soon I fell in love with its larger limestone rivers, which possessed larger trout and hosted incredible hatches. However, as excited as I was to begin "matching the hatch" for larger and more educated brown trout, I always made it a point to continue spending time dry-fly fishing the small mountain streams, which provided an experience you cannot find on larger waters. They demand your full attention, or otherwise your rig could end up in an overhanging tree. Up to age sixteen, I lived and died by the dry fly on small streams (even if it meant catching no fish), but that soon came to an end.

Along with the move came my opportunity to meet Joe Humphreys, my fly-fishing hero and a master nymph fisher whom I had read about for years as a child. I was fortunate to receive countless lessons on the stream from Joe, who often took me up into the mountains to fish the same brook trout streams he had fished during his childhood. Although I enjoyed dry-fly fishing, I soon learned that nymphing was the way to catch fish consistently throughout the year, even on small streams. No longer would I leave a small stream early when there was little dry-fly activity. Nymphing gave me a way to fish small streams 365 days a year.

It is true that most anglers traveling to the mountain streams are likely looking for small wild trout eager to accept a dry fly—just as I was. There's just something special about watching a small wild trout come up and inhale a large attractor pattern off the surface. However, what one desires is not what one always gets, and though trout inhabiting small streams are likely to eat a dry, any number of variables can shut down surface feeding. Small-stream fishing usually requires some walking on the angler's part, and once I arrive, I refuse to allow poor dry-fly fishing to drive me off the stream. It's time to work nymphs.

For the purposes of this discussion, a small stream refers to a moving body of water less than 20 feet wide with a tight canopy making for difficult casting. Not all small streams require small-stream tactics, which are designed for fishing in tight quarters, including the use of a shorter rod and leader. A small stream meandering through an open meadow is technically a small stream but has few casting obstacles such as overhanging trees, and here you can still use at least a 9-foot fly rod and standard nymphing leaders. The long rod gives you better line and leader control, as it enables you to reach and lift them over nagging currents. The only time I resort to a shorter rod and leader is when overhead room for the cast is restricted.

Small-stream tactics are useful for all water types, including freestone, tailwater, spring, and limestone. These tactics are not limited to the more popular small, high-gradient freestone rivers but are appropriate for any waters, large or small, where casting is limited. Trout seek cover as a means of protection from predators. Large rivers often contain overhanging trees or difficult casting areas, and you can use the small-stream tactics discussed here in those conditions as well. Once you've made a small-stream presentation, the drift, line control, and strike detection are similar to the tactics used on larger rivers, so in this chapter I focus on techniques for delivering flies in tight quarters.

SMALL-STREAM GEAR

In areas with little casting freedom, you need to use a shorter rod and leader. I prefer a 7- or 8-foot medium-fast rod rated for either a 4- or 5-weight line. Some anglers like to use a shorter rod with a smaller line weight, but a 7-foot rod allows for better line and leader control, and it also serves as a longer lever to produce longer casts. A 5-foot fly rod will not match the 7-footer for line and leader management, such as when you need to hold line off nagging currents. If you're able to control the size and shape of your loop (discussed below), you will find that a 7-foot rod is an ideal small-stream tool.

Also, a lighter-weight line will not be able to generate the same energy as a 4- or 5-weight with a shorter casting stroke. Casting stroke is defined as the path the rod tip travels during the accelerated movement. The longer the path of the stroke, the more energy you create, and vice versa. In small streams, casting motion is often limited, and sometimes a shorter casting stroke is your only option. This is where you need the heavier taper of a 4- or 5-weight line to make up for the power lost with the short stroke. Though casts less than 15 feet are common on small streams, there are times, such as in low-water conditions, where distance is necessary, so you need a line weight that will load the rod quickly and create sufficient power to cast over 40 feet in tight brush.

The leader is as important in small-stream fishing as on larger waters. The main differences between small-stream and traditional nymphing leaders are the length and the lack of a sighter. I use a 7½-foot 4X aggressive knotless nylon leader, but I cut off the 4X nylon tippet section and attach 4X fluorocarbon tippet. Though fluorocarbon reflects less light, the material is more resistant to abrasion, and small-stream fishing often requires placing the line and leader over rocks or other in-stream obstructions to achieve a natural drift. Also, knotless leaders grab less debris, which can be an issue when placing the leader over obstacles to achieve a drift. The Umpqua Power Taper is a favorite of mine for small streams, as the aggressive butt section helps turn over nymphing rigs with a limited casting stroke.

For my small-stream rig, I avoid using a built-in sighter, as this would increase the number of knotted sections as well as the length of the leader. Instead, the line and leader connection serves as my reference for strike detection. With the short leader, the fly-line tip is close enough to the nymphs to watch it for a strike. However, if you feel you need a sighter, you can build a short one (less than 10 inches) into the leader. Take care not to disturb the leader taper, as it will play a key role in turning over your nymphing rig in tight conditions.

Devin Olsen rigging a dry-and-dropper rig on a small tributary of the San River in Poland. You need to make longer casts during low flows, and a dry-and-dropper rig allows for better line and leader control when casts exceed 30 feet. GEORGE DANIEL

As water levels drop and trout become more wary of artificial patterns, one effective tactic is to replace a gold or copper bead with a black one. JAY NICHOLS

SMALL-STREAM RIGS

The dry-and-dropper is an excellent rig for small streams when trout are eating on all levels. The high-floating dry fly acts as a suspension device and also as a general attractor. Because of the limited casting stroke and the need for the rig to turn over quickly, I rarely tie more than one nymph off the dry fly, as multiple-fly rigs are difficult to turn over and also tangle more easily. On average, the length of the dropper from dry fly to nymph seldom exceeds 2 feet, and it most often is 16 to 18 inches. A weighted nymph is preferable to an unweighted nymph with split shot, as the combination is far more likely to tangle than a single nymph. Most small-stream fishing is done during the warmer spring, summer, and fall months, when trout are likely to move up and down the water column while feeding, so dredging the nymph right along the bottom isn't always necessary. Though this is not exactly dry-fly fishing, it's the next best thing.

However, there are times when trout in small streams are likely to hold tight to the bottom. Cold or high-water conditions often require you to go deep with nymphs. In this case, one heavily weighted nymph fished with tight-line tactics is best, rather than two nymphs or an unweighted nymph with split shot, again because it has less propensity to tangle.

Above: This is the perfect scenario for a snap T retrieve—an angler casting over an obstruction. GEORGE DANIEL

Left: In pocketwater, even on small streams, I use as long of a leader as possible to reach over nagging currents. CHRIS DANIEL

SMALL-STREAM TACTICS

One significant difference between small-stream and larger-stream tactics is the time you spend on each section of likely holding water. My experience has been that fish in small streams are more eager to eat a fly on the first drift through, whereas in larger, more bug-rich waters, it may take multiple casts to move a fish. This is why on small streams, I present no more than five times to each area before moving on to the next spot. I like to move fast when small-stream fishing, as I believe the more water you cover, the more trout you're likely to catch. And with a small stream, it's easy to cover all likely holding spots in a short amount of time.

The main difference, however, is that you are making shorter casts and frequently have to deal with brush. Several tactics should be in your arsenal when you are casting and retrieving around brush. Roll casting with weights and the rolling tuck are techniques for fishing in tight situations where there's no room for a backcast. You can use the snap set where overhead brush prevents you from setting the hook with the usual tactics. If your fly becomes stuck in brush, the snap T retrieve is the best way to get it out, especially in heavy growth. The bow-and-arrow cast is for nymphing in tight brush, and Joe Humphreys's tactic of "taking it to the level" works great for casting under brush.

Roll Casting with Weight

A common occurrence on small streams is that you won't have enough room behind you for a backcast. This is especially the case in low-water conditions, where you cannot wade into the middle of the river without spooking fish. You are likely to find yourself in this casting situation from time to time on large rivers as well, especially when the water is too deep to wade and you are forced to stay close to the bank. Roll casting with weights can be a good solution.

At the 2006 World Fly Fishing Championships in Portugal, the small mountain streams were thick with cover, and low water forced successful anglers to remain close to the bank and blend in with the surroundings. But staying close to the bank meant that we could not backcast to load our rods. I decided that roll casting with weights would be a good approach to deal with this combination of heavy brush, low water, and spooky trout, and I made 40-foot-plus casts using a dry-and-dropper rig to present my nymphs. As luck would have it, I was able to measure three trout during my first session on the Ceira River, and all because I was flexible enough to cast weighted flies in tight brush where other competitors struggled. This type of flexibility will also allow you to nymph in areas most anglers pass over. It will not only give you shots at fresh fish, those

You can use a long rod in tight casting situations—if you're able to understand and control where the rod tip travels during the casting stroke.
JAY NICHOLS

You can use a bow-and-arrow cast when nymphing small streams or areas with overhead canopy. This photo shows Devin Olsen taking the rod to the level on an unnamed mountain stream in Poland. Position the rod tip below the obstacle before coming to a stop on the forward cast.
GEORGE DANIEL

that are rarely hooked, but also provide better opportunities for catching big fish. Big fish like cover, and most anglers pass over many big-fish habitats because of their inability to cast nymphs in difficult spots. The ability to roll-cast with weight permits you to catch more fish and also provides you with opportunities to present your fly in big-fish spots.

The only difference between roll-casting just the fly line and a fly line with weight is in the timing. When using weight, you need to speed up the timing of the cast. With the traditional roll cast, you pull the line straight back and off to an angle. You then slightly lift your rod hand above your head and pause until the line naturally forms a D shape off the rod tip, which takes roughly one second. The D shape creates the tension you need to begin the forward casting stroke, and you cannot make the cast until this occurs.

The problem when roll-casting with heavy weights is that while you are pausing and waiting for the D to form, the weights begin to drop through the water column as soon as they are no longer under tension. The deeper the flies drop, the more energy is required to deliver the fly. If a heavy rig drops deep enough through the water column, it can be almost impossible to create enough energy to break the surface tension with the rig and still make an accurate delivery. Thus you need to keep the fly as close to the surface as possible before making the

forward casting stroke. The higher the nymph rig is in the water column, the less resistance there will be to the forward casting stroke. This is why you need to speed up the timing when roll-casting with weight.

Accuracy is a must when trying to pinpoint a cast so your nymphs land exactly where you want them. The first step in accuracy, especially when casting weights, is to anchor your backcast 180 degrees from your intended target on the forward cast. That is, in order for your flies to hit the target, your rod tip must travel in a straight line during the casting stroke from where the flies straighten out on the backcast to the intended target on the forward cast. To put this in perspective, point your rod tip toward the spot where you want your flies to arrive during the forward presentation. Now focus on the direction in which the butt section of the rod is pointing, and imagine a line continuing straight back from the butt of the rod. The end of this imaginary line is where your backcast must arrive before you make the forward casting stroke. Your forward casting stroke needs to travel along this straight path to accurately present the flies.

ROLL CASTING WITH WEIGHT

To roll-cast with weight, start by pointing the rod tip at the nymphing rig. Make sure all slack is removed from the line and leader so that the rig will move as soon as you begin to move the rod tip. Keeping your rod hand low and your elbow close to your body, begin to elevate the rod tip to point upward at a 45-degree angle. Your hand should be extended fully outward away from the body. At this stage, angle the rod tip slightly away from you to allow the loop to form away from your body.

Maintaining a stiff forearm, begin to accelerate the rod tip backward just enough to keep the flies skating on the surface of the water. Again, the rod tip is angled away from your body during this movement. This is an accelerated motion where you are speeding up through the drift.

Continue drifting your rod hand back toward your head while still keeping a steep rod-tip angle away from your body. For this short, 25-foot cast just about all the line should be off the water, with nothing but the flies skating on the surface.

Continue the drifting motion, and come to a stop when the rod is angled upward but behind you. The rod tip should still be angled away from your body. Pause to allow the line to fall behind the rod tip to load the rod. Hold the pause until a D shape forms between the rod and line. This D is what will load the rod during the forward casting stroke. If you're using heavy weights, the pause should last no longer than it takes for the D to form. If the pause is too long, the heavy weights will drop too deep through the water column, making it difficult to create enough energy to bring the rig near the surface and deliver it to the target.

After the D forms, direct the rod tip back directly over your head with your rod hand, while also sliding your elbow close to your body in preparation for the forward casting stroke. At this point, your rod hand is just out of sight and at eye level. The rod tip is still angled back to maintain the D shape.

In this case, I noticed that my rod tip was angled slightly downward on the backcast, so I simply repositioned it closer to vertical. A steeper rod-tip angle allows you to lift more line off the water with less effort.

Now your rod hand begins to drift outward to the target, while your elbow begins to drop as if you were performing a karate chop. The elbow leads the cast, extending outward to the maximum length. When your elbow can lead no farther, your forearm takes over the lead by continuing to drift outward.

Your rod hand stops on the forward stroke at about the same time as it becomes clearly visible.

The thumb pushes outward during the final phase of the cast to turn over the rig. This photo shows the rod tip pointed toward the water, but the finger is pointed at an angle outward. The position of the rod tip here is due to the bending effect of the rod unloading. However, note the direction of the loop as it aims outward.

All casting motion has stopped, and the weighted rig begins to unroll toward the target.

Begin to elevate the rod tip as the loop continues to unroll toward the target.

Hold the rod tip in this position until all line and leader have landed on the water. Then begin to elevate the rod tip or strip in line as the nymphs start drifting downstream.

ROLLING TUCK

The rolling tuck is a variation of the original tuck and was invented by Joe Humphreys. One of Joe's favorite aspects of fly fishing is fishing in brush, and he created the rolling tuck to deal with such situations. Many small streams have deep pockets where you need to use a tuck cast so your rig will quickly reach the bottom. This cast is not limited to small waters, however, but can be used on any river where your "backdoor is closed," meaning there's no room for a backcast. The mechanics of the cast are the same as for roll casting with weights, except in the presentation stage.

Begin by slowly sliding the line on the water, using the rod tip to create a D-shaped loop. The line needs to hang off the rod tip behind you to create the tension necessary to make the forward casting stroke. Your rod hand should be slightly elevated above head level.

Now begin to accelerate your rod hand toward the target, letting it continue to drift forward and then bringing it to a sudden stop. The rod tip should point outward and not downward toward the target.

The rod tip begins to unload as the line starts to travel toward the target. At this stage, hold the rod tip stationary as the loop unrolls.

The rod should be positioned near chest level at this point. This is vital, as your rod hand needs to lift upward during the next step. After coming to a stop, the weights begin to unroll toward the target. It's essential that you bring the rod tip to a sudden stop and pause for a split second before you begin the upward lift. In this photo, the nymphs are starting to unroll toward the target, and the end of the line is almost vertical. Wait until you see the line standing straight up before beginning the upward lift.

The loop continues to unroll toward the target as you keep your rod hand stationary.

Once the line begins to angle toward the target, start to lift your hand upward toward the sky. The rod tip is angled toward the sky too. Imagine that you are attempting to stab the sky with the rod tip. This is the motion your hand makes with the rod tip to create the tuck.

Once your hand is fully extended upward and tension occurs on the rod tip, this forces the weighted rig to kick under the rod tip, which remains locked in position while this occurs.

The nymphs enter the water directly under the sighter. This is the steep angle necessary to allow the nymphs to drop quickly through the water column.

The downer-and-upper movement drives the nymphs deeper by increasing the force and angle at which the nymphs penetrate the surface. The thumb/finger (whichever is placed on top of rod handle) drives upward during this last stage, increasing the rig's momentum toward the stream.

SNAP SET

When overhead brush prevents you from lifting the entire fly line off the water to set the hook, you can use the snap set, which will also help keep your nymph from snagging in the brush if you don't connect with a fish. This hook set requires fly line on the water, as you use the weight of the line to create enough tension to set the hook. Because of this, the few times I've used it have been when suspension nymphing with a short leader. Essentially, you energize the fly line so that it jumps vertically off the water just a few feet, which creates enough tension to set the hook.

This hook set has some disadvantages, however, and I use it only as a last resort, since it has less power than the usual methods of setting the hook, and I don't think it secures the hook as well as simply lifting the rod tip or using a strip set. Another issue I have with the snap set is the delay between seeing the strike and actually moving the fly to set the hook. In a regular hook set, there's only one motion: lifting the rod tip in a particular direction. This allows a quicker reaction to the take of a fish than with the snap set, which requires two movements: an accelerated upward motion followed by a downward motion. As a result, I feel that it's not as effective at setting the hook. However, there are times in tight brush where lifting the rod tip will virtually ensure that your flies become tangled in the overhead cover, so it's still a good tactic to know.

Begin with the rod tip close the water, and make sure there's little slack on the water. The connection between rod tip and fly line needs to be tight to ensure that the short rod movement energizes the fly line. If there's a belly of line on the water, keep your rod tip pointed at the belly to create a tighter connection.

The first part of the hook set is an upward motion of the rod tip. Hand movement is minimal, just enough to lift the rod tip to a 45-degree angle to the water to begin lifting the line and leader, up to the suspension device, off the water. If you lift the suspender off the water, you are using too much power. As the length of line on the water decreases, the rod movement should be shorter. A micromovement of your wrist and forearm is all that's needed to move the fly line.

Just as in the traditional casting stroke, where you make an accelerated movement to a stop, you must pause to allow the line to begin lifting off the water before the next accelerated motion begins. The pause is critical, since the rod tip needs the tension of the fly line to start the next accelerated motion. In this case, the fly line needs to form somewhat of a loop above the rod tip to create tension on the rod tip for the downward motion of the next step.

Once the rod tip is loaded, the rod should move in the opposite direction, directly down toward the water, and come to an abrupt stop.

This downward movement of the fly line forces the suspension device to snap off the water, creating the tension to set the hook. Less energy is needed for smaller amounts of line; more energy for longer line.

SNAP T RETRIEVE

A popular method for retrieving a snagged fly from brush is to wiggle the rod tip back and forth, attempting to snake the fly over the obstacle. This works only about half the time, however, whereas the snap T retrieve works close to 90 percent of the time. This is because the snap T retrieve pulls the rig farther away from the obstacle, making it easier to free. The snap T retrieve is executed similarly to the snap set, but here you direct the loop of line toward you rather than straight up off the water. Also, the stroke length is longer than in the snap set, because it takes more energy to move the rig toward you

instead of just lifting it several feet vertically off the bottom. I learned this from Frank Smethurst, host of the fly-fishing show *Trout Unlimited: On the Rise*, while he was filming an episode on a small trout stream. Frank used this tactic to retrieve flies in some of the thickest brush I've seen. Though Frank takes no credit for developing the retrieve, he was the one who introduced me to this application of the snap T, and it has saved me many a fly and helped me keep a clear head in situations where I otherwise would have gotten frustrated when attempting to retrieve my fly.

In heavy brush, the line often is draped over an obstacle while you're presenting your fly to the trout. When you retrieve, there's a good chance the fly would hang up on the brush if you simply attempted to slide it over the obstacle, especially with a weighted rig. Instead, the rig needs to ride high over the obstacle to avoid snagging. This is when you want to use the snap T retrieve. First, as with most casting motions, the line needs to be tight and the rod tip pointed low to the water. Extend your rod hand outward toward the fly, with your elbow positioned close to your body.

Keeping the line tight, begin to move the rod tip in a vertical path toward the sky. The flies will start moving parallel to the flow. The rod tip usually should reach head level at the end of the casting stroke. Accelerate your stiff forearm upward during this movement as your hand directs the rod tip toward the sky. Again, this is an accelerated vertical movement to get the belly of the fly line near the level of the rod tip before making the downward casting motion. Now accelerate your hand to a sudden stop, and pause to allow the line to unload toward the rod tip.

After the pause, the line unloads upward toward the sky. Begin to drift your rod hand downward, but at an angle toward the rig. This motion is similar to cracking a whip, but in this case, you want to snap the nymphing rig over the obstacle. The casting motion will create a whiplash in the line, forcing the rig to travel toward you instead of directly upward. That is, the belly of the line is moving upward, but the sudden downward thrust kicks the tip with the fly line back toward you.

Accelerate the rod tip down toward the water, and bring it to a stop immediately before it reaches the surface. This begins the whiplash reaction in the tip of the fly line.

The back-and-forth motion kicks the fly line up over the obstruction. The longer the stroke as the rod tip travels upward and downward, the higher the fly line is lifted off the water. Hence, a higher obstacle requires a wider movement.

Continue to hold the rod tip still until the line falls on the water.

You are now ready to retrieve your line for another cast.

Bow-and-Arrow Cast

The history of the original bow-and-arrow cast is unknown to me, but the modification of the cast discussed here was originated by George Harvey sometime around the 1940s. George was not only an incredible angler, but also a true innovator.

With a traditional bow-and-arrow cast, you kick out an amount of line approximately the same length as the rod, maybe a bit longer. Next, you pinch the line under the reel seat with your rod hand, grab the fly, and begin to pull back on the rod tip. This movement bends the rod, similar to a drawn bow

ready to fire an arrow. Holding it in this position, you point the rod tip toward where you want to deliver the fly. Once released, the rod tip unloads the line and directs it to the target. However, with a short length of line, you can only cast the fly so far.

During low water, distance is a must. While fishing low water in the brush, George needed to cast farther, so he developed a technique to shoot the line a greater distance with a bow-and-arrow cast by creating a series of loops in his hand instead of grabbing directly onto the fly. The photo sequence below describes how to execute George Harvey's modified bow-and-arrow cast.

A bow-and-arrow cast may be your only option when nymphing in tight brush. Point the rod tip out instead of down to allow the tip to unload without knocking the water's surface, which is a common cause of breaking a rod tip.

BOW AND ARROW

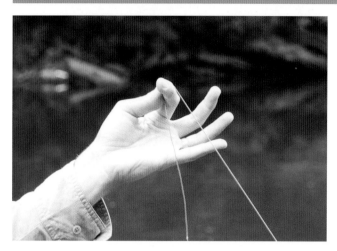

1 Note: Typically, the line hand gathers mostly leader material and maybe several feet of fly line. However, leader material doesn't show up in a photo as well as fly line. We used bright-colored fly line in place of leader material so you can easily see how the loops should look in hand. The first step is to gather line in your line hand. Begin by making a large loop over the top of your index finger. Then pinch the line between your index finger and thumb 8 to 12 inches above the fly. The line hanging vertically in the photo represents the 8 to 12 inches of tippet material leading to the fly.

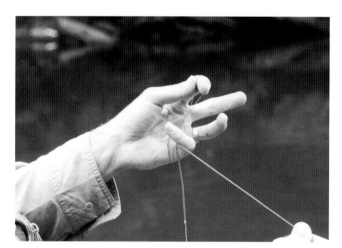

2 Keeping the line pinched between the index finger and thumb, begin to pull line inward with the pinkie finger on your line hand. Stop once it traps the line, holding it in place.

3 With the pinkie finger holding the line in place, use your rod hand to create another loop of line over the index finger of the line hand.

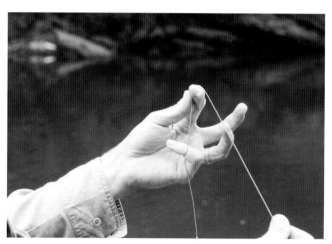

4 Once you've made the second loop, pull the pinkie finger out of the preformed loops while keeping the loops pinched with the index finger and thumb of your line hand. After you pull out your pinkie finger, a loop will be hanging.

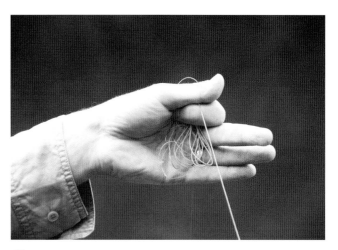

5 Begin the loop-building process again with the pinkie finger of your line hand gathering in another loop of line, and continue building loops until you have the length of line you need to make the cast. The loop size depends on how big of a loop you're able to construct in your hand. For example, one full loop that I create in my hand averages 8 inches in total length. This means that three loops equals 2 feet. Knowing this, I calculate the length I need minus the length of the fly rod and the amount of line between the rod tip and my line hand.

6 Once you've gathered enough loops to achieve the desired length, continue to keep the line pinched between your index finger and thumb. Your goal is to have a series of loops lying on top of one another, which will allow the loops to come off your hand without tangling. Loops that are not stacked correctly will tangle during the release.

7 After pinching the coils of line and leader in your hand, make sure the length of line still out of the rod tip is slightly less than the length of the rod tip. I like to have my line hand positioned between the stripper guide and the cork to eliminate all unnecessary slack. Trap the line with your rod hand so that no additional line will slide through the guides as you begin to draw it back. The next step is to begin drawing back on the line while pointing the rod tip upward and outward, since the unloading rod tip will flex downward. If you were to point the rod tip downward while it was unloading, the recoil would cause it to hit the water. The slower the action of the rod, the greater the recoil. Depending on the rod grip, your thumb or finger should be angled out and up, which means the rod tip will also be pointing in the same direction. If you need to get under brush, you likely will have to drop lower in the water to lower your profile. Now extend your rod hand out and point the rod tip toward the target. Next, start to draw back the line with your line hand, creating a bend in the rod, until your hand is directly in front of your face.

8 With the line hand drawing fully back on the rod, the bottom three fingers on the hand are facing upward and not attached to anything. You will use these three fingers to create even more bend in the rod and increase energy built into the bend of the rod by pulling them inward on the line.

9 With the back three fingers, begin to pull down onto the tensioned line and inward toward you, which will increase rod bend.

10 Keep pulling your fingers inward until they can move in no more.

11 Continue to hold the rod tip steady, and release all the coils simultaneously when ready.

12 Begin drawing your line hand back until the rod is fully loaded.

13 This photo shows a medium-action rod that is fully flexed up to the midsection. Keep the rod tip and hand angled upward, as this will allow the rod tip to unload without smacking the water's surface. Continue to draw back your hand until it is near your ear. The line should be pinched between the thumb and index finger, and the back three fingers should be free to move.

14 When your hand is fully drawn back near your ear, reposition the back three fingers so that they are directly on top of the fly line, pulling the fly line in toward you and loading the rod even deeper. Line control goes from the index finger and thumb to the back three fingers.

15 Once the rod is fully loaded, drift your hand slightly away from your ear, perpendicular to the target, to keep the loops of line farther away from you so that they won't catch on you.

16 Now, holding the rod tip steady at the target, simply release the coils all at once.

17 Still holding the rod tip steady, allow the nymphing rig to unroll to the target.

Here's a variation where you bring your hand back even farther.

Remember, a longer cast demands additional rod load.

TAKING IT TO THE LEVEL

At some point while fishing, you will need to cast under an obstacle, even if you fish larger rivers. Fish seek cover as both a means of protection and a place to find food, especially in summer, when trout are conditioned to feed on sunken terrestrials. Overhanging obstructions on or near the water are fish magnets, because they offer trout protection from overhead predators. As anglers, we know this is where we need to present the fly, but the question is how to get it there.

One of the best methods of casting under overhanging brush is one I learned from Joe Humphreys, who calls it "taking it to the level." While fishing tight brush, you need to consider the level at which you want your fly to enter the water, and then take the rod tip to that level before coming to a stop. The level of the rod tip determines the level at which the loop is formed and therefore the level at which the flies enter the water when the rod tip comes to a stop. The stop on either the forward cast or backcast unloads the rod tip at that precise moment, and the loop forms at the exact level at which the rod tip stops. You need to make sure your rod tip will be low enough to clear any overhanging obstructions. For example, if a hemlock branch is hanging 3 feet over your target, then your rod tip should be close to the 2-foot level before coming to a stop.

Drifting the rod tip is the key to taking it to the level. The term *drift* in this case has nothing to do with how your fly moves on the water. Instead, it refers to the forward or backward motion the rod tip takes before accelerating to a stop. This is a pulling and not a pushing motion. During the drifting motion, you need the nymphing rig to keep the rod tip under tension long enough for you to take the rod tip to the level at which you want the fly to go under the obstruction before coming to a stop. Also, the slower the pulling motion, the more time you have to position the rod tip. I like to keep my index finger on the rod blank during the casting stroke; when that finger feels the resistance of the weights, I know I'm correctly drifting the rod.

A common problem when fishing in the brush is that anglers try to force the cast and not take the time to set it up. As the saying goes, "good things come to those who wait," and successful casters are those who are patient enough to set up the cast. Keep in mind that you're fishing to relax and escape the real world. To force myself not to rush the cast while fishing in the brush, I use a slow breathing technique, taking one complete breath during the entire casting sequence. I inhale deeply on the backcast and do not begin my forward casting stroke until I begin to exhale.

Begin by drifting the rod tip toward the target. This will bring the weighted flies near the surface. Continue to drift the nymphs near the surface until your rod hand becomes visible in your peripheral vision.

Now begin to pull the rig with your forearm toward the target while keeping the rod tip at a low angle. Do not break the wrist. Keep a stiff arm and pull the flies toward the target with an accelerated movement of the rod tip.

Continue pulling the weights until the rod tip points at the target, and then come to a sudden stop with the rod hand. Note that the rod tip is below the level of the overhanging limb. This will allow the loop to unroll under the obstacle.

Begin elevating your rod hand after coming to a stop to start reaching over tailing currents and prepare for line and leader control.

Small-stream nymphing demands constant awareness of your surroundings. I prefer to position myself closer to either side, as this provides more open space for the rod tip to travel during the casting stroke. Some presentations require feeding line downstream. Note how I store the coils on my knee.

SMALL-STREAM ACTIVE RETRIEVE

Native or wild trout in mountain streams often are more aggressive feeders than their large-stream cousins and will often take flashier flies fished with an active retrieve. While dead-drift presentations have a time and place, keep the technique below in mind.

Make a cast directly upstream, and place the rod tip close to the water's surface immediately after the presentation. Pinch the line with your line hand, and hold the line away from the rod as if preparing to make a single haul. Your rod hand should be fully extended toward the target to provide the line hand with more leverage before actively retrieving the fly.

Once the fly sinks to the correct level, begin moving both the rod tip and the line hand. The rod tip remains close to the water's edge through the drift to allow for a horizontal drift. If you were to lift the rod tip, the flies would move vertically. Sometimes this is a desired result, but I often prefer to swim my flies horizontally to the stream bottom, especially on small streams. While the rod tip is moving horizontally downstream, begin to slowly pull the line back with your line hand as if making a slow haul during the retrieve.

Note the slight bend in the rod. This tells you your nymphing rig is anchored on the stream bottom and you're pulling the flies faster than the current. The rod tip should be pointed slightly away from the nymph to provide some give during aggressive takes. Never point at the fly, as there's very little give with this angle, often resulting in broken tippet knots.

Continue to simultaneously move the rod tip and pull with the line hand. The speed and direction of the retrieve are based on what the trout and their food source are doing at the moment. For example, in muddy water, where visibility is poor, I use a slightly slower motion to give the trout more time to locate my small streamer pattern. However, if stonefly nymphs begin migrating toward the streambank, I may speed up the presentation.

Continue to rotate your shoulders downstream while the rod tip leads and the line hand pulls. The drift is short, and you usually need to begin the forward cast as soon as the rod tip drifts directly across from your body.

Index

Page numbers in italics indicate illustrations and sidebars.